Chapters

1. 1982 Alienation, Inspiration
2. 1983 Thatcher Rules but No
3. 1984 Running for the Miners and with Whistler.
4. 1985 Riots, Diets and Disquiet.
5. 1986 The Bad, the Good and the Scilly.
6. 1987 Same Old Tories but a Different Running Story.
7. 1988 Cross Country, Cross Words.
8. 1989 Barriers and Walls, Grief and Joy.
9. 1990 Capital Gain, Corporate Win, Prize Delight.
10. 1991 Sleepless in South Liverpool.
11. 1992 Older, Wiser, More Knackered, Olympic Gold.
12. Epilogue

✝

Chapter 1

1982 Alienation, Inspiration, Initiation

In many ways this is a love story.

The sky was a perfectly painted cornflower blue and the air pinched the skin. It was Sunday, late winter and a beautiful morning. Unfortunately the same adjective could not be attached to 'the game'. I disconsolately wandered to the side of the pitch and sat on the damp grass, a safe distance from the motley group of spectators whose number wouldn't have contravened the Riot Act, but whose behaviour would.

I was 31 and trying to play football. Here the word 'trying' could have conveyed so many shades of meaning and most of them would have been accurate. At that moment the main thing preventing me from playing was the fact that the majority of the players had become a tad bored and decided to switch sports. A mass bout of mixed martial arts was taking place around the centre spot. A mesh of flailing bodies moved as one, bouncing off an invisible barrier delineated by the centre circle. Steam and abuse floated upwards fouling the pure atmosphere. From a distance it looked like a Neolithic tribal dance to encourage the awakening of spring. It wasn't. It was a scrap, a set-too, unnecessary posturing; I'd seen it all before.

In the past, admittedly, I too had been caught in the gravitational pull of this type of dervish dance, joining in on the fringes, but it was becoming a regular feature which spoilt the games. During matches in the Huyton and District Sunday League in the early 1980s, a delicate touch on the ball was now much rarer than an indelicate crunch of the balls and a quick one-two did not necessarily require the involvement of a football. Don't get me wrong, I loved playing the game and enjoyed the fact that it allowed physical contact. A precursor to involvement was accepting that accidents of mistiming and over-enthusiasm could lead to injuries. They were part of the game. For me, what didn't belong were the premeditated acts of violence, where the perpetrator all but reached into a back pocket to retrieve his business plan, neatly written in blood. This behaviour appeared to be on the increase.

In 1979, three years earlier, I'd been a victim of this sort of admirably organised assault. At that time, I was playing for a pub called the Tenterhook, in the Kirkby Sunday League. Situated on the edge of the Tower Hill Estate (a deprived area in Kirkby, which was a deprived area in Knowsley, which was a deprived area in Merseyside and so on) the pub was aptly named because it didn't have what you would call a 'chilled ambience'. The atmosphere kept you on the edge of your seat, back to the wall with one eye on the exit and both hands on your glass.

On that day, playing for the Tenterhook, I'd been repeatedly scythed down by the opposition full back. Frustrated and annoyed, I lost control and gave him a taste of his own medicine, studs lunging into his shins, over the ball. I immediately felt remorseful. A bad injury could have serious consequences, especially for those players who were lucky enough to have a job. Time off could result in hardship for individuals and their families. A clearing of the mad, red mist allowed me to become mindful of this. I approached my opponent and apologised. We agreed that neither of us wanted the violence to escalate, shook hands and played the rest of the game fairly.

This would have been a happy ending were it not for the fact that the psycho of their team (there always seemed to be one nominated nutter in each side, more than one if you were unlucky) had been watching our private little drama unfold and was evidently dissatisfied with the peaceful outcome. He waited for his opportunity to make a retribution contribution. With five minutes of the game to go, I made a pass to one of our forwards. Full of self-congratulation, I was gazing after its elegant arc when I was suddenly overcome; not by the emotion of the moment but by the inability to stand. Our violent vigilante had decided it might be better if I observed my pass from ground level. Sad to say, I was too busy writhing in agony to subject it to further technical appraisal.

Above and around me a tempest raged as my team mates tried to get at the misunderstood maniac and his team mates tried to protect him, I suspect not for the first time. After the storm had subsided, the outcome was amazing leniency from the ref for the perpetrator (possibly influenced by the fact that Mike the Psycho knew where he lived) and a fracture of the ankle and ruptured ligaments for me. Thanks.

This trend for foul play and leniency towards it was not specific to Merseyside. It was a national malaise, encouraged by the antics of so-called professional players and administrators in the Football League. These players were not good role models unless you were auditioning for the role of the long-lost Kray triplet. As usual, it was a case of the few spoiling it for the many. Fast forwarding again to 1982, this generally wasn't a great time for peace, love and understanding. With the Falklands conflict in full swing, an atmosphere of jingoism and machismo was being whipped up in the country by the government, aided by newspapers like The Sun. Its 'GOTCHA' headline while reporting the sinking of the Belgrano was typical of the paper's determination to make light of the cost and consequences of war.

I was just trying to play football, to keep fit, to get an exercise buzz, not to prove I was hard, which, let's face it, would have been like the Krays trying to prove they were sensitive types. For me, risking being side-lined unnecessarily with injury due to unsporting actions (as predator or prey) somewhat defeated the object of getting involved in the first place.

Other factors were also preventing me from trying to play. I was the wrong side of 30. It's a fact that, as you get older, you tend to become more rubbish at playing football. This state of rubbishness becomes all the more apparent if you were not that good to begin with, no matter how good you thought you were. It is also true that the more rubbish you become, the crapper your team mates become. One of the immutable laws of football is that if you are having a bad game it is always your team mates' fault. They won't pass to you or, if they do, they don't give you the right pass. In fact, they don't carry the ball up to you, place it next to your foot and swing your leg to get the desired effect; bastards.

On the whole, having team mates in your team can be extremely annoying, because they tend to be self-centred individuals, who are only interested in what the team can do for them not what they can do for the team. In fact, just like you.

Pitches in the lower amateur leagues in the '80s also presented a unique set of challenges. Today you hear of top teams going off to remote areas of the globe to play international games and when they don't do well they complain that the pitch was uneven or that the grass was too long. They claim that this prevented their expansive passing game. Boo-hoo; at times we couldn't see the ball never mind pass it. It was also not uncommon for the long grass to hide deep potholes which required, at best a ladder, at worst an emergency call to cave rescue to aid extrication.

Sometimes there might be no posts or just the charred remains thereof (especially impressive with metal ones). Some pitches might only have a caster sugar hint of appropriate marking while others could display a bewildering web, made by a joy rider's tyre tracks. (It occurred to me that maybe if we apprehended the motorised trespassers we could give them a plan of the pitch and they could demonstrate their skills by marking the lines accurately.)

For some of the Sunday games the opposition didn't turn up; for others the ref didn't; sometimes half your own team might not or turn up at the wrong place. I always turned up but often found it a waste of time because the game had to be cancelled due to one of, or a permutation of, any of the above factors. In addition, the heathen habit of playing on the Sabbath could generate its own problems. It was not uncommon for the excesses of the previous night to come to fruit, in one way or another, usually with synchronised vomiting at the side of the pitch after about five minutes of play. Some of my team even had to attend church to atone for their Saturday sins; well, that was the excuse they gave for nonattendance. It was more likely that they were still getting a few more sins in before a grilling.

"This is a very unpredictable, inconsistent and unsatisfactory way to exercise and keep fit," I muttered verbosely as I watched the hair and acrylic fly in the centre of the pitch on that particular sunny Sunday morning in 1982.

"Too right, lad," said one of the opposition subs who sat down beside me and offered me the joint he was smoking.

By then I had been living in Liverpool for about seven years. I had been playing for various teams in the local Sunday leagues for about five of those years and by 1982 I was playing in Huyton, an area dominated by sprawling council estates on the eastern edge of Liverpool. My team was 'imaginatively' named Liverpool Social Services, worryingly abbreviated to Liverpool S.S. Most of the team were social workers with the occasional friend, like me, dragged in to make up the numbers.

It was a year when national figures for unemployment had risen to record post-war levels of well over three million and the Merseyside area had suffered more than most. Many of our opponents came from areas where poverty was the norm and some mistakenly thought our team was from the Social Security. This added an extra edge to many games we played in, especially if someone's benefit giro hadn't arrived. There never seemed to be an appropriate opportunity to correct this erroneous belief, or indeed for me personally to avoid a tarring with the 'social' brush by explaining that I was, in fact, a primary school teacher. I'm not sure it would have made much difference; besides why spoil the fun? Seriously though, you would have thought someone could have come up with a subtler, snappier team name.

That scrappy Sunday game was a watershed for me as over the past year I had started to lose my passion for football and have my head turned by, what was to become, another love. The increasing awareness of my decreasing skill, added to my dissatisfaction with the macho ethos and general chaos messing up the game, finally convinced me it was time for a change. I was about to switch allegiance to a different sport which had begun to have a greater level of exposure.

The opening bars of 'Chariots of Fire', Vangelis's theme music for the film of the same name, still cause a skin prickle and a tear duct response when I hear them now. The film was released in 1981 and some scenes had been shot in Bebington Oval. This was an archaic athletics stadium with a cinder track, situated on the Wirral, over the Mersey from where I lived and close to where I worked in Rock Ferry. As I watched the film, which was about the 1924 Olympics, beyond the story line and historical backdrop, I was attracted by the different type of sporting code revealed. Here competition could be fierce and yet a respect for opponents could still survive. The greatest competition was against yourself, with no buck to pass; any pain involved was self-inflicted and I liked the long shorts.

In the same year this film was released, inspiration also came from London where Chris Brasher and John Disley had returned from observing the New York Marathon. Blown away by the atmosphere and inclusiveness of the event, ordinary folk mixing with elite athletes to complete the seemingly superhuman feat of running 26 andabit miles, these two Brits were determined to replicate the Big Apple event or even better it. The result was that the first modern day London Marathon took place. As I watched the race unfold on the television I was struck by three things; firstly, the possibility that I could have a go at this amazing race; secondly, the fact that the spirit of the race fitted in with my feelings about sport; thirdly; a ball thrown at me by my three-year-old daughter who wanted to go to the park.

Road running appeared to me to be the people's sport; no matter what ability, anybody could enter and although it was a competition, the overriding atmosphere was one of comradeship and cooperation. At the highest level, this was illustrated by the sight of the two race leaders in the 1981 London Marathon crossing the line together, in honour of the inaugural event.

Subliminal marathon messages were also being sent to me from an unlikely source. Released in May 1982, 'Combat Rock' by the band the Clash, was, and still is, one of my favourite LPs. Shortly after it was recorded in April, leading band member Joe Strummer disappeared and the Clash had to cancel their planned tour. Jogging Joe was found three weeks later in Paris with his girlfriend, two days after they had, apparently, run in the Paris Marathon. Joe Runner claimed that his training regime had included drinking ten pints of beer the night before the race. The thought occurred to me that if a dissolute punk rocker could run a marathon, then so could I (but maybe I'd have to go a bit easier on the beer).

Declining the spliff offered to me at the side of that sun-kissed, puke-fringed, long-grassed, poorly defined, potholed, football pitch cum boxing ring, somewhere in deepest Knowsley, I resolved that I would train for a marathon. As London had responded to New York, many cities across the UK were responding to London by setting up their own marathons. Liverpool was one of those cities. September 1982 was to see the first Mersey Marathon in the new era of road running. The marathon boom could be heard across the counties of Great Britain and I was all ears and a couple of legs.

As the year wore on I was confident that I would be able to take the 26 miles in my stride (well maybe more than one) and that my renowned stamina and fitness would carry me comfortably across the line. Such was my confidence that I hardly bothered training. I knew I could run 26 miles, I'd already done it. OK, so that was over seven days and was my top weekly mileage prior to the event but surely that would be enough, wouldn't it?

No sooner had I started training seriously than it was time to ease off. The race date jumped off the calendar every time I passed it, somehow entering my body and loosening my bowels. I was beginning to have 'whose stupid idea was this' dialogues between my manself and mouseself (who was squeaking a lot of sense) but by now too many relatives and friends knew I had entered. Pride was involved and the fateful day arrived quicker than Christmas on Planet Mercury.

Sunday 26th September

And finally after all the years, well weeks, OK then, days, of hard training the moment had arrived; time to do battle with the blackstuff and take on 26 andabit miles of Liverpool's challenging road surfaces. Nerves meant I ate little and defecated much. The start was in Speke, home to what is now called John Lennon airport. My friend was driving me there. This added to my stress. I not only had to worry about getting to the finish but also about getting to the start. The problem lay not with the driver, who was, generally, on a good day, sane(ish) but with the vehicle, a Morris Marina, rated by many as one of the worst cars of all time. I was not a connoisseur of the car market but even I could tell it was a heap.

(Crap Marina)

If I could choose my dream job it would be as a car-model-namer. It doesn't appear to require thought, logic or common sense, qualifications which I have none of, in abundance. Although totally suited to this job I could see that I would be up against stiff competition when someone could manage to come up with the name 'Marina'. That required a special madness. If you took the name literally, it is unlikely anyone with connections to an actual marina would have touched one of these cars with a barge pole. I couldn't see it being a must-have for the yachty set. Stripping the word back to its roots, perhaps the name evolved because it did well in underwater trials. This would also explain why it was so rubbish on the land.

It was certainly a crap car which, incidentally, also accurately described the colour of this particular model. A photograph shows me standing next to the vehicle in question before leaving that morning. My hand is laid carefully on the roof, to avoid knocking anything off. I am trying to look confident, but there is fear behind my eyes. Fear of the car's inability to finish the journey or mine to finish the race? I cannot remember; a mixture of both perhaps. (I would just like to take a moment here to thank my friend for the lift again. He loved that car and had no idea I held it in such low regard. He probably would not have taken me to the race had he done so.)

Miraculously, the Marina got me to the start area but by then, nerves a-jangling, I wasn't sure whether to feel grateful or not. The changing/baggage area was an empty warehouse, previously a car showroom (no doubt once full of dull Marinas). Here I sorted out my running apparel. I wouldn't say I was professionally kitted out for the race but my limited training had allowed me to come to a few conclusions about what to wear and what not to wear. On one 'long' training run, being a chilly day, I had set off wearing tracksuit bottoms over my shorts, two t-shirts and a nylon jacket. On my return I looked and felt like I'd been running through the jungles of Borneo and had contracted malaria. This experience suggested to me that no matter how cold it was, within reason, wearing a large number of layers was not conducive to efficient, long distance running. Race day, my ensemble comprised of; shorts (football-style, baggy, black, nylon, by Umbro); vest, (beige, shapeless, cotton, by M & S); socks (football style, black, nylon, by the Army and Navy

Stores); running shoes (slightly too worn, by Brooks*). Sartorial inelegance personified.

* (Brooks was the maker's name not the shoes' previous owner who had worn them slightly too much.)

The most important part of my outfit was my professional knee bandage. The off-white tubigrip was a universal sporting symbol representing lack of confidence. It screamed, "I have not trained enough, will probably fail to finish but at least I'll have a visible excuse."

At the start, huddled at the centre of a splodge of humanity, five thousand people in all, I was almost overcome by the potent composite perfume of sweat, embrocation and urine. I just wanted to stay there (who wouldn't?). It was warm and there was little discomfort, other than nasal. Regrettably, I was rudely awoken from my miasmal musing by someone firing a gun. (People not from Merseyside insert your own joke here about Liverpool and guns but we've probably heard them all, the jokes not the guns.)

The sudden firing of a 25lb blank shell from a field gun signalled the start of the race but also caused many people to leap in the air and some to dive for cover. Eventually however, the main direction taken was onward as into a valley of dread staggered the five thousand.

One mile, two miles, three miles, this was easy! With the wind behind me and wings on my heels I travelled through the suburbs of South Liverpool, past the end of Forthlin Road and Paul McCartney's old house. Paul was out at the time. He was busy recording the hit 'Ebony and Ivory' with Stevie Wonder. It was destined to spend seven weeks at number one in the Billboard charts. Although I didn't expect to get into the top twenty myself I felt on song. Carried away by the moment, I had mentally torn up any vague pre-race pacing plan. I had a ticket to ride, and I didn't care. I headed towards oblivion with a great grin on my gob. At about eight miles we reached Sefton Park.

The image of Liverpool back in the '70s and '80s, often perceived and invariably promoted by people who had never visited or spent time in the area, was one of a grey northern city blighted by poverty and dereliction. It was true that parts of Liverpool were desperately poor but this could also be said of many northern conurbations. For me, this didn't prevent it from being a beguiling city with grandeur clearly evident behind a somewhat weary façade.

What many didn't realise or recognise and probably still don't, is how green Merseyside is. Much of the greenery is a heritage of its rich mercantile past where swathes of private land were bequeathed to the public in the nineteenth century. There are over ten square kilometres of parks and open spaces in the city. The English National Register of Public Parks described Merseyside's Victorian parks, collectively, as the most important in the country. This includes Birkenhead Park, the first to be publicly funded and later partially used as a template for Central Park in New York. The city of Liverpool has ten listed parks and cemeteries including three Grade II, more than any other city outside London.

As I ran around Sefton Park I felt in familiar surroundings. Situated only half a mile from the flat I rented at that time, I often used the two andabit miles of the perimeter as a training track, as did hundreds of others. On a pleasant Sunday morning it was not unusual to experience a jog-jam, not something to put on your toast before a run but congestion caused by the heavy traffic of running bods. Fortunately Sefton Park's 235 acres, had space to accommodate the volume of foot traffic.

Resisting the temptation to go home and have a cup of tea, I was still feeling reasonably fluid myself as I exited the park and passed the end of my road. We ran towards town, along the faded elegance of Princes Avenue, through the grand Georgian Quarter and then strode downhill, past the ten mile mark at the Anglican Cathedral, whose giant glowering tower was often shrouded in mist, adding to its gothic menace. At that time, work to finish the cathedral had only been completed four years previously. In spite of an early start at 8.00 am in 1901, it was 77 years in the building. The finished item was the biggest cathedral in the UK, the fifth largest in the world and one of the most behind schedule.

Having run through the garrulous crowds in the town centre and on towards the sparsely populated commercial area in the north of the city I started to feel the early pace. 11 miles had gone but now there were no bantering crowds or interesting architecture to occupy me. The mind had nothing to do except consider the body and it was not impressed. Mind's voice said, "Well, you got a bit carried away didn't you? I thought we had some sort of plan? Now look at what sort of mess you've got us into." Body said nothing but started to sulk.

My feet had earlier skipped over the road surface, brushing it with a lover's light kiss, now they were plonking deliberate smackers on it like a tipsy great aunt at Christmas. The tarmac began to suck my feet down. At 15 miles I ran into a wall, and then another. Neither was the metaphorical wall that runners claim to hit when they haven't done enough training or have gone off too fast and which can be used as an excuse if people don't believe the old tubigrip ruse.

First we turned into a wall of wind. On any training run, a head wind can be an irritation but, 15 miles into a marathon, facing 30 mph gusts felt like running through frogspawn. The second wall appeared as we turned on to the Dock Road. The Dock Wall loomed up on our right and all manner of warehouses, of different vintages and in different states of repair, on our left.

Built in six stages between 1816 and the 1840s, the dock wall was intended to protect the docks from illicit ingress and egress and probably undress. It is a magnificent structure many miles long and of mixed design, having been constructed by a variety of architects over the 20-odd years of building. In 2012 an application for 'listed' status was drafted, hopefully to save and perhaps even restore some of its outstanding features, including the crafted entrance gates at various points along its length. At that moment in 1982 I wasn't enjoying its granite gorgeousness, in fact, it was like running inside a ridiculously long prison exercise yard and I was an innocent man being punished.

In the heyday of the docks, the wall had 33 water fountains embedded in the structure. Of these only seven remain; five in cast iron and two in granite. The dock owners reasoned that the availability of fresh drinking water would discourage their workers from going into the pubs, which had mysteriously sprung up along the Dock Road. They obviously knew their men well! Maybe if they had pumped free beer into the fountains the plan would have worked.

For me, dehydration had started to kick in and the water stations seemed too far apart. (Where were the beer-fountains when you needed them?) The sun had come out and the combination of wind and warmth was beginning to make me feel like, and probably look like, a prune on legs. At about 19 miles the route passed the Three Graces, the impressive buildings which dominate Liverpool's famous waterfront skyline. If I had looked up I would have seen the huge clocks of the Liver Buildings, bigger than Big Ben's dials. I could have checked my time. I would also have seen the Liver Birds looking down at me looking up. None of this happened because by then my sights had lowered and all I could see was the road as I tried to head butt my way through the mythical, metaphorical marathon wall. The Liver Birds were probably shaking their heads at the pathetic sight of all those staggering ants below and wondering what to have for dinner.

Turning back up the hill, past the Cathedral again, I was in theory, 'almost' there; six miles from the finish. Was this fact a cause for celebration and an uplifting of spirits? Was it hell! I was in Hell. I was in desperate straits on the home straight. The primary emotion I felt was despair, except for the occasional feeble glow of anger when some misguided spectator shouted, "Keep going, only six miles to go." That little word 'only' was hugely open to interpretation. I was too exhausted to express anything on the clay mask that my face had become.

I plodded on. "I will not walk, I will not walk, I will not walk," one hundred times after school. The head teacher of the primary school I worked in had turned up on the route to give me support. He saw me coming from a long way off and was cheering enthusiastically. His enthusiastic demeanour morphed slowly into one of concern as I got nearer and he got a better look at the state I was in. He was probably already mentally planning supply cover. "I will not walk, I will not walk, will I not walk? Why not walk I?"

By now I was running so slowly that I probably could have walked quicker. The dye in my shorts was running faster than me. My kit was soaked in a mixture of sweat and the water I had thrown over myself in an attempt at self-resuscitation. Nearly everything chafed. Even my brain seemed to be rubbing against the inside of my skull. The one place I had applied Vaseline was on my nipples because I'd seen someone do it on a TV programme which may or may not have been about running. Inexplicably, I'd never thought to lubricate inside my cranium. By now my body seemed to be melting, draining into the earth, as I sank lower and lower. It felt like I was running with my arse stuck in a bucket. I was tempted to turn my head to check if I was leaving a trail of slime to mark my gastropodan progress but my head became too heavy to hold up, let alone turn. I saw nothing but road surface and heard only fuzzy disembodied noises from the crowd. My body and mind started to separate and, worryingly, go their own ways. I no longer had any perception of time or place.

Seconds became minutes, minutes became hours and… well you get the picture. Two thousand years later I finished and was finished, left in emotional limbo. Bedraggled, dark ringed eyes staring lifelessly out of a drawn, pallid-skinned skull, I dragged my body through the finish funnel. A year later, Michael Jackson would imitate my style in his 'Thriller' video.

After I was swaddled in foil, as if ready for cryogenics, my blood suddenly disappeared. I don't know where it went but my skin turned grey and I had an irresistible urge to lie down and call it a day. The Marinaman and my partner stood over me being chirpy and supportive but all the time I could sense they were mentally calculating how long they should leave it before getting medical assistance. I can truly say I had never experienced anything like it before. After about 20 minutes Mr Blood came back from his holidays but he wasn't too keen to throw himself fully back into work. Soon I was on my feet, walking, after a fashion, talking, after a fashion and dressed totally out of fashion. My tracksuit hung from me like an encumbrance, extra weight on a body I was already having difficulty carrying around.

Loaded carefully into the Marina, I was delivered back home safely. I now felt like the car's colour and this classic vehicle was in better condition than me. Eileen, my partner, waited on me hand and foot that afternoon because mine felt like they had weights attached. It was only later in the evening that I managed to regain the capacity to think without my head spinning. Then I started to reflect on my performance. It would appear that I had achieved a reasonable first marathon time of under three and a half hours (3:26:10). Had it only been that long? Although I did not want to think about it too much (things were still raw, literally) I knew with better pacing and more training I could beat that time.

I woke next morning and thought I was paralysed. Making a greater effort, I realised that, thankfully, it was only muscle stiffness but, shockingly, in every muscle in my body. Even my eyelids were stiff. Muscular damage of this degree was new to me and had never resulted from any other sporting activity. I somehow got to work to complete the school day, moving like Frankenstein's monster. The kids thought it was hilarious. "I will not laugh at sir, I will not laugh at sir;" fifty times at break.

Later, struggling home, I needed several old ladies to help me across the main roads. On the way I stiffly bought an evening paper, the Liverpool Echo, containing the marathon results. I noted that I'd managed to finish in the first 450 out of 5000, which I thought was creditable. There was also a picture of the winner. He had won in a time of 2:27:15. He looked old enough to be my grandad. On reading the caption under the photo I found out he was only 42, ten years older than me. At that time I didn't realise that training to be a successful marathon runner could not only make you feel like you were at death's door but also make you look like you were through the door and having a cuppa with Mr G. Reaper. It was at that point I decided that if my grandadalike could run a successful marathon then I could. I vowed to be back next year, better prepared.

In the paper, next to the marathon results, the leader comment caught my eye. It read; 'Pressure on Foot'. I thought it might be about the latest medical research into metatarsus trauma caused by long distance running but it turned out to be a report on the Labour Party conference in Blackpool where the leader Michael Foot was being pressurised to rid the party of the Militant Tendency.

At that moment I didn't realise how much marathons and militants were going to figure in my Liverpool life over the next few years.

Chapter 2

1983 Thatcher Rules but Not Merseyside OK

I played football with Derek Hatton. There, I've said it and I'm not ashamed. And why should I be? He was a perfectly affable bloke to have a kick-about with. He was supposed to operate in midfield but had a tendency to stray to the left wing. Now he doesn't even get picked.

Most of this is true. The last two sentences are bad jokes, but also true. For those people who don't get it, Derek Hatton was a prominent and much vilified member of the Militant Tendency, a Trotskyist group working within the Labour Party, which came to prominence in the politics of Liverpool in 1983. We'd played 5-a-side football together when we were both employed in Knowsley, Merseyside, working in the community in the late 1970s; but more of 'Militant' later.

For those who also haven't realised, the title of these memoirs pays homage to a television drama series which was first screened on BBC2, in five episodes, during October and November 1982, just after my first marathon. 'The Boys from the Blackstuff,' written by Alan Bleasdale and set in his home town of Liverpool, was a national success. So much so, that it was repeated on BBC1 and won the BAFTA for Best Drama Serial in 1983.

It was so popular that one of the main characters, Yosser Hughes, became a kind of cult anti-hero with his catch phrases being bandied about the length and breadth of Britain. Yosser, in his desperate search for employment, would parrot the phrases, "I can do dat. Gizza job," every time he saw someone doing any kind of work. As a consequence of the programme's success, anyone quietly engaged in gainful employment in a public place could expect to be scared shitless by some wit bawling these phrases at them in a bad Scouse accent. (After seeing my 'grandad' win the 1982 Mersey Marathon, even I thought, *I can do dat. Gizza jog.*)

The British Film Institute described the series as: "a warm, humorous and, ultimately, tragic look at the way economics effect ordinary people." Indeed, economic conditions were having a dire influence on the life of many people in the North at that time. Coming to the end of the first four years of Thatchergedon, a person was lucky to have a job but considered a pariah if they didn't.

I felt a little ambivalent about 'Boys From the Blackstuff', glad that it highlighted the blight of unemployment but uneasy that it put Merseyside in the spotlight and gave more ammunition to those only too willing to put Liverpudlians down with negative stereotyping. Theoretically, this drama could have taken place anywhere in the North. The pilot episode, just called 'The Black Stuff,' had been about a tarmac laying gang from Liverpool, working in Middlesbrough, in the Northeast of England. I had made the reverse journey, being born in Middlesbrough and spending 19 years there before eventually arriving in Liverpool in the mid-1970s. Having grown up in an unfashionable northern 'backwater', I knew all about the endemic regionacist ridiculing of industrial towns by commentators exercising cultural hegemony from the nation's capital city. I also had a wide knowledge of whippet training, tripe recipes and the history of cloth caps, ecky thump.

It seemed to me that for some the series could easily confirm a one-eyed view of Liverpool. The truth was that it was a fiction, a drama, just like 'Inspector Morse', the television police series, set in Oxford, based on Colin Dexter's novels, screened between 1987 and 2000. The difference was that watching 'Morse' wouldn't make visitors wary of going to Oxford in case they fell victim to the town's many murderers, who were killing people on a daily basis by throwing them from the top of the dreaming spires, or off punts on the river Isis or sometimes by squashing them between two of the heaviest books, (weight-wise) in the Bodleian Library. Oxonians weren't all condemned as homicidal. In spite of its gory themes, 'Morse' was almost an advert for Oxford. We saw frequent glimpses of many an amazing building, usually as someone plummeted from its highest point. The programme rarely featured areas of the town which, in truth, had deprivation and social problems to match those of many northern conurbations. To be fair it wasn't Morse's job to highlight the problems of the working classes, unless they were servants slaughtering their employers. He was too busy cleverly solving murder mysteries and crosswords while wading knee-deep in bodies and banging on about opera and classical mythology. 'Blackstuff' realistically covered serious issues and depicted Liverpool, in spite of its catalogue of impressive architecture, as grey and gritty. Morse, in spite of a murder or six, portrayed the Oxford cityscape invitingly. 'Blackstuff' didn't do the same for Liverpool even though less carnage took place. At the end of the day the programmes were both dramas but their aims were different. One was mainly to entertain, the other to inform and make a point.

In the recent past Liverpool has produced much literary talent. Many have written with a social conscience and often about injustice in their city. If other places had an equal number of high profile, vocal advocates for the poor and exploited, maybe they too would come under the same unfavourable scrutiny from detractors.

The country may have liked the 'Blackstuff' series but it obviously wasn't keen on the message because, in May 1983, Margaret Thatcher was back as prime minister. The headlines read: "Tories swept back to power in a landslide." Post-polling day I optimistically misread the morning headlines as: "Tories swept away by the power of a landslide." And did Merseyside go along with the rest of the country in this massive political swing to the right? Of course it did…not. Bucking the trend, as usual, there was an overall swing to Labour. Terry Fields, a member of Militant Tendency, actually took the Broadgreen constituency for Labour from the Conservatives. On winning the seat he announced that he was, "a worker's MP on a worker's wage" and always donated much of his MP's salary to the labour movement.

In May, Labour had also ousted the Liberals in the city council with many members of the Militant Tendency elected. Derek Hatton, my co-footballer, was now playing up front, as Deputy Leader. All this had happened in spite of a vitriolic campaign, by the local Liberal Party and the Labour Party nationally, to try to prevent Militant members standing as Labour candidates. Of course there was blanket condemnation of Militant by the Tory government but they were in the habit of maligning anyone with political ideas more liberal than Machiavelli. Whatever anyone else thought, it seemed that the Liverpool electorate were not going to be told how to vote. They wanted representatives who would challenge the government. The city was out on a limb again.

In 2012 I went to see an exhibition of work by Liverpool born artist John Kirby who, although no longer a resident of the city and not having had a particularly happy time living here as a young man, still expressed an affiliation with his birthplace. In a film interview he said something which rang true. He described Liverpool as a 'Marmite' city; you either loved it or hated it. Many people outside the city regarded the population as a bunch of recalcitrant wastrels and bolshie bastards (no wonder I fitted in).

This view wasn't restricted to the tabloid press and misinformed individuals. Cabinet papers, released in 2011 under the 30 year rule, revealed that, in the aftermath of the 1981 riots, Geoffrey Howe, the Chancellor, warned PM Thatcher against putting money into Liverpool because it would be like "pumping water uphill" and he told her it was, "much the hardest nut to crack." He recommended a "managed decline". Not keen on all that pumping and cracking, Thatcher was inclined to agree.

A distorted view of the city's population, promoted by many self-inflated windbags, was that Liverpool people perpetually regarded themselves as victims. Apparently the sense that they were always singled out for unfair treatment was ingrained in the Liverpool psyche. However, people who stick their necks out do get singled out. I can't recall any of the other cities which had witnessed riots in 1981 being recommended for this special 'managed decline' and I'm not a Scouser. In fact, part of Howe's plan was to divert funds to cities like Birmingham where the Tories saw more potential for money and votes.

These proposals may have gone through were it not for (in part) opposition by Michael Heseltine who had been appointed to look into the economic and social causes of the 1981 riots. The recommendations in Heseltine's cabinet paper (although given a lukewarm reception in the Cabinet itself) served to halt the influence of Howe's ideas, just as he seemed about to organise for Liverpool to be detached from the UK and shoved into the Irish Sea; out of sight out of mind. (It is rumoured that this plan was abandoned amid fears that the floating city might get caught on unfavourable currents and end up beached next to Bournemouth.)

Unlike the economy, after the elections, my running began to look up and I found a partner to run with. His name was Whistler. For the '82 marathon I had done all of my training, what there was of it, alone. I had started to 'up' my mileage in preparation for the '83 reprise. I desperately wanted to improve and finish in better shape but I still wasn't taking a wholly serious approach to training apart from in the area of alcohol consumption. I confess I was fond of the odd glass of beer. Previously I had gone out willy-nilly and consumed alcohol for recreational and relaxation purposes. Now it had become a scientifically proven component of my training regime, to loosen muscles, deaden pain, rehydrate and replace carbohydrates. Admittedly, this modus operandi wasn't accepted by most of the athletics coaching fraternity but after a few pints what did I care?

For some time I'd toyed with the idea of having a running buddy who could, maybe, help me push myself a bit more. On one long run I was thinking about this possibility when I turned around and nearly jumped out of my shorts. There he was, Whistler, gliding silently beside me, like Marty McFly on a hoverboard. To this day I don't know where he appeared from.

Whistler was a rock climber who had decided to come down to earth. I seriously can't remember when or how we started running together but we did. He was a university lecturer but he was only a little older than me. I'm explaining this to avoid giving the impression that he was a shaggy bearded, shag tobacco smoking egghead, wearing baggy-arsed cords and a shagged-out tweed jacket. Although, to be honest, I'm not sure how he dressed for bed.

For a university don he was a man of few words, each well weighed before being dispensed. He too was new to this running lark and so, both being educationalists, we were able to swap and discuss important theories picked up from various experts in the media and from other experienced runners; for example, complicated ideas about how to eat food without missing your mouth and the technicalities of putting one foot in front of the other with the aim of moving forward without collapsing like a tranquillised elephant. These conversations were short, as were many with Whistler.

Ideas weren't the only things Whistler picked up through running. I first noticed his 'habit' when he almost caused a pile up at rush-around hour in Sefton Park. He executed an emergency stop in a particularly narrow section of the perimeter in order to bend over and pick up a grey, left hand, gardening-type glove which lay on the floor like a dead cephalopod. The air was immediately filled with the growl of Vibram on gravel, the scritch of overstretched Lycra and a gale of expletives, as peak-hour plodders swerved to avoid the sudden gluteal obstruction Whistler presented.

When I had enquired of him politely, "What the hell do you think you're doing with your arse, you arse?" he confessed to his sin of an odd acquisitiveness. He admitted he had a collection of gloves at home, nearly all left-handed. But not to worry said he, in response to my increasingly concerned frown, he didn't have a glove fetish because he also harvested many other random objects on his runs. The only rule was that he had to be able to carry 'finds' back home comfortably, without his legs buckling.

He never invited me to view this collection but I did imagine a dimly lit attic festooned with soiled articles of clothing, broken wheel hub covers, eyeless teddy bears, pink prosthetics, random road-kill, bottles half full of yellow liquid and a copy of 'Lady Chatterley's Lover,' all dangling from the rafters on old piano wires. I had no desire to check out my imaginings.

Whistler lived in a shared Victorian mansion near the entrance to Sefton Park. In 1866 the Liverpool Corporation announced a competition to design a public park which was to be developed south of the city centre. It was won by M. Andre of Paris and Mr Hornblower of Liverpool. It was decided to name the park after the Earl of Sefton who had originally sold the land to the Liverpool Corporation; quite right too. I can imagine the negotiations. "Here you are. Have a load of money for this crappy bit of waste ground and, you know what, when we've spent a load more public money on making it look half decent, we'll name it after you. Thank you for being you, your Earlship." Next time I sell my house I'm insisting that a blue plaque goes on the wall!

The site was, at the time, agricultural land with no trees but by the time the park was opened in 1872 it had been transformed into the magnificent space it is today, with woods and cascading water courses. In order to recoup some of the outlay for the construction of this public facility (and the money paid to the Earl) a number of private villas were built adjacent to the park, of which 84 remain. Some are of great architectural merit; others are of interest because of their eccentric style and solid craftsmanship. Whistler lived in one of the latter. It was a bloody huge, rambling affair with comical, conical towers and more chimneys pointing skywards than American missiles aimed at Havana. It was Whistler's Camelot in which he housed his kingdom of found objects. He had come to own the house, with a few friends, almost accidentally.

The building had previously been a council nursing home but became surplus to requirements when caring private enterprise started to take over looking after our elderly. The house was to be sold by a process of sealed bids. Whistler and his friends had put in a ludicrously low bid just for a laugh. Their laughing mouths must have frozen in shock when they found out their bid was accepted. They were now struggling to maintain the crumbling gothic behemoth, which wasn't quite so funny.

Looking on the bright side, Whistler had lots of room and an extensive attic, for his …err… collection. It was also handy for our runs. I would jog round the corner from my flat, call at his at a prearranged time and carry on the run with him. One day, in school half-term, I had the luxury of being able to get a long run in, midday, midweek. Having arranged to call, I rapped on the big old door and he appeared, also wrapped. He was wearing a rather natty tartan dressing gown. "Come in," he said and wandered off muttering something else I couldn't hear. We walked through the baronial hall into a capacious communal kitchen. Here stood a vast black cooking range which would not have looked incongruous in the bowels of Buckingham Palace. I thought I could hear a fire crackling somewhere but the range was cold. It may have just been the sound of dry rot spreading.

"Sorry, I have to make a call," Whistler said suddenly.

The phone was in the hall and as I was standing near the door I was just able hear his half of the conversation.

"No, I woke up this morning feeling terrible…….. Yeah, headache, sore throat, temperature…… Yes, I will." His voice seemed quieter and sicker than it had a minute before. "Do you think you could put a note on my door telling the students I won't be in...? Thanks. Yes I will."

As he came back into the kitchen I spoke, "Sorry I didn't realise you'd…"

But before I could finish the sentence by saying, "…contracted pneumonic plague," he'd whipped off his dressing gown to reveal a full running kit. A roll of drums and a clash of cymbals wouldn't have been out of place but it may have been hard to hide the tympani under the bedroom wear. "Let's go then," he breathed mirthlessly. It's an old adage but in this case true, it's the quiet ones you have to watch!

With Whistler's help my training had been going well. I was managing to run 50 miles a week (sometimes) and my long runs were 18 miles (occasionally). I knew I was getting serious when I was enticed into a sports shop by my dandy alter ego. He lured me in and bullied me into buying some running shorts. Unlike in 'Chariots of Fire', running shorts in the '80s were extremely short and this pair were also extremely bright red. Less flamboyant me reasoned that the shortness was acceptable. It would mean less weight, which could be crucial (especially if I started running three thousand miles a day). I couldn't think of even the most implausible excuse for the redness but Alter E had handed over the money and pushed me out the shop before I could protest.

Summer had arrived and I was forced to take a break from pounding the streets. Eileen, my partner, and I had been together for four years and we made the rather bold move of deciding to go on holiday with her mum and dad. To be truthful she decided, then it was decided I should agree. On the positive side, I realised it would give me a chance to recharge my batteries after the combined trauma of three terms teaching and relentless tarmac treading. I could also wear in my shorts. Little did I know that two incidents on holiday, involving the red shorts and inappropriate footwear, could have seriously jeopardized my nascent running career.

We were staying on the west coast of Italy in Marina Di Pietrasanta, a seaside resort near Pisa. Things were going fine in our ménage à quatre; there had been no need for recourse to lawyers, the local carabinieri or Mafia hitmen and all wills remained unchanged. In the first week we took a day trip to Lucca, a pretty little walled town famous for its olive oil and its... err... walls. It was a hot day and we decided to rest in a shaded spot above the town, on the walls the town was partly famous for.

All was quiet except for the distant thrum of traffic and the percussion of cicadas as the noon sun shimmered in the haze-paled Tuscan sky. We flopped on the stone seats set into the oft-mentioned walls and tuned in to their renaissance resonance. Sporting my red running shorts I lay back, admiring them from above. Suddenly I was getting too much resonance. Was it the heat? My eyes seemed to be playing tricks, as the stitches in the fabric of my shorts appeared to be moving. Then I felt the first Lilliputian stab of pain in the groin, then another, then more, then more to the power of ten. I eventually realised. Bloody red ants! Fiery little buggers! I leapt up and started to beat myself ferociously about the crutch. It wasn't until the majority of the crimson miscreants had fallen lifeless to the floor from an area marked private, that the pain of the self-flagellation also started to kick in. That sort of bruising would be hard to explain. Fortunately Eileen was there to witness the cause. She and her parents were hugely supportive; they cheered me throughout my excruciatingly inaccurate haka, singing 'dead ant' dead ant' to the 'Pink Panther' theme tune. I believe to this day that the ants were attracted by the colour of the shorts. They thought they were boarding the mother ship to return home. They must have been disappointed by what they found. I could almost excuse their biting.

After my ordeal I walked a bit funny, sorry, funnier, for a couple of days while the formidable formic acid and haka haematoma were dispersing. Running would have been out of the question. In future years this would have been a blow because I would have been trying to slip out for a run whenever the opportunity arose. But in 1983 I was not, as yet, completely addicted and had no intention of wasting good drinking time by running.

In the second week of the holiday we went on another trip, as you do, this time to Pisa and its famous leaning tower. From afar the tower looked like a wedding cake gone horribly wrong. At the base it looked like an even bigger wedding cake gone wrong; looking up at it almost made you fall backwards. I should have known it would be tempting fate to go up the tower with a woman called Eileen.

(Releasing the red ants from the red pants)

As we climbed up the inside of the structure it was a bit disconcerting that the spiral steps leading to the top were so narrow and slippery. Over the centuries countless feet had worn dips in the treads, concave grooves big enough to pour half a bottle of Chianti into; but why you would want to do that I don't know. On the stairs there was no handrail. At the top I believe there was a low rail but we never got that far to find out.

For some reason, partly because, other than up, we didn't know where we were going but mainly because we were thick, after nearly three hundred odd steps, we took a wrong turning and came out on the highest external loggia. If you look at a picture of the tower, the external loggias are the layers, with pillars, beneath the top of the cake. Here there was no guard rail and the surface, although a few feet wide, protested against friction. This may not have been such a problem if it were not for that stupid lean.

The tower was closed in 1990 because the lean had reached 5.5 degrees and I imagine this was also the angle of preference in 1983. I know this incline doesn't sound too extreme and it probably wouldn't have been were it not for the forces exerted by gravity and the power of the brain to bend perception.

On an inexplicable impulse, driven by stupidity rather than bravery, we decided to walk round the tower on this narrow, frictionless, unfenced loggia in our highly suitable, smooth-soled, leather sandals. The first quarter of the journey was not too bad because we had emerged on the side which was leaning back but after that we found ourselves starting to lean increasingly outwards. Gravity was encouraging us to take a closer look at the vertiginous view and perhaps even to make a more intimate inspection of the terra cotta Tuscan topsoil below. Leaning back against the wall only forced our feet further outwards as we inched ourselves around, sandals shuffling swishily, slipping on glassy white marble. Eileen froze and I had to try to coax her round even though I'd developed disco legs. I envisaged breaking my record for the 50 metres, vertically. In this case it wouldn't just be the record that I would break. They would be scraping Peacock pizza off the piazza in Pisa. This lurid mental image didn't help the nerves.

After what seemed like 360 hours we completed the 360 degree journey and jellywobbled back down the steps. I thought my legs would never recover. We went to a bar to calm our nerves. A few hours/beers later my legs had gone again.

I am aware that some readers may complain that these holiday anecdotes have nothing to do with running. In defence I would say that the running shorts were a prominent element and that my legs, undeniably useful in running, also featured. More pertinent though, I feel, is the fact that these tales are cautionary and flag up the many and various dangers that holidaying presents when training for an important running race. My advice is, where possible, stay at home.

Somehow I made it through the holidays and I could concentrate on the marathon. Outside running, two things happened in September which were to have lasting repercussions for many people. Ian McGregor was made head of the National Coal Board. This would indirectly cause me to become much more politically active than I had been since university days. The government also privatised cleaning, catering and laundry in the NHS, starting the erosion of the Health Service which still seems to be the mission of so many politicians today, mostly those who can afford private health care. A school term had started and I had to get my priorities right. At that time my mind was firmly fixed on improving my marathon time.

Sunday September 25th

It may seem hard to believe but after a year the Marinaman's Marina was still going strong and it got me to the race again even though the organisers tried to fool it by changing the start/finish area. This had been relocated to more attractive surroundings; a wide green sward of parkland at the foot of Woolton woods in South Liverpool.

The weather was perfect for running, an overcast, mild day with no wind to talk of. Looking round I tried to guess which (by their outfit or demeanour) of the other runners were newbies or which were old hands and legs like me! Then I had to remind myself that, since schooldays, I had only ever run one running race and that was twelve months ago. Still, I felt in control. And what a difference a year makes. I started conservatively and ran within myself all the way round. Although the start/finish area was in a different place on the route it was basically the same course and I could ask myself at similar points, how I felt compared to last year. The answer came back each time, 'so much better'.

If I placed pictures of myself finishing the '82 and '83 Mersey Marathons side by side it would possibly constitute the easiest spot the difference competition ever. Even a two-year-old could do it, presuming that they understood the task and weren't too busy trying to poke a breadstick into a wall socket. The only similarity to be found was that I was obviously still clinging to vestiges of my past as a non-serious runner in that my faithful vest was still clinging to me (in threadbare cotton, by M&S, now of uncertain hue).

Nor could the post-race experience have been more different. One important fact this year was that blood decided to stay. In fact, it was whooshing around me in swashbuckling style. I am pictured holding my medal to my mouth with one hand and biting it (the medal not the hand) whilst toasting myself with a pint of beer in the other. And who said men couldn't multi-task? The previous year the most I could muster was taking in the minimum amount of oxygen to avoid expiration before the next inhalation. Apparently I wasn't the only person in better shape because the St John's Ambulance only treated 350 casualties, half as many as in 1982.

I was also experiencing another unfamiliar sensation; the much vaunted runners' high. I was buzzing. I felt like a million dollars and I was talking at a million miles an hour but making even less sense than usual. Earlier, I had ambled casually over the finish line under a banner on which 'Tetley Bittermen' was printed in red lettering (matching my shorts). But I was not a Bitterman because the clock read 3:07:14; a huge PB (personal best) by nearly 20 minutes. Almost as soon as I had finished, my endorphin fuelled, electric brain was planning the next marathon and calculating the increase in speed necessary to run under three hours, the Holy Grail for most modest marathon runners. The answer came back quicker than a flash drive; approximately 16 seconds per mile. A tough ask believe you me but, the way I felt, not out of reach. I then suddenly realised that all the things I thought I was thinking I was blabbering.

(Spot the difference; '82 surrendering, '83 multi-tasking.)

"Are you ever going to shut up? I think I preferred you in last year's comatose state," said Eileen. Marinaman smiled and nodded.

As autumn settled on Sefton Park, the horse chestnut trees glowed like beacons against the bleaching sky. Orange leaves tacked lazily from tree to ground in order to mirror the branches. The perimeter was further illuminated by the occasional tree in a defiant red (the leaves vainly attempting to mirror the majesty of my shorts). I was running silently alongside Whistler, in a reverie, imagining future glory, when he suddenly spoke. The sound of his voice never failed to take me by surprise.

"What do think about ten?"

Ten what, I thought, ten pounds? Was he making an offer for the shorts? 10 o'clock? Was he suggesting a time for our next run? Ten gloves? Was he putting a figure on the most left-handers he'd picked up in one month? I stopped the mental conjecturing and asked him.

"Ten what?"

" Miles," he assibilated.

"I thought we were doing thirteen."

"No, a race."

"A ten mile race?"

He nodded. A little door of possibilities opened in my head. I'd never thought about other distances. Like many other newcomers to running, for me it had all been about the marathon and its challenge, not about other, far less insane distances.

"Preston Fire Brigade 10, October 23rd."

He could be so clinically informative when called upon.

"It's a date." I enthused.

"True." He quietly conceded.

And so it was that I began to diversify in running distances. This ten-miler was to be the first of many races under the marathon length; 5k, five miles, 10k, ten miles, half marathons and 20 miles, occasionally four or eight miles. It may seem a bit obvious but it had just dawned on me that one of the ways of improving my marathon speed would be to run shorter distances as fast as I could. Also, every distance would provide its own challenge. I was suddenly excited by the thought that I wouldn't have to wait another year before bouncing along the blackstuff again.

Whistler and his partner shared a Polo, a car that is, not a mint. I shall call his girlfriend K2. She was a climber who had some strange views which I can only presume were a result of her spending too much time on high ground. She definitely had an altitude problem. She wasn't keen on running or runners. She argued that it was a middle-class activity compared to climbing. She wasn't exactly the salt of the earth herself so I took her comments with a pinch of it.

Climbing she believed was democratic, all for one and one for all and buy one get one free. But, at the same time, she thought it an esoteric sport unlike road running which was just like walking around to the shops, only usually quicker. She gave me the impression that she and other climbers looked down on road runners which I suppose they couldn't help doing, being so high up. In my view running was a way of testing yourself without risking life and limb. Climbing was scary. I know, I had been up the Tower of Pisa in leather sandals. Some climbers seemed to think that the danger element in their sport made them superior to other athletes. Arguing against K2's warped perception was futile and only created friction between her and Whistler. However, in my opinion her comparison of the sports was obviously flawed even, as I found out, when including the peril element.

Subsequent extensive research (I read it in a magazine in the dentist's waiting room) revealed to me that it was a myth that running was safer than climbing. Climbing was actually relatively safe. You were much more likely to die during a surgical procedure than while climbing. (It's especially hazardous to be involved in both at the same time.) In the US, research of 11 million runners showed that, between the years 2000 and 2010, one out of 259,000 people running half and full marathons dropped dead, while, in the UK, a study revealed that one climber died for every 320,000 climbs. So I suppose you could use (manipulate/skew) these statistics to claim that running is the more dangerous sport. So that must mean that we runners are the real dare devils not mountaineers. So, climbers, get down off your high horses, but do be careful.

Addressing the subject of democracy, the thing I loved about running was that I believed it to be one of the most accessible sports. You didn't need a long list of elaborate or expensive paraphernalia to partake. All you needed was appropriate footwear. Theoretically even this wasn't essential. In 1960 Abebe Bikila won the marathon in the Rome Olympics in bare feet, his own!

Running was also democratic because it helped people to get out and help others. The amount of money raised for charity by individuals sponsored to run many distances in many outfits and in many weird ways was huge. By 2010 it was calculated that since the first race in 1981, £500 million had been raised for charities in the London Marathon alone. I liked to run my races with no frills but didn't have any problem with other people forever trying to come up with different ways to complete the distance. (The fact that Michael Jackson had unveiled his 'Moonwalk' on a Motown 25 TV special in 1983 perturbed me a little. I anticipated serious headaches for race organisers trying to encourage MJ look-alikes to travel in roughly the right direction on the course.) At the end of the day if you asked a group of runners why they wanted to complete a marathon or why they wanted to do it in a certain way their answers would probably all be different. That was the beauty of it.

Whistler was waiting in their car when I arrived at his house on the Fire Brigade Ten race day. I opened the passenger side door and immediately gave him a withering look as the fetid internal air wafted up into my face.

"Sheep shit", he stated sheepishly.

My look said, "Oh yeah."

"She blames me for bringing it in, I blame her. We both refuse to clean it up," he explained.

I raised my eyebrows and got in. We took off, heading north, engulfed in a pungent fug. To be honest, the odour had an ammoniacal quality and, as I'd had a few hoppy relaxers the previous night, it acted like smelling salts to wake me up. It wasn't long before my nerves also started to work and I added my own nuances to enhance the car's internal atmosphere; crapulous caromas.

On arriving at the ten mile race venue, the Fire Service Headquarters in Preston, the first thing I noticed was that everyone seemed calmer than pre-marathon. The number of entrants was much smaller. Groups of runners were chatting away and it all felt quite intimate.

I ran with Whistler; this was the first time I had done so in a race. As we progressed I felt comfortable and was enjoying the experience. At about eight miles he gasped, "We're nearly doing sub-six minute miles." He was plainly suffering a little more than me and, as I knew that getting under an hour for 10 miles was quite a respectable achievement, I decided to push on in the last two miles.

I still felt easy and had plenty of energy left. I completed the race in 59:56 and was quietly pleased. Whistler did 1:00:07 and was quietly quiet. My time convinced me that I should step up my training further. A marathon time of less than three hours seemed to be possible. I also felt that I was capable of doing more than one marathon in a year. After some consideration, I entered for the Wolverhampton Marathon in March of 1984. The fever was beginning to take hold.

Chapter 3

1984 Running for the Miners and with Whistler

"To all Duranies we say respect the Marathon in Everyway as the best thing that has happened to your town."

This strangely patronising quote is part of a message from the popular music group Duran Duran, which appeared in the 1984 Wolverhampton Marathon programme. On the last day of March I was preparing to take on the 26 andabit mile challenge again and had received my number and a programme through the post. As I read through this communiqué from the stars I asked myself two questions: Firstly, why did Duran x2 feel the need to make 'every way' a compound word and then give it a capital letter (..respect the Marathon in Everyway)? Was this done for emphasis or was it a typing error? Lead singer and heart throb, Simon Le Bon was notoriously cack-handed on a typewriter. Or was it possible that Everyway was an area in Wolverhampton, on the marathon route, which was known to be generally unsupportive of long distance foot races? Perhaps many of the residents were allergic to 'Fiery Jack' or maybe their apathy or antipathy stemmed from the fact that Everyway was the centre of Wolverhampton's mountain climbing community? Who knows? I obviously didn't.

My second query was; what kind of place has a marathon at number one on their 'best thing to happen to our town' list? I racked my brain but only came up with Edinburgh of the Seven Seas, capital of Tristan da Cunha.

As I scanned this message, asking myself these unanswerable questions, I became bored and my eyes drifted up to the soft focussed photo of the dreamy pop quartet above it. I enjoyed imagining what havoc would be caused to their bouffant barnets by running into a 40 mph headwind. Tempestuous whiplash and temper tantrums would ensue, no doubt. But, hey boys, respect backatya for the support and the attempt to get the 'Everyway' folk on board.

Meanwhile, back on the road, I carried on with my intent to run more races under the marathon distance in order to compliment my training and to experience a different kind of running. I had entered my first ever half marathon, in Ormskirk, some three weeks before the Wolverhampton event.

Ormskirk is a market town thirteen miles north of Liverpool's city centre. It was once the hub of commercial activity for the flat agricultural lands of West Lancashire and is still the regional administrative centre for the West Lancashire borough council. Harold Wilson, Labour prime minister in office twice between 1964 and 1976, was MP for Ormskirk from 1945 to 1950 before becoming MP for Huyton. Ermm… and that's about it. Oh, except that the town boasts the distinction of having a church with a tower and a steeple, both at the same end. This gives the visual impression that, in days gone by, the tower and the church suffered a head on collision. Apart from these thrilling claims to fame, it's a quiet township and a suitable place for a running event because the roads are relatively traffic-free and comparatively flat.

I completed the course in 1 hour 19 minutes and 44 seconds and felt reasonably satisfied with my first crack at a 'half'. I also noted how much easier it was to race at this distance compared to the full marathon. The formula for calculating estimated marathon times from half marathon performances does not always produce accurate results, mainly because of the multitude of disasters that can befall a runner in the mysterious and unpredictable twilight zone that is the last six or so miles of the full distance. However, it has been claimed that if you multiplied your current half marathon time by two and then added 10 to 20 minutes this would give you some idea of how you might be able to perform in a marathon. Using this formula I was definitely on for a sub-three hour marathon in three weeks' time (barring being attacked by wild ice-axe wielding climbers or incensed embrocation allergy sufferers at the 19 mile mark in the Everyway suburb of Wolverhampton).

Just to the southeast of Ormskirk lay the coalfields of Lancashire. A decision made early in the year by the new head of the Coal Board, Ian Mcgregor, backed by the Thatcher government, would soon have a profound effect on communities there. The proposal was to implement an accelerated closure of coal mines, with the aim of making the industry more 'efficient'. Five days before the Ormskirk Half, the National Union of Mineworkers, faced with what they felt was an attack on their industry, communities and jobs, called a national strike. This was one of two political events, in this year, which would capture my imagination and stir my emotions; the other being the Zola Budd fiasco.

Late in March, however, I was focussing on Wolverhampton. Amongst all the preparations, at the back of my mind, deep in the section labelled 'Miscellaneous', was an intermittently flickering light bulb of awareness, which occasionally illuminated the knowledge that my elder sister, who I had not seen or contacted for at least a decade, now lived in Wolverhampton. We had drifted apart, as brothers and sisters can do. This information about her general whereabouts had not yet been transferred to the 'Facts I Must Act On' section of my brain. So, for the moment, I switched the light off.

Whistler had a friend; in fact he had several friends, unlike me. This particular friend lived in a house on the banks of the river Severn in the Ironbridge gorge, Coalbrookdale, Shropshire, close to Wolverhampton. 'Coalbrookdale at Night' *(1801)*, Philip James de Loutherbourg's painting, is one of the great images of the Industrial Revolution. It depicted a scene, previously idyllically rural, (carthorses and a human figure in the foreground hint at this past) now dominated by incandescent furnaces. It created an image of hell on earth. The place has, somewhat simplistically, been described as the birthplace of the Industrial Revolution. It certainly played an important role in the development of the mass production of good quality iron from the late 18th century.

When I was born in Middlesbrough in 1951, iron and steel producers Dorman Long were one of the town's main employers and the industry figured prominently in my family history. My father was an electrician at the steel works. (One of his favourite jokes from a limited and unconvincing portfolio went like this; I worked for Dorman but not for Long.) Both my grandfathers were also steel workers at this firm before nationalisation in 1967. My maternal grandfather's father and grandfather were iron workers. My great, great, grandfather was specifically a puddler. This was a dangerous and exhausting job which involved stirring molten pig iron to get rid of impurities. My ancestors were forced to leave the industrial area surrounding Coalbrookdale when iron and steel production declined. They moved to Middlesbrough, on the coast, where the industry had grown because of easy access to cheap imported iron ore. So I suppose you could say iron was definitely in my blood (isn't it in everybody's?).

Coalbrookdale was no longer a vision of hell. Nature had fought back as soon as industry vacated the area. It eventually became a peaceful and attractive World Heritage Site with 'living' museums to illustrate and explain the area's tumultuous and significant history. The Ironbridge area is of course named after its wooden church. Just kidding, it is the site of Abraham Darby's unique, single span, cast iron bridge. Opened in 1781, it not only provided the benefit of a safe river crossing but also became a monument to the skills of the pioneering ironmasters.

Whistler suggested we should roll the Polo down to Coalbrookdale the Saturday before the Wolverhampton race, avoiding a 90-odd mile drive in the morning before the start. His friend had offered to put us up. I had no objections as long as he didn't put us up too high. Whistler and his friend were out of the same mould. Saturday night by the Severn was not a wild or raucous affair and words hung in the air for minutes rather than seconds before they were replaced sparingly. This atmosphere conserved energy but drained my ebullient spirit. It left me far too much time to think about the race. I became nervous.

The friend's house was in a fairly secluded spot on the river but far from quiet, as the water roared down the gorge. Flooding was a perennial problem here and, as many of the older houses were built on industrial waste tips, subsidence was also a worry. I was beginning to wish I had been put up higher. After a fitful sleep, filled with dreams of running for my life, one step ahead of a raging torrent, I was pleased to wake up on Sunday, in the same place, geographically if not mentally. In fact, I was just pleased to wake up. A two hour drive down the motorway might have been less stressful.

Race-day bowels soon set in. A light breakfast was followed by three heavy visits to pebble dash the porcelain and unload the carbs.

This had become the pre-competition norm. Whistler's friend's toilet had an interesting location in that it was virtually suspended over the river, with a great view of its sweep. As I sat, enthroned, I could see canoeists riding the fierce flow. I hoped they wouldn't be fatally distracted, catching sight of me, caught with my pants down, going through a similar process.

The time came, unbelievably slowly, to leave Whistler's friend and he managed an understated goodbye gesture, more of a tic than a wave, as we left the dale. Conversation with my chauffeur on the short journey to Wolverhampton was restricted to talk of where the start was, where to park, what to wear and race pace. Whistler always had a clothing dilemma in temperatures below 67.5° F. To wear or not to wear, a thermal long-sleeved T shirt, or a 'lifer' as we often called them. I tended to go for the beige, cotton vest (M&S) whatever the weather. My theory was that you always warmed up after a mile or so of hard running and a 'lifer' would eventually make you sweat too much and therefore dehydrate. Whistler, on the other hand, thought it was essential to keep the upper body warm; physiologically, because it made it function better and psychologically because he was a southerner. There was a light drizzle. He went thermal, I went vest. We decided on three hour finish pace.

Finally, all the nervous faffing about over, the race was under way. Just after halfway, we were a little slower than sub-three hour pace but I still felt fresh. I could sense the barely perceptible signs of Whistler struggling. I turned and told him I was going to have a go at breaking three hours. He nodded with a face which spoke much more than his mouth usually did. It said a mixture of 'go on, leave me you bastard' and 'there's no way I can run any faster'. One thing you do learn in marathon running is that, if you are going for a time, you have to run your own race. Well, that was my excuse for abandoning him.

As I forged ahead and exerted a little more pressure on myself I noticed how many people I was overtaking, runners who had started too quickly. Towards the 23 mile mark I went past a gnarled veteran who looked 85 but was probably only 32. He turned and gasped, "If you keep that up you'll break three hours." This prophecy from a striding soothsayer spurred me on further and, to my delight, actually came to pass as I continued to pass. Making my last effort down the finishing straight I could see the clock reading 2:58 andabit. I eventually finished in exactly 2 hours and 59 minutes.

Whistler came in grumpily with 3 hours 10 minutes and 17 seconds. My 'well dones' fell on deaf ears. The truth was that, although he had run well, I think he sensed an ability gap was opening between us. On the way home I talked enough for both of us and made up for the three of us the previous night. In a manic monologue I was meeting the weekend's required word quotas with plenty to spare.

Looking back at the eight-page-results-souvenir produced by the Wolverhampton Express and Star I came across this enlightened report on Leslie Watson's winning of the women's race:

"Lesley's 98th Marathon

Turning heads as she led the ladies home was stunning 34-year-old Lesley Watson. A real catch for anyone who can keep up with her, unmarried auburn haired Lesley finished in two and three quarter hours. Running her 98th marathon she crossed the finishing line to cheers and wolf whistles from the crowd lining the ring road." (They couldn't even get her name right!)

In the name of gender equality I decided to write a piece in a similar vein about my own triumph. Here goes;

"Drawing gasps of admiration from the adoring crowds, gorgeous 33-year-old Toni Peacock strode manfully across the line in 665th place. Sorry ladies, but swarthy dark haired divorcee Tonee, who finished in two hours and fifty nine minutes, is already spoken for. Running only his third marathon, he crossed the finish line to shouts of 'Cor, love the red shorts, sexy legs' and jeers from jealous local mountain climbers."

Surprisingly, the report on the male winner was nothing like this.

Over the next few months my running was destined to be intertwined with politics. If, for some reason, anybody had asked me to describe my politics in one word I probably would have replied 'emotional'. To misquote Robert Zimmerman, I didn't 'follow leaders, I watched the parking meters' (I'm not sure why because I didn't have a car).

THE FIGHT GOES ON – Tony Peacock and Shirley Jackson of the Liverpool 8 Miners' Aid Committee prepare for the Saturday collection of food outside Leo's. The miners' strike is nearing eight months now and continued support is essential if they are to win their fight for jobs.

(Collecting money for the miners in Liverpool 8)

I admired certain people in politics but never revered them. I agreed with certain ideas but not necessarily how they were put into practice. I supported certain causes but not necessarily the means by which they were promoted. I was never particularly interested in joining a political party, or group. To paraphrase Marx (Groucho not Karl), I wouldn't want to belong to any party which would accept me as a member. At the end of the day I believed we were all equal and no-one perfect, especially me. My politics tended to be issue-based and my commitment tissue thin.

The miners' strike was an issue I was committed to in a peripheral way and I'm sure it was an event everyone had an opinion on. What I saw was a large number of union members withdrawing their labour, not for more money, but in an effort to save their jobs and communities. The way the dispute developed and was dealt with resulted in extreme hardship for the strikers and their families.

I never truly believed that the miners were going to win the struggle against a government whose real aim was to crush their union but I wanted to do a little bit to help support their dependants. For the first time, in a dispute like this, the restriction of welfare benefits normally given to families in need was used as a weapon against strikers. Clause 6 of the 1980 Social Security Act stopped strikers' families claiming 'urgent needs' payments. This was a direct attempt to force union members back to work through their children. Most of those involved in the strike had to rely on donations to survive.

As a supporter of the Liverpool 8 Miners' Aid Committee I helped to collect gifts of food, door-to-door and outside supermarkets in some of the poorest areas of Liverpool. The response was remarkable. It strengthened my view that those who understood deprivation were more willing to help others in the same boat. A particular example sticks in my mind. At one house an old man shuffled to the door. When we had explained our presence he turned away and after some rummaging in the kitchen, came back with a white sliced loaf. 'It's all I've got,' he said. I told him to keep it but he insisted that I accept his donation, saying he wanted to do his bit. Reluctantly but humbly I accepted his offering. I could see it meant so much to him that I did.

We had a few harsh words from a few people while collecting but the vast majority were supportive. This was in an area where riots had exploded three years previously. You could see they understood what taking away employment did to a community. Those in power didn't or couldn't care less.

Another way in which I planned to help was by being sponsored for running a marathon with the proceeds going to the families support fund. I hurriedly entered the Birmingham Sunblest People's Marathon, scheduled for May 27th, hoping for more than another white loaf. The running of two marathons with only two months between was going to be a stern test for me but one I could not afford to fail. There was more than my Mother's Pride riding on it.

Wanting to maintain some intensity in my training before Birmingham I entered a half marathon which was organised by the Greenbank Centre, a local disability training facility on the edge of Sefton Park. The course included five laps of the 2.3 mile perimeter of the park which, as previously related, I was already intimately familiar with (left-handed gloves and all). Having never done so many laps continuously I was worried that I might be overcome by dizziness and go crashing into a tree rather than hitting the wall.

Arriving at the start, it was evident that there was a small field of runners. It seemed that the race hadn't been particularly well advertised. Not many fast runners appeared to know about it. I say this with certainty because, well under 90 minutes later, I was amazed to find myself finishing in third position. This was the highest I had come in any leg race since 1966 when I had won an 800 metres race at school. To be honest that wasn't even an official race. I was in a group of kids forced, by a burly bellowing PE teacher, to run two laps of the track for forgetting our kit. My surprising turn of speed, on that occasion, had been generated by the desire to get back to the warmth of the changing rooms.

After my third place in the half marathon I experienced a combination of shock and elation which might have killed a lesser athlete but I cantered the mile home to tell Eileen that there was a desperate need to break open the ale, in celebration. On reflection I may have been a little hasty dashing off so quickly because, it transpired that, not only had the centre laid on a 'Disco and Bar' but prizes were to be presented by Liverpool FC stars Craig Johnson and Bruce Grobbelaar.

Just over a month later and three days after my appearance in the Birmingham Marathon, goalkeeper Grobbelaar would be performing his famous 'wobbly legs' routine intended to put off Italian player

Graziani, in a penalty shoot-out to decide the outcome of the European Cup Final between Roma and Liverpool. It appeared to work. Graziani missed and Liverpool won. It's rumoured that Bruce got the idea for the 'spaghetti legs' distraction from watching me finish the Green Bank Project Microtech Half Marathon. (If I'd gone to the disco I could have performed a real pasta pins master class for him.) I cannot verify if there is any truth in this rumour even though I'm the person spreading it. Nevertheless, it was a momentous day for me, a first three finish and my photo in the local paper. It has also been suggested that Craig and Bruce were gutted that I'd left early because they didn't get my autograph (same source).

When I received my number for the Birmingham Marathon it was accompanied by a useful booklet on training and preparation for the event, produced by Tom O'Reilly and John Walker. The information which most interested me was the section on suggested kit for training:

"Two sets of clothing would be our minimum recommendation to someone running on a regular basis, this should comprise of: two to four T-shirts (including both long and short sleeves), two vests, three or four shorts, four pairs of socks, one or two track suits and at least one good wind proof wet suit and gloves, these are a must for adverse weather."

This list left me agog. There were more garments here than in my entire everyday wardrobe. It was also confusing. Were three or four shorts the same as one and a half or two pairs of shorts? And why was a wind proof wet suit a 'must' for adverse weather? Up North we usually made do with a layer of goose fat covered with brown paper. The list did, however, get me thinking. Maybe my somewhat limited kit list of one red short(s) and one vest (M&S) needed revision; but perhaps at a later date when I'd won the pools.

Looking at the pamphlet recently it still left me slightly agog but mainly aggrieved. The added ag was caused by the half page advert for a Marathon Bar on the back: "Packed with Peanuts, Marathon really satisfies." Why, oh why, oh why, the bloody change of name for one of my favourite confections? Snickers? Sounds like knickers worn by a snake, ridiculous! My eyes still fill with tears of sadness, frustration and anger! Well, err, yes, moving on.

The Birmingham Marathon was to be a significant occasion for me. To begin with there was money riding on it; this was the first, but certainly not the last time I was to be sponsored for wearing my joints out. Secondly, it had become a family affair. Eileen and her clan hailed from Birmingham and they were all loyally turning out, mainly to check that I was fulfilling the criteria for receiving their sponsorship monies.

We were staying at Eileen's mum and dad's and the race finished near her brother's house in Chelmsley Wood, where we planned to gather, après-ski-daddle. She also had three sisters many of whom were there, but I can't put an exact number on it. However, most importantly for me, it was a family affair because Laura, my six-year-old daughter (from a previous marriage, as they say) was also there. The first time she had been to one of my marathon races.

Laura's mum and I had decided our marriage was a mistake shortly after Laura's birth. Maybe we should also have listened to Marx's opinion on marriage, 'don't make the same mistake once' (again Groucho not Karl). When things were obviously going wrong I made the decision that, even though the marriage had failed, I wanted to try to make my fatherhood successful. I wanted to be fully involved; easier said than done. That weekend, however, everyone was there.

An unwelcome and unpleasant visitor had also arrived. He shall be known as Flemming Green. In other words I had developed a really crappy cold the previous week and, to be honest, I felt like I had custard soaked cotton wool packing my sinuses, a thicket of brambles on my chest and a Showaddywaddy song in my heart. I felt like a million dollops. I'd never tried to run a marathon race with a bad cold and all sensible medical advice warned against it. But the show-waddywaddy had to go on.

I started gingerly to check out how my body felt. Riding on a flood of phlegm and sputum, I couldn't feel anything so I just kept going. The only thing I remember well about the run was seeing all the relatives gathered, in the drizzle at 20 mile, barely sheltered by the air-raid bunker architecture of the Swan shopping centre. That little huddled group, in front of a backdrop of grey skies and concrete high rise, seemed to have a radiating glow around them, like Baby

Jesus in a porridge advert. For a few fleeting seconds I basked in their relative comfort. My daughter watched my not-so-stately passage with worried eyes and, I was told, burst into tears immediately after I'd run past, demanding to know where I was going. To be honest even I wasn't sure of that. I do know I was digging deep for the miners. The finish couldn't come soon enough so it didn't. As I stumbled over the line I managed to raise my snot heavy head to look at the clock. It read 2:57:13, a PB, nearly two minutes quicker than Wolverhampton. This time should have induced a sense of surprise and pleasure but I was too drained to feel either.

International marathon man Charlie Spedding had been the official race starter and was also there to see the earlier finishers cross the line. He had recently won the London Marathon and been selected to run for Great Britain over the marathon distance at the Los Angeles Olympics, later in the year. He would go on to win a brilliant bronze medal there. The Birmingham Mail reported him as admitting that he had 'itchy feet' when he fired the starting pistol. *Charlie,* I thought, *I can recommend an excellent anti-fungal cream for that.*

I was just thankful and hanky-full for a 'job done' with the bonus of a personal best. I sat on a chair in the middle of Eileen's brother's kitchen with the commotion of cooking and a cacophony of chatter from assorted sisters swirling around me. Unable to conjure up conversation or indeed movement, I was an inert island in an ocean of prandial pandemonium. The Sunblest UK People's Marathon was done but I felt like a lump of raw dough. Nevertheless, it had been worth finishing because, as a result of my efforts, I raised nearly a £1000 for miners' families, a big chunk of which came via a friend of Eileen's who, being a shop steward on the Liverpool docks, offered to take my sponsorship forms to his generous union members. I remember well his battle-scarred face as he locked his battleship blue, unblinking eyes on to mine while counting a wad of ten pound notes into my hand. Not an easy manoeuvre and extremely scary. God knows how he would have looked at me if I hadn't completed the run? So a good result all round.

The summer of '84 was predominantly sunny. (It does happen occasionally!) This was good news for one large patch of South Liverpool because, in May, the International Garden Festival was opened by the Queen. Its gardens had been constructed at Otterspool, a reclaimed and greened landfill site, by the banks of the river Mersey. The staging of the event had been encouraged by Michael Heseltine, in his unofficial capacity as 'minister for Merseyside'. This was one of several initiatives in response to the 1981 riots which attempted to attract business and jobs to Liverpool and the surrounding areas. The general feeling locally was that these schemes were just gestures, unsustainable and of no long-lasting benefit to the community.

Heseltine was a dove in a government dominated by a cabinet of hawks. Official papers released in 2011 confirm that, in actual fact, the main government response to the riots in '81 was to give police forces better equipment and more powerful weapons to deal with public disorder.

The festival was brief but beautiful, a bit like a runner's high or my red shorts. Sumptuously created gardens from around the world embellished a majestic setting with panoramic views of the wide and mighty Mersey. Over the river, across the Wirral peninsula and beyond the river Dee, the hills of Clwyd and the mountains of Snowdonia could often be seen, carved clearly on the crystal morning sky or glowing scarlet like a sleeping dragon as the sun set over a Celtic sea.

Being only a mile or so from our flat we occasionally went down to the gardens in the evenings when the main crowds had dispersed and the price of entry was lowered. Many locals, especially those unemployed, could not even afford the discounted entrance fee. There were 60 individual gardens outdoors and indoor exhibits in the domed Festival Hall. We were often attracted by the tempting fragrance emanating from the Dutch gardens. The bar there was selling Oranjeboom beer, cheap.

Over the opening period from May to October 3,380,000 visitors passed through the gates, then after that err …none, because the gates were locked. It seems that there had been no real thought as to who was going to maintain the gardens afterwards. They had been privately developed on a short term basis and no one seemed interested in keeping them open for the public in the long term. The Militant dominated council would or could not step in as they were already at loggerheads with the government over funding. Half the site was given over to the building of private houses and the festival hall was used for a variety of purposes before it was closed in 1996 and then demolished in 2006. The once beautiful gardens were left to grow into a flimsily fenced-off wilderness. This fact was to lead to embarrassment for the council although it was not really their fault.

In 2000, a delegation from China arrived in Liverpool to oversee the construction of a magnificent arch to be built at the entrance to Chinatown, which is located near the city centre's southern edge close to the Anglican Cathedral. The area was home to the oldest Chinese community in Europe. The structure was to be the largest, multiple-span arch of its kind outside China. The much admired and grandiose Chinese gardens built on the festival site in 1984 had been funded by the government of the Peoples Republic (of China not Liverpool). The 2000 delegation were naturally keen to see how the gardens had 'matured'. After giving up on the idea of trying the old magical mystery tour trip-trick of slipping LSD into their green tea and driving them about in a windowless bus, shame-faced local officials had to show the disappointed Chinese visitors a scene of dereliction and neglect. The Garden Festival had been a short term wallpapering job to mask the real problems of the city and the cracks had soon appeared again.

On June 18th the government's investment in police resources after the '81 riots was put to 'good' use. When about 5000 miners picketed the Orgreave coking plant near Rotherham they were confronted by over 5000 newly equipped policemen, mostly South Yorkshire's finest, who appeared to be led by men who lacked the human touch, to put it mildly. (This impression would be tragically reinforced in another 'crowd control' operation by this regional police force later in the decade.) The officers with shiny new truncheons drawn, repeatedly charged the miners, inflicting serious wounds on several individuals.

A colliery worker, in Liverpool to raise funds for miner's families, tried to explain to me what it felt like to have been at

Orgreave. He described how the picket line, manned by strikers dressed for summer in jeans, T-shirts and trainers were set upon by police dressed for battle, wearing full protective body gear and boots, wielding batons and shields, many mounted on horseback. He admitted to having been frightened for his life. Some miners organised themselves against the charges and tried to defend their lines. Can you blame them?

This account may seem one-sided but the fact was that as early as 1991 the South Yorkshire Police were made to pay out £425,000 to 39 miners arrested at the incident. That was probably just the tip of the iceberg. It was almost as if the police were being used to wage class warfare against union members who were just trying to protect their livelihoods and communities.

By June I had already run two marathons but that year I had got a touch of marathon fever, which is a bit like boogywoogy flu only you have the runs for longer. Against all the normal logic of how many marathons a person should run in one year (the common view was that two was more than enough, some thought once a lifetime was) I planned to run three more. The first marathon of the three was intended to have been run for altruistic reasons. Whistler was desperate to run under three hours and had entered the Manchester Piccadilly Marathon because it was a flat, fast course. He also now considered me to be a sub-three guru since my twin triumphs in the West Midlands. He asked me to pace him to achieve his goal. I cheerfully agreed to take on the task. Even as I nodded and smiled, accepting the job, I was thinking that running your own race was the key.

In the end, all Whistler's plan achieved was to boost my confidence and regrettably dent his further. I stuck to my task, running even pace and trying to encourage him to as he got slower and slower and his knee lift got lower and lower. By 22 miles it was obvious that we weren't going to go under three hours and Whistler was tiring rapidly. I, on the other hand, was full of beans running at that pace. So much so that I got distracted from my support role and started to take the lead. I confess to showboating a little; bantering with the crowd, signing autographs, drinking champagne, kissing babies, conducting civil ceremonies and generally making an arse of myself. Whistler sank deeper and deeper into the slough of despond. We finished in 3 hours 14 minutes and 46 seconds. He was really disappointed, having posted a slower time than in Wolverhampton, whereas I had just run a decent marathon hardly breaking sweat, wind (in spite of being full of beans) or the bank of energy. Maybe I came across as a little too pleased with myself and not sorry enough for him. Looking at the results I didn't even allow him the courtesy of finishing in front of me. Two weeks afterwards our roles were to be reversed but with a somewhat different outcome.

Due to the fact that, for some unfathomable reason, I had been ignored by British selectors and not chosen for the marathon team to run in the LA Olympics, I decided to enter an equally prestigious event, the Wirral Charities Marathon. This was scheduled for July 15th, two weeks before the opening ceremony of that City of Angels sideshow. After my merry Mancunian meander I was crackling with confidence. Whistler suggested that he could join me at half way for encouragement in the last thirteen miles. I could hardly refuse his seemingly charitable offer in this charities race even though as I nodded in acceptance I was thinking, *I'm going to run my own race*. I also had a niggling suspicion that in some way he might want to get revenge for my dereliction of duty in Manchester. In this race the professor would become the freshman as I faded. Would he take this opportunity to display the same lack of respect as I had appeared to? Would he take advantage of my tiredness? Was all this running making me paranoid? After some thought I dismissed my concerns on the grounds that Whistler showboating was as likely as the Pope pole-dancing.

The Wirral peninsula punches squarely northwest into the Irish Sea like a sandstone fist. Known generally to Scousers as 'over the water', it is joined to Liverpool by three tunnels, two road and one rail. The river Mersey washes its northeastern shore, still busy with some mercantile activity and chemical industries. The river Dee flows by its low southwestern cliffs with their Arcadian airs and graces and salty air and grasses. The two river coasts were like chalk and cheese but all sandstone. The race was due to start and finish at Parkgate in the far southwest of this huge Jurassic jetty.

Parkgate is a seaside fishing village with no sea. Postcards produced in the early 1900s show bonneted children paddling in pools on a sandy beach. In 1984 there were still fisherman's cottages, but only by name not by present occupants' occupation. The tidal waters of the Dee were now a mile away, across grassy marshland created by silt, constantly deposited by the river and forcing its flow ever closer to the distant Welsh coast. A once wide, generous, estuary gradually reduced to a mean channel; a once flourishing fishing village now sedately reminiscing about the good old days. The last mile of the race would be run alongside the village's sea wall with no sea.

I arrived courtesy of a Merseyrail train under the river and a bus from Birkenhead (the Wirral's main town which faces Liverpool across the Mersey); from gritty city to pastoral pastures in forty minutes. I felt confident but not complacent. I knew that the course followed country lanes repeatedly zigzagging up then down, from sea level to higher ground, for the whole distance. It was not a course to attempt to conquer too quickly. Setting off steadily I was soon running rhythmically. The miles passed smoothly. As I reached the half-way point, Whistler suddenly jumped out of the bushes. *You could get arrested for that,* I thought. I was well into my running but he was just starting. Initially, I sensed he was struggling to tag on because he seemed to be a stride behind me. I was running my own race, as I had promised myself.

Little by little Whistler settled into a steady cadence and I gradually got more ragged. It wasn't that I was really struggling but I did become aware of the difference in our energy levels. This wasn't helping me. I also imagined he might be enjoying the shoe being on the other foot whilst still wearing both shoes on the correct feet. It was fortunate for me that, in my short experience of long distance running, I'd discovered I usually had the ability to focus internally and block out most external distractions. On this occasion that included Whistler. I knew I was slowing but I also knew I was going to finish. With this knowledge I told myself I would complete the course as quickly as I could without blowing up. A couple of people passed me and Whistler tried to encourage me to tuck in behind them but I let them go and stuck to my own pace. Once we were by the sea wall I was seadog tired but knew it was nearly over. The little climb back up to the finish at Parksfield was a big effort but when I crossed the line my tiredness wasn't too overwhelming and was soon superseded by elation when I discovered I'd achieved yet another PB of 2:53:00, knocking off over four minutes. That equated to nearly ten seconds a mile faster. This might not seem much to a non-runner but is, in anyone's book, if you have to do it twenty six times.

After the finish Whistler commented on how he'd found it hard to keep up with me at 13 miles but it had got easier. He said that he'd tried to pull me along towards the end but that I hadn't responded. I knew he wasn't trying to take the piss and was telling me all this genuinely because you couldn't meet a gentler bloke. He had tried to tow me along at a pace I would have struggled with but wisely I had resisted. This cautious approach had allowed me to run faster than ever before!

Looking at the results I realised that I'd finished 24th out of just over 400 and less than ten minutes and only 14 places behind the running legend, Ron Hill, former European and Commonwealth marathon champion. I bathed in a warm glow of reflected glory for days. Ron was not only a great runner but also a great innovator in terms of running clothing. He produced his own range. He had trained hard as a runner but also trained as a textile chemist. This allowed him to experiment with and produce different fabrics for running garments. His comfortable leggings, called Tracksters, later became an ever-present item in my sporting wardrobe and beyond. I loved them so much I would have worn them out to the pub if Eileen had let me.

In an unconscious homage to Ron's presence in the Wirral race I had finally ditched the old M&S vest and had worn a modern lightweight mesh variety, the type he had pioneered in his early days. He was also partially responsible for me starting to write a running diary which I kept up primarily from 1985-1988. Having read his autobiography, 'The Long Hard Road,' I had been fascinated by its detail. This encouraged me to try to include as much information as I could in my diary writing. Much respect to Ron.

Ron Hill inspired me; Zola Budd made me cry. Yep, an elfin 17-year-old runner reduced me to tears; me and Mary Decker. I had been a passionate opponent of the abhorrent apartheid system in South Africa since I was a teenager. Although not actively involved in any campaigns I had always tried to make the anti-apartheid point even when it wasn't easy to. As a schoolboy who played rugby up to county level I'd argued against most friends and team mates in favour of the 'Stop the Tour' campaign when the all-white South African rugby team toured Britain in 1970. I'd also debated the evils/benefits of apartheid, eyeball to eyeball, with an extremely aggressive uncle who was a shipwright who'd left Middlesbrough's declining shipyards to work in South Africa. I can still see the veins standing out on his reddening neck after being challenged by me, his smart-arsed nephew. He had been a highly talented amateur footballer but with a reputation for unpredictable bouts of violence. I was lucky to survive the 'discussion' with him unscathed. I had felt passionate enough about it to take the risk. I'd also uncharacteristically got into a scuffle at school with a South African boy who had joined my class and was always expressing his opinions on why the 'bleks' should be kept in their place. After our set-to he'd had the audacity to accuse me of being a bully. In the second year of my degree course I had also been involved in a sit-in, protesting against the University's investments in apartheid South Africa. I felt it was crucial to isolate this evil regime and let black people in South Africa know that they had supporters in other countries who agreed with their struggle for freedom. The sporting ban, in place at the time, was a way to demonstrate this, along with all the other sanctions.

So I shed tears of frustration and anger when the governing body of the sport I was now involved in decided to select Zola Budd, a white South African, to represent the UK in the 3000 metres in the LA Olympics. The Daily Mail, well-known crusader for freedom, helped persuade the Thatcher Conservative government, well-known champions of civil rights, to fast track Budd's application for British Citizenship, in the name of justice and fair play. To be honest the fact that Thatcher was an unashamed supporter of Apartheid meant that little persuasion was needed.

I didn't really feel resentment towards Budd, she was a gullible young women manipulated by others, but I was bitterly angry about the way others used her and the system. This unusual bid for citizenship hadn't been for humanitarian reasons, to save someone from being incarcerated, tortured or killed. The main justification seemed to be that Budd had broken several world records on the track. Obviously those involved in managing her application saw an opportunity to get reflected kudos from any Olympic bling she might manage to pick up; as they might say in LA, 'way to go with that Olympic Spirit'.

My fury and frustration subsided after I penned a letter to the Amateur Athletic Association (but didn't send it) and USA's Mary Decker hit the deck, after colliding with Budd, in the 3000m final. A bewildered looking Budd trailed in seventh, roundly booed by the partisan American crowd. What is still often overlooked, in all the drama that ensued, was the brilliant silver medal snatched by UK's Wendy Sly. So here I am, not overlooking it. Well done Wendy!

Zola Budd continued to run for the UK for a few years before going 'home'. She didn't perform well on the track but won the World Cross Country Championships twice in that time. She was never wholly accepted by the British public and never really looked comfortable in the team vest.

The UK total medal haul in track and field at LA amounted to three gold, seven silver and six bronze, with Sebastian Coe in the 1500m, Daley Thompson in the Decathlon and Tessa Sanderson in the Javelin all receiving gold. But I also remember watching an impressive performance by the appropriately named Shirley Strong, in the Women's 100 metres hurdles, when she dipped over the line to take silver. "Yes, well done," I shouted at the TV screen. I got no response but, little did I know that, in just under two years' time Shirley would be saying 'well done' to me in person.

 The long, dry summer had come to an end and I had to go back to teaching and, more importantly, refocus on my third Mersey Marathon! By the time race day arrived I had been running well and improving my times in bounds and strides. I had high hopes. But the marathon is a mystery, a puzzle in which all the pieces might seem to be the right shape but on the day they just don't bloody fit. I have a picture of myself completing the race, as I have for most of my marathons; proofs are sent by the official photographer in the hope that competitors will buy the full size version of their discomfort and disillusion. I am walking under the finish banner. I have obviously run to the line not over it. My body language shouts depressed spirits and jadedness. Some (like Eileen) would say that I always expected too much. But running is a sport which is based on a mixture of unrealistic optimism and constant disappointment.

I had just run my fifth marathon of the year and it was my second fastest, thirteen minutes faster than last year's Mersey; glass half full. The problem was that I had run a marathon on a much harder course two months previously and run forty seconds quicker; glass half empty. I needed a full glass so I went to the pub.

On October 12th an event occurred which David Hughes of The Telegraph newspaper described as; "the most audacious attack on the British government since the Gunpowder Plot." The Brighton bomb, blew up a large part of the Grand Hotel while it was hosting the Conservative Party conference; tragically five people were killed and thirty one injured. The intended target, Margaret Thatcher, the prime minister, emerged unscathed from the rubble. The bomb was planted in a brutal attempt to remind the British government that the IRA were still waging war against them and would continue to do so on Irish and English soil until their cause was recognised. Claiming responsibility, the IRA promised that they would try to kill the PM again, stating; "Give Ireland peace and there will be no more war."

History has shown that violent acts against the State can often galvanise rather than intimidate those in power. The bombing certainly had no effect on the government's approach to Ireland other than harden it (if that was possible) and in this country it resulted in Margaret Thatcher being more popular than ever. Whatever she felt inside, she showed no external signs of vulnerability in this extraordinarily stressful situation. She was admired for her lack of emotion. The bombing also deflected negative attention away from this ruthless British government, which was bad news for anybody in the country standing up to them. No emotion, meant no concern, meant no sympathy. It seemed to me that this was the government's general approach to the serious problems facing many of its electors.

On November 27th Band Aid a 'Super Group' set up by Bob Geldof released 'Do They Know Its Christmas'. This recording was sold to raise money to help famine relief in Africa and became the biggest selling single of all time in the UK. Geldof promised that all the proceeds would go to the cause. Totally out of touch with the groundswell of public support for the project, Margaret Thatcher and her government had other ideas, insisting that tax should be paid on the sales. They subsequently reneged, presumably when someone from the real world advised them it might affect their election chances. The single raised £8 million.

More mundanely my marathon year had ended on a bit of an anti-climax but in my last race of the year (the Preston Harriers Ten Miles in mid-November) I managed to record a PB of 58:04. Good, you would think, but I'd noted in a running log at the time that I'd 'gone off too fast' and yes, you guessed it, I was 'disappointed with the time.' In 1984 I'd run five marathons, five half marathons and a few other races. I'd competed a lot, perhaps too much, but I knew that if I wanted to improve my marathon time I'd have to increase my training mileage from the fifty-five miles a week I'd averaged since the beginning of October.

As the year drew to a close it seemed to me that George Orwell's fictional representation of 1984 hadn't really been accurate but, like the book, the last 12 months had given us little to laugh at but much to ponder. On a lighter more aerated note, I had finally got rid of the bloody threadbare, cotton vest (by M&S)!

Chapter 4

1985 Riots, Diets and Disquiets

In January 1985 two funny things happened. The first was the launch of the Sinclair C5. Like a daddy-longlegs, it had a brief and awkward life and, ultimately, it was difficult to see the point. The C5 was an electric, three-wheeled vehicle launched by inventor Clive Sinclair on the 10th of the month. By this time Clive was already a Sir, knighted in 1983 for services to industry. He had made his name and a large amount of money from his contributions to the development of electronics in the UK. His 'slim line' pocket calculator was a huge success and, after modest interest with earlier models, the ZX Spectrum home computer captured a big chunk of the market. Spookily, its life span, launched in 1982 before being withdrawn in '92, mirrors the period covered by this memoir. I am hoping for similar commercial success.

I was exposed to the ZX and it to me, as part of my teaching job, because as an educationalist I had to be, ahem, teetering at the cutting edge of technology. However, showing the children the wonders of IT quickly lost its appeal. While the ZX interminably whirred and clicked its annoyingly modern way to being loaded up, via a cassette tape, a decidedly old fashioned riot was breaking out in the classroom. Personally, I didn't think these computer things would catch on. Credit to Sir Clive, though, he shifted five million units worldwide over the ten year period of the ZX's production. It was widely seen as being responsible for launching the IT industry in this country.

And so, riding on his wave of success, boffin Clive decided to encourage us to try to ride over the crest of a hill in an electric vehicle. The C5 was a recumbent, battery-assisted tricycle, which had pedals but could, theoretically, operate independent of human power reaching speeds of 15 mph. The fact that it was not capable of exceeding this speed meant that the driver did not require a licence. It was doomed to failure.

Now don't misunderstand me, I am totally in favour of electric cars. It was a mystery why automobile research and development hadn't come up with a decent one sooner. (Could it be because most of their funding came from the petro-chemical industry? Perish the thought and the planet.) Being a keen cyclist, I was in favour of any idea which would reduce the pollution and motorised mayhem which plagued our roads. However, to get the rest of the fickle public on board, I felt that an attractive alternative needed to be offered.

Although the C5 sold at a reasonable £399 plus £29 delivery it had too many features which made it totally unattractive to habitual motorists. It was open to the elements (even less attractive when you are recumbent), the aerodynamic close-to-the-ground design meant its presence was not always obvious to other vehicles and it wouldn't go up hills unless you pedalled like an amphetamine-stoked hamster.

At that time I could fairly easily run about 10 miles in an hour. I was possibly outperforming the C5, fuelled mostly by cereal and beer. I certainly would have sailed past it going up a hill and my battery lasted longer. Everything considered it would appear that those purchasing this machine had a death wish. The driver certainly ran the risk of being squashed under an HGV, like a crane fly beneath a two-year-old child's Startrite. Less dramatically, chances of an early demise from pneumonia would be heightened by repeated lap-dampening. Finally and crucially, heart attacks were a distinct possibility, as a result of the strain from furious uphill pedalling in an attempt to keep up with arrogant runners. Although limited in its appeal, in the area of shortened life expectancy, at least the C5 offered a range of choice.

The vehicle was made in Merthyr Tydfil, at the Hoover factory. This led to the urban myth that it was powered by a washing machine motor. What was true, however, was that (as our transatlantic friends might say) it sucked. It was a commercial disaster and production was stopped on August 13th after 8 months. However, as Sir Clive quickly worked out using his pocket calculator, it sold 17,000 units which was the best result for an electric vehicle until the Nissan Leaf sold 20,000 in 2011. In my opinion, this time delay in the appearance of another viable electrical conveyance was caused, not only by the grip the oil companies had on the industry, but also because the C5 gave electric vehicles such a bad name for over a quarter of a century.

What of Sir Clive? In 2012, while he was still busy reinventing himself with his foldaway 'A Bike' and threatening us with another electrical vehicle, his personal life seemed to have followed, what some might describe as, a thematic course. From inventing a predecessor to the lap top and then a trike that got your lap wet, he went on to marry a 33 year-old lap dancer in 2010. When asked what qualities he saw in his bride, the quick-witted, 69-year-old, erstwhile chairman of Mensa responded, "Well, she is a former Miss England, isn't she;" brilliant. It is unlikely that you would need a calculator to work out what she saw in multi-millionaire Sir Clive but you might have to use one to work out 'how much' she really liked him.

And on the theme of the rich, big brained and narrow minded, an event (or non-event) in Oxford University was the second thing to amuse me in January 1985. As it is, always was and (bar a revolution) probably always will be, Oxford and Cambridge Universities function as elitist nurseries where many politicians suck their dummies and fight over who is going to be milk monitor before heading off to big school at Westminster. Margaret Thatcher, milk snatcher, went to Somerville College, Oxford in 1943. It came as a surprise when, on January 30th 1985, her nomination for an honorary degree by the University's Hebdomadal Council (don't worry it's a different world with a different language) was rejected, 733 votes to 319, by Congregation, its governing assembly. An unprecedented number of voters turned out after a 'No To Thatcher' campaign by the student union. Many who voted were scientific and medical dons, who were rarely seen venturing out of their labs in daylight never mind getting involved in academic debates. They had emerged from deep inside their departmental cells, frizzy haired and blinking owl-eyed, cages suddenly rattled by the effects that government cuts were having on their research funds.

I laughed. She was too busy bashing the plebs to see the patrician flanker coming. I wondered if she had already bought her scarlet and crimson gown and velvet bonnet, the fancy dress for a Doctor of Civil Law. She was probably ironing it while Denis was down the offie getting the champers in (or vice versa) when the news came through. Ah well, at least the booze wouldn't have gone to waste with Denis around. Of course, her public reaction was the usual; unemotional with a disdainful edge.

    I don't want to give readers the impression that I didn't like Mrs Thatcher. I actually owed her a debt of gratitude. Unbeknownst to the Metallic Monster she got Eileen and me together. We had both been invited to an election celebration party in 1979. The celebration turned into a wake as the Conservatives swept to power, with an 8.1 % swing, led by Finchley's fiercest. In spite of having just met, Eileen and I were of the same mind. The only course of action in the face of this great disappointment was to have a drink and a dance. As we walkchatted home together to our respective abodes, the dawn chorus was in full swing. The birds were in fine voice. They either hadn't heard the news or favoured the right wing, which would also explain why they were flying in circles. As we walked through Princes Park in Toxteth, the day's first sunlight glistened on dew-coated grass and the lake held a light mist above its surface. It didn't dawn on us that within the year we would be living together on a road adjacent to this park.

Princes Park is another of Liverpool's grand, green areas. It spreads over 45 hectares and is only a five-minute walk from its sister space, Sefton Park. In 2009 it was upgraded to a Grade II Historic Park. From 2011 it has been home to Liverpool's only 'parkrun', one of the series of weekly, Saturday morning, 5k runs held in parks throughout the country.

This park was originally a private development, open to the paying public and financed by the selling of the Georgian-style mansions, built on the perimeter. Opened in 1842 it was acquired by the council in 1918. The designer, Joseph Paxton, was an interesting character. He was born in 1803, the seventh son in a farming family. Leaving the farm he managed to blag his way into a gardening job at the Horticultural Society Gardens at Chiswick. Displaying enthusiasm, dedication and obvious ability, he soon came to the attention of the Duke of Devonshire who not only owned a London pad nearby but also Chatsworth House in Derbyshire. (It really annoys me that the aristocracy are not forced, by law, to live in the counties they're named after.) In the course of time, young Joseph impressed enough to be appointed head-gardener at Chatsworth and proceeded to redesign the gardens, a process which included the construction of the Great Conservatory, in 1837. The unique designs he produced for these glasshouses are seen as forerunners of today's greenhouses. It is said (by me) that his structures came with care instructions which had a whole section on the dangers of stone throwing by people inside but no mention of the possibility of someone setting one alight, which is what I managed to do to my dad's greenhouse when I was eight.

The news of Paxton's extraordinary vision spread and he was soon to be commissioned to design many parks, gardens and glasshouses. Princes Park in 1842 was followed by Birkenhead Park in 1847 and the remarkable Crystal Palace in 1851. In 1850, American landscape designer, Frederick Law Olmsted, visited Birkenhead Park, which was the first publicly funded civic park in the world. So enamoured was he of the wonders he beheld there, it is claimed that he incorporated (copied/stole) many of the ideas in Paxton's creation when helping to design New York's Central Park. So Birkenhead is basically New York without the sky-scrapers or maybe it's the other way round. As fate would have it, the running of the New York Marathon through Central Park would be something I would never do! It would have been an appropriate link but the next marathon stop for me was in the cosmopolitan melting pot that was Wolverhampton, for another crack at 'the best thing to happen to their town'.

I was determined to hit '85 running and desperately wanted to improve my time. I started keeping a proper record of my training and later in the summer also began to keep a diary. I recorded each week's mileage and the miles for the whole month. January's weeks' totals were 76, 78, 78, 59 and 320 for the month. This was more than acceptable, considering it had been exceptionally cold with lashings of sleet, snow, ice and slush. After training in such conditions I usually ended up aching in places I didn't know I had. My body was making tiny little adjustments to stabilise itself and then, the next day, letting me know how much it had been working behind the scenes. I tended to be a bit cavalier in my approach to running across ice. I believed that if I ran fast enough my body would gain momentum and therefore enough balance, to progress safely. If this technique failed it also meant that if I did go down to meet the cold hard ground it was with far greater velocity. The usual result was that my iced buns turned into hot crossed buns.

Mathematicians amongst you will notice that my mileage was slightly less on the fourth week of January. This was because I eased off a little, to rest before a half marathon in Helsby at the end of the month.

Helsby is a little town/big village with a split personality. It lies between Runcorn and Chester and, depending on which way it looks, has two distinct characters. When its southward Janus face looks out, it imagines itself as rural. It sees a spread of pasture and dairy farms. Visible in the distance is a sandstone ridge, which carries the 34 mile Sandstone Trail from Frodsham in Cheshire to Whitchurch in Shropshire, through bucolic surroundings. This track is one of the most popular long distance paths in the Northwest. It treads quietly over the leaves and pine needles of the vast and ancient Delamere forest (where I was to be roughly treated by mendacious wood spirits in 1991). From here it travels further south, passing by the towering medieval Beeston Castle, perched on a landlocked island and surrounded by the pastoral, patchwork sea of the Cheshire plain. The southward, Janus face smiles, satisfied with this view.

But then northward face frowns. It sees a totally different sight. Not so long ago the vista would have been dominated by the vast open space of the doglegged, tapering end of the Mersey estuary. The view to the horizon would only have been interrupted by the distant buildings of Liverpool, 13 miles away as the gull flies. These days the first visual impediment is close, close enough to hear; the buzzing M56 motorway. Then, to the left are the chimneys and tanks of the Stanlow oil refinery and to the right is the appropriately named Rocksavage, with its chemical and fertiliser plants. North facing Janus sees industry. At night it is like a blazing inferno, a modern-day Loutherbourg's 'Coalbrookdale'.

I had seen a vision like this before. It is a mighty frightsight to come off the North Yorkshire moors at night and see the Teesside industrial complex spread out on the plain below. A forest of stacks, belching effluvia and multi-coloured flares, bedecked with a legion of flashing lights; it is like Satan's grotto. When I was a child, living on the southern edge of Middlesbrough, foul odours were frequent, and not just produced by me. The bouquet depended on the wind direction. From the north they came from Billingham ICI, from the east they came from Wilton ICI; different odours but equally rank. We were spoilt for choice. I suppose it is appropriate that we Teessiders should be nicknamed 'Smoggies'. Film producer Ridley Scott also saw this vision and translated it into a post-apocalyptic view of urban life in his cult film 'Blade Runner', released in 1982.

The Helsby half-marathon was always popular with local runners; not because they were fans of Ridley Scott or aficionados of industrial architecture and fragrances but because it was fast and flat. So many fast times were run there that it was reckoned (by me) to be one of the most scrutinised and re-measured courses in the whole of the world of running.

The course followed country lanes which intersected the flatlands of the marshy estuary shores and the industrial sites which had grown up there. Fortunately, the hedgerows were high enough to make most of the hideous denaturalisation invisible. Unfortunately, also invisible was the content of the atmosphere that runners dragged into their lungs. The warning, 'residents are advised to stay inside and keep their doors and windows shut,' was not exactly unheard of around these parts. In May 2001, 26 homes were evacuated in nearby Weston because of toxic fumes leaking from a chemical dump. North Cheshire Health Authority tests at the time found kidney abnormalities in half the residents from this area.

For this year's Helsby Half, overnight snow had turned to mush on the surrounding lanes. The course measurers drew back their curtains, heaved a sigh of relief and snuggled back into warm beds, for there would be no contentious fast times this day. A multitude of idiots from the running fraternity, including me, got up and ran the race. It was like running in Slush Puppie, the popular chemical concoction for children. This is not to be confused with running in

Hush Puppies which would have been an altogether more comfortable experience. I noted that the icy sludge underfoot had a similar range of colours to the aforementioned ice crystal confection. Worryingly prevalent was a radioactive green. I finished the race in one piece although my socks had disintegrated. I was hoping my lungs had fared better.

I wasn't disappointed with a time of 1:18:11 considering the conditions and the tiredness in my legs from the miles run that month. What was significant was the fact that, later on that Sunday afternoon, I went out and ran a four mile warm-down. Running twice a day would soon become a regular feature of my training and another step in being totally absorbed by this damn sport.

79, 90, 68, 90, 74, 65, 61, was the sequence of weekly miles I ran through February and March before the Wolverhampton Marathon. I was running twice a day most days. This often required me to get up at some unsophisticated hour to run three miles before work. It was always a strange experience and almost became an extension of sleep. The body slipped into automatic mode once the first serious obstacle of getting out of bed was overcome. All I had to remember was to put some clothes on.

If I couldn't run in the morning I would nip out of school and run at dinner time. I would return with minutes to spare and throw my work clothes back on, mostly the right way round, before marching into the classroom fully prepared; maybe not to teach well but hopefully to get an improved time in my next marathon.

Training for a marathon needs a decent weekly mileage but also requires the added ingredient of a 'long one' each week. As well as 'upping' the miles overall I had also lengthened my long run. I had managed a 21 miler with Whistler a few weeks before and then, perhaps inadvisably, did a 25 mile run eleven days before marathon race day. I had run this training 'jaunt' at a faster pace than I had run in my previous year's Wolverhampton Marathon. Anyone with half a brain would have realised that this long run was too much, too fast, too late. But I had less than half a brain, over three quarters was now being taken up by a feverish, obsessional totting up of the 'miles run' column. Thrown into this mix was another half marathon in Ormskirk where I had bust a gut to be rewarded with a half marathon

PB of 1:15:12. Another significant goal of a sub-75 minutes half had come within reach. There was no doubt I had done enough training but the question was had I done too much. Only time would tell.

On March 3rd the Miner's Strike formally came to an end. Some pit workers had already gone back to work independently, forced by extreme poverty and a year without wages. Government ministers later admitted that they had inflated (lied about) numbers of miners returning to work in order to dent strikers' morale. In some areas a distinction is still made between those who returned to work after a couple of months and those who clung on until forced to return for the sake of their families.

Many miners in Nottinghamshire, who had remained at work, had broken away from the National Union of Mineworkers to form the Union of Democratic Mineworkers (UDM). They had been lauded by the government but condemned as strikebreakers by the majority of pit workers. The UDM later claimed that the Conservative government had promised them that their mines and jobs would be safe. As a reward for showing loyalty most of their pits were also closed during the 1985-1994 period.

Ten people had died during the conflict. A taxi driver was tragically killed when a concrete post was thrown through the windscreen of his car while driving 'strikebreakers' to work; two miners served prison sentences for manslaughter. Six strikers died on the picket line, two of these deaths are still viewed with suspicion. Three children from miners' families died while scavenging for coal on a spoil tip in the winter. No-one was deemed responsible for nine of the deaths.

In 1994 a European Union inquiry into poverty classified the mining village of Grimethorpe, in South Yorkshire, as the poorest settlement in the country and one of the poorest in the EU. The question for me was; does the government have a duty of care for its people? I concluded that these were obviously not this government's people. This was more 'managed decline.' Many miners walked back to work in procession, brass bands playing, banners proudly streaming, in a last act of defiance against a gloating government.

Running was definitely a distraction preventing me from dwelling on the dire economic and social conditions faced by many people in the UK. I was lucky enough to be in a secure job. I was also fit and healthy and I was determined to run myself ragged to prove it. The line between fitness and illness was narrow. When I was running at my peak I seemed to find any bugs available and invite them into my system. I didn't have to look far. Primary schools were not exactly known for being germ-free zones; in fact, baby bugs went there to learn their trade before going out into the adult world. Many seemed to choose my body to make the transition. In the week before the Wolverhampton Marathon, while easing off, I remarked in my training log that I felt 'absolutely knackered, no energy'. This could have set off alarm bells had it not been for the fact that it was common for me to feel more tired when running less. I'm sure most people have had a similar sensation, feeling more lethargic when on holiday. You stop working hard and your body automatically shuts down to recover. I wasn't quite sure how I was feeling on the eve of the race. Would my intense three months training pay off?

The Wolverhampton Marathon was a funny race. Not least because of the pronouncements of the eccentric organiser Billy Wilson. Talking about the race volunteers in the foreword of the '84 programme he had stated;

"WE are (I suggest) all members of an exclusive club known as "THE ONE PERCENT". The membership is worldwide and it is secretly exclusive because no person could ever 'buy' or even 'fanny' their way in. The cost of membership is high, i.e.:- unswerving devotion to your duty. Love and patience with mankind. Pride in your birth place or community abode.."

There was more but it got increasingly messianic and difficult to follow. In the end you couldn't work out whether you were entering a marathon, answering a maths question or joining a cult. As I read the message I became increasingly unsure of Billy's number skills and the demands he made of his volunteers. He had obviously got hold of one of Sir Sinclair's calculators and pressed the wrong function on the keypad. 'An exclusive club known as The One Percent..?' One per cent of what Billy? Maybe the takeover of the world by his cult had begun and this was the total of world conversion, so far. Or maybe it was just the smallest percentage he could think of to represent exclusivity. And what acts would he expect people to perform in order to try to 'fanny' their way into his organisation? I can only imagine the disappointment if you were rejected by Billy, after a hard days 'fannying'.

His personal message in the results supplement after the '85 race was not only equally weird but also prophetic, in an 'asking for trouble' sort of way. It started;

"CONGRATULATIONS! A never ending stream of them, that's all we've had. What about the criticism? So little, I don't like it! It makes my job more difficult if our organising body sit back on their laurels! Well, as I told you all, the Wolverhampton Marathon brings that 'magic tickle' to the back of your tongue. So talk among your friends and spread the word of this wonderful future city."

In the '84 programme Billy had described the marathon as producing a 'boiling fever', now it was a 'magic tongue tickle'. To be honest, I felt it was time for him to book an appointment with his GP to look into these symptoms and maybe while there ask the doc to check his laurels, which shouldn't even be rested on, never mind sat upon. As for worrying about the lack of criticism he need not have worried. He'd have more than he could cope with after the '86 race, including mine.

But getting back to the '85 marathon, for me it was a disaster. I tripped over and fell at four miles. Having dusted myself off and got going again I was rewarded with a ripping stitch at eight miles. I was forced to stop to ease it. Although still making it through 20 miles in a respectable time of 2:05 I ground to a halt soon after. I then did something I had never done in a marathon before, I walked. I did so on and off for the last one and a half miles. I managed to stagger to the line in just under three hours but after all the expectations I felt hugely disappointed. I was hot and dehydrated. Amongst all the explanations (excuses) for what, I felt, was a poor performance, one stood out for me.

I don't know whether I had been straying too far south too often of late, or whether I had been running too much with Whistler but something had caused me to make an uncharacteristic decision before the race which I believed had really cost me. I'd had a pre-race attack of extreme neshness and decided to wear a long sleeved thermal underneath my vest. Never again! I don't know what I was thinking but they can't have been positive or logical thoughts. It was probably the final mistake of many in my preparation which needed only one to ensure my downfall. Oh yes, and there was the downfalling.

When I got home I was annoyed with myself. After all the training I still felt I had something to prove. I made a decision born of frustration. I entered another marathon, the Stratford-upon-Avon, Shakespeare Marathon which was only three weeks away. Would I be able to recover in time? It was a question which my less than quarter-of-a-brain didn't have room for. Would it be a case of all's well that ends well or love's labours lost?

Four days before I was about to throw myself at the Wolves and be eaten up by disappointment, one of my old favourites had reason to be cheerful. Soul singer Stevie Wonder received an Oscar in 'The Most Original Song' category. The song 'I Just Called to Say I Love You' was from the film 'The Woman in Red'. In his acceptance speech, 'Little Stevie' dedicated the award to black activist Nelson Mandela, still imprisoned by South Africa's apartheid government. In a bold response, the South Africa Broadcasting Corporation banned Mr Wonder's song from the country's airwaves. Stevie must have been tempted to 'just call to say I love you' for boosting record sales.

He'd already had a tune banned in South Africa, in 1982. This was a duet with Paul McCartney 'Ebony and Ivory,' the recording of which, as I have already explained, prevented Paul from being outside his house to cheer me on in the '82 Mersey Marathon. This song was voted 59th best Billboard hit of all time in a 2008 poll. It was also destined to appear on many 'worst song of all time' lists. It was voted worst duet in history by listeners of BBC 6 Music, in 2007. Deriding it for cheesy sentimentality, a significant number of music fans wished a reason could have been found for banning it in the UK.

Also in 1985 Michael Jackson had taken a break from crutch clutching to grab the publishing rights for most of the Beatles music, from recording company EMI. This was a bit harsh on Paul McCartney because he was a rival bidder; felony and irony. This shrewd purchase was to go towards saving Jackson's estate from the huge debts accrued before his death in 2009. Incidentally, those debts included £315 million loan owed to Barclays Bank. (Note to self; if needing a huge loan from a British Bank; 1. Wear dark glasses and don an obviously fake nose. 2. Walk awkwardly backwards into a local branch, 3. Sing in wobbly falsetto, hand in hand with a chimpanzee.)

It was also at about this time that Eileen and I did decide to take out a loan, to buy our own house. We walked into the building society conventionally, unaccompanied by anthropoid apes, which was probably why our initial request for £300 million was downgraded to £20,000. We were persuaded to take out an endowment mortgage which, we were assured, was a safe investment. They told us we would be chimps to turn this offer down.

Since 1980 we had lived 'over the broom' around the corner from Princes Park. Here we had a lovely, big, two bed-roomed flat on the top floor of a Victorian villa. The property was owned and run by ETA Housing Cooperative. This organisation consisted solely of the people who happened to be living in the house at any given time. Previously the house had been owned and lived in by a rich, eccentric hippy. He had shared the space with a group of friends who were his paying tenants. On leaving Liverpool he gifted the building to the people he was sharing with. The only condition was that they ran the house as a co-op. This sounded like a great idea.

Again just to set the record straight, I am totally in favour of co-ops, in principle. But one of the main problems with co-ops can be the type of people they attract. There had already been a high turnover of residents in the house before we moved in. This trend continued while we were living there. Most were lovely people but not all were of reliable character or, indeed, particularly cooperative. Eileen and I soon found ourselves reluctantly acting as secretary and treasurer, respectively, of ETA. This meant we were responsible for collecting rent, keeping accounts, organising meetings to decide how to use rent money and for arranging repairs to be done on the house. None of these tasks were particularly easy and we found chunks of our time being increasingly taken over by them.

No-one seemed to know where the name ETA had come from. It had been suggested that being the seventh letter of the Greek alphabet, it represented the seven original members of the co-op. There were other possible theories (mostly mine; OK, all mine). In Spain, ETA was also an acronym for a Basque separatist group known for violent, direct action. We were certainly a separate entity but violent direct action was not a trend in the house; unless you count the time a resident on the ground floor flew into a rage about the lumpiness of his mattress. He chucked the offending item into the back garden and, although a teetotaller himself, drenched it with a bottle of his girlfriend's favourite whisky and set fire to it. And there was also the time an occupant of one of the first floor flats smashed a pane of original etched glass in the front door because she'd forgotten her keys. She then left the door gaping for anybody to enter. (It was presumed that someone else would deal with it. That someone was usually me or Eileen.) These were direct actions of a sort but annoying rather than particularly violent, besides none of us were Spanish.

There were two other alternative translations of ETA which I think fitted the group better. Firstly, there was the Japanese version, a word which translates as a member of a class of outcasts who did menial and dirty tasks. According to the Thatcher government this described most of the North of England. The English version of the word is also an acronym for 'estimated time of arrival'. This was what so many of the tenants seemed unable to give us when we asked for their rents. Whatever the reason for its name, we had decided it was time to leave the organisation. The responsibility for trying to maintain the property and keep the co-op viable negated the benefits of living there. We were fortunate enough to be financially solvent early in 1985, so we decided to start looking for a small terraced house to buy and the bank was going to give us all the money; how generous.

Meanwhile, forsooth, the Shakespeare Marathon didst loom. The three weeks leading up to the race I decided to take it easy, which is not surprising as I was still recovering from the Wolverhampton disaster. I decided to change my routine and did not run at all on the Friday and Saturday before the early Sunday race start. We travelled to Birmingham on Friday to stay with Eileen's mum and dad. The information which came with my number contained particularly wise words; it was almost like the writer had heard about my last performance and was lecturing me on my transgressions: "Run in clothes that allow free circulation of air so as to avoid overheating. Wear clothes you have used before and feel comfortable in." Damn right! It also added; "Make sure you grease well those parts that may chafe, i.e. thighs, armpits, nipples, crutch etc." The last body area may have been added especially for anyone doing it in Michael Jackson fancy dress and the 'etc.' to cover runners with other special requirements.

On the Sunday morning we made the short journey south from Birmingham to Stratford-upon-Avon, the Bard's birthplace. The word 'marathon' does not appear in any of Shakespeare's plays but 'run' appears 198 times, 'running' 32 times, and 'wall' 65 times (30 of these in 'Midsummer Night's Dream'). 'Ale' appears a disappointing 15 times and 'beer' a small six. Shockingly, there is no mention of Vaseline, carbo-loading or fartlek.

The configuration of this marathon was two laps through the Warwickshire countryside. This would allow plenty of time for thought because other distractions, like people or buildings, would, on the whole, be absent. It was not an easy route due to its openness and the inclusion of quite a few sneaky inclines. Keen to get going and confused by inaccurate mile markers, I started off a little fast and got the dreaded stitch at eight miles. I did, however, manage to combat this without stopping and eventually got into a comfortable cadence. Half way through the second lap I felt strong. My reversion to a more conservative pace had conserved energy. The confusing mile markers meant I was uncertain as to exactly what pace I was actually running. I was amazed and delighted when I crossed the line in ninth place with a PB of 2:48:30; knocking four and a half minutes off my '84 Wirral Marathon record and dipping under 2:50 for the first time. I now felt justified in taking the decision to run Stratford so soon after the Wolverhampton comedy of errors. (I promise that will be my last Bard bon mot, for the mo.)

On Sunday May 5th, two weeks after the Stratford Marathon, I ran in the Liverpool Half Marathon and two weeks after that in the

Chester Half Marathon where I recorded a time of 1:14:39, the first occasion I had run under 1:15. I had competed in five races, two full and three half marathons, in 8 Sundays. I had run pretty much flat out in all of them, hardly giving my body time to recover between, but I was still improving. I believe that one reason I continued to improve was that I was recovering by keeping some of my training miles relatively slow. Help had come from an unexpected source.

I knew I had caught the running bug but I hadn't realised that it was going to be contagious. Eileen, who had avoided almost all physical exercise at secondary school by apparently having a weekly menstrual cycle, had suddenly been 'bugged'. Deciding to try to get fit she had started running. I had accompanied her on the first of her tentative, short runs. To my surprise I had found that these short runs were also benefiting me and had got me out of the habit of thrashing myself every time I went out for a run. As her jogs got longer, I was able to include them in my longer outings by carrying on after she had finished her desired mileage.

I think this would be a suitable point to explain how I had managed to devote so much time to running without causing friction in my relationship with Eileen. A simple explanation of the situation was, Eileen had her politics and I had my running but also Eileen had her running and I had my politics. We shared interests. There was only a difference in emphasis. I encouraged her to join me in my world of running and she did the same to me with her world of politics. We both pursued our main interests vigorously but not exclusively. The rest of our time we shared. Through her we developed a circle of political friends and through me a circle of running friends. Sometimes the two overlapped. To conclude; Eileen was not a running widow and I was not a political widower. There was rarely any conflict. We were lucky.

In May and June my mileage totalled 618 miles. 68 of those miles had been run with Eileen. Slow recovery miles are often dismissively called 'rubbish miles' by some athletes. Many feel they are useless in terms of improving form and will virtually eradicate them from their schedules. In my training schedule they seemed to do the trick because at the end of June '85 I returned to the scene of my showboating run with Whistler, the Manchester Piccadilly

Marathon, and obliterated my personal best by 8 minutes when I recorded 2:40:30. It was apparent that another contributory factor, aiding this pleasing progress, was the running of fairly even splits. The first half I ran in 1:19 and the second in 1:21. Even splits are the key to running a marathon to the best of your ability. In future races this was a lesson which I would remember but, usually, only after I had failed to learn from it. Over ambitious expectation is so often the downfall of marathoners, even the most experienced.

As summer approached I was amassing my mileage in several ways; running in the morning, running at dinner time and running in the evening, sometimes a combination of two or even all three. In June I had run over 100 miles in a week for the first time. I was running with Eileen and still occasionally with Whistler but I was also doing the fast stuff on my own. My improvement suggested that I must have been doing something right.

While I pursued my sporting activities, two tragedies occurred in May. Both occurred, in part, as a result of conditions which had been allowed to develop in this country's principal sport. Considering that they provided a huge amount of revenue by paying for live entertainment, football fans were still treated little better than cattle. Inadequate and unsympathetic marshalling saw them herded into and penned inside crumbling and unsafe stadia. Many grounds were tinder boxes waiting for a spark.

Valley Parade in Bradford was one of these antiquated grounds. The stand, built in 1911, was a wooden structure with an asphalt roof and had changed little since it was originally erected. The materials used in the stand's construction, a build-up of rubbish underneath the seats, unavailability of fire extinguishers and the locking of exits from the stand, all contributed to transforming the innocent dropping of a match, or perhaps a cigarette end, into one of the worst disasters in sporting history. On the May 11th during the match between Bradford City and Lincoln City, this stand took little more than four minutes to be engulfed in flames. 56 died and 265 people were injured. Half of the fatalities were aged under 20 or over 70.

Many heroes emerged from the crowd that day. Fans and staff trying to rescue or help those injured or at risk. Terry Yorath, manager of Bradford city, the home team, was injured coming to the aid of others. His family, including 12-year-old daughter Gabby, had escaped from the stand unscathed. Gabby went on to be a main presenter for BBC's 'Match of the Day' and presented a moving Radio 4 documentary about the disaster in 2010.

By the end of the month another football related catastrophe dominated the headlines. Another dilapidated stadium, more inadequate safety precautions, more insensitive marshalling of the crowd but this time the ignition point was not a casually dropped match but an explosion of disproportionate aggression between opposing supporters. It was the European Cup Final, Juventus versus Liverpool FC. Of all the conditions which may have contributed to the death of 39 people (32 Italian, four Belgium, two French and one Irish) the crucial factor, which led to panicking fans being crushed by a falling wall, was a hostile charge by some followers of Liverpool FC.

As a boy I was a football fan of my home team Middlesbrough FC. I was a regular at Ayresome Park. Today I still follow their results but I am not a fan in that I don't go to matches or put my life on hold on Saturday (or Sunday) afternoon. I like to see them win but don't descend into a deep trough of depression if they don't, which is a good job considering their results. I had lost interest when it appeared that the humour of the terraces was being spoiled by a poisoned minority starting to use the area as a meeting place to express their offensive views. Although the arenas weren't, the games were once generally fit for family entertainment until parts of many grounds were taken over by groups of disaffected, predominantly white males. In these groups only the mob members mattered and everyone else was fair game. I believed football was a sport to be enjoyed by all and not a place for fanatics whose aim was to make sport of anyone who wasn't like them.

In reporting on matches the expression 'football's a man's game' often got wheeled out by commentators to explain aggression on and off the pitch. Some 'hard men' became legends. For 'hard' read, those who regarded skilled play as an anathema and broke rules and bones to stop it. They were allowed to practise their base craft relatively unfettered. Tabloid headlines were often about violence on and off the pitch, not football.

In my view the real news was that it was and is just a game. No more important than that. It should be a game for everyone and anyone. It is a game of great skill and beauty but where the basic skills are easily achieved if not the beauty. The fact that I was still 'trying' to play footie until aged 60 is a testament to its universality and my love of it. It is a game which can get physical but certainly no more than rugby league or union. Yet fans watching these other ball games rarely appeared to feel the need to replicate the physicality of the game on the terraces. Somewhere along the road, football was infiltrated by a minority who sought a vicarious thrill from brutality and hatred on the pitch and terraces. My view was that not enough was done by clubs or government to discourage or re-educate these individuals. Government policies and attitudes espousing the importance of self-aggrandisement had left some young people directionless, lacking the moral compass provided by a more unified, community-based society. Football terraces were a place for some alienated individuals to gain personal recognition through group infamy. This minority enjoyed disproportionate sensational media attention. However at the end of the day, whatever contributed to the behaviour of certain people at Heysel, it was unacceptable and ultimately led to a human disaster of far-reaching consequences.

The bonding sense of solidarity felt among many football fans is undeniable. The difference between the two tragedies that month was that the Bradford disaster revealed how football people in a community could work together sacrificing their individual safety to help others while Heysel revealed how some 'followers' of the game could sacrifice other people's individual safety with acts aimed to prove blind allegiance to and a distorted pride in their group. Many English football clubs had a reputation for their ultra-violent elements. Liverpool FC was not, to my knowledge, one of these clubs. However, the actions of 'supporters' on that day left an indelible stain and gave anybody who was prejudiced against the city an even bigger stick to hit it with. The scenes at Heysel could have been acted out by 'followers' of many teams in England. They were a result of the existence of a small but virulent sub-culture in the game and a reflection of society's woes condensed. It happened that the fans were from Liverpool and being an advocate for the city had just got harder.

I've no idea how fans who were involved on that day felt but I expect the real fans were and still are mortified. I felt that the club itself was slow to react, taking too long to come up with an appropriate response. It wasn't until May 2010 that a permanent memorial to commemorate the dead of Heysel was erected at Anfield, Liverpool FC's football ground. The European Union of Football Associations' (UEFA) response wasn't much better. May 2005 eventually saw a memorial unveiled outside the new Heysel stadium. The old ground was never again used for football games after that fateful night in May 1985 and was eventually demolished.

The Heysel disaster is well remembered both in and outside Liverpool but the seemingly less contentious but equally tragic Bradford disaster not as much. Coincidentally, Liverpool's Gerry Marsden, of '60s pop group Gerry and the Pacemakers, accompanied by Paul McCartney and others, went to number one in the charts, in June, rereleasing a version of Rodgers and Hammerstein's 'You'll never Walk Alone'. The record was sold to raise money for the Bradford Burns Unit which had dealt with many of the injured from Valley Parade. As is well known, the tune had long been Liverpool FC's anthem.

July 1985 saw me running the Chester Motor Auctions Half Marathon as Eileen's co-driver. It was her first half marathon and a hellishly hot day. Most men don't need the excuse of hot weather or a thirteen mile run to break out into a sweat. Just the thought of hard work will cause most to produce rivers of perspiration and brimming armpit ponds. Some women however seem reluctant to sweat. ("It's bloody physiology not reluctance," retorts Eileen. Damn, I didn't realise she was looking over my shoulder.) They seem to see it as an undesirable attribute which, in terms of socialising with other humans, I suppose it is. However in terms of long distance running it is a necessary evil. It keeps the skin cool in high temperatures. Eileen was one of these reluctant sweaters. Maybe all those missed PE lessons had clogged up the pores. Anyway, she preferred to gradually go through all the shades of red in a paint colour chart rather than perspire. ("I'd rather bloody sweat," splutters Eileen, flushing. Damn, she's still there.)

On finishing the race, running with her, my skin was damp and cool; hers was dry and hot, in spite of blood being desperately pumped to the surface to keep her temperature down. She hated running in the heat so to her credit she managed to complete her first half marathon in just over two hours. She received a medal and, coincidentally, a blood blister on the bottom of her foot which was the same shape and circumference as the medal. Two prizes in one race! For some reason she wasn't as pleased with the foot award.

I enjoyed running in unfamiliar places when I got the chance, so whenever Eileen and I went away I always tried to get out for a gallop in a different milieu. This statement could possibly be seen as an excuse for the fact that I was now totally addicted and would have probably turned into a gibbering wreck if I didn't get my daily foot fix.

The week-end after Eileen's inaugural 'half' we went to her parents' in Hall Green in the southern suburbs of Birmingham. I was trying to keep the running ticking over before my fourth Mersey Marathon in September. It was another warm day on Saturday and while Eileen spent time at the shops of Solihull with her parents and one or two of the many sisters, I headed off south, running into the Warwickshire countryside. I lolloped through the lanes sedately, aware of the high temperatures. When I entered the village of Tanworth-in-Arden it seemed as if the sun had finally got to me. Had I been running so slowly that I had arrived a century earlier? Everyone was in Victorian dress. As I shuffled through the streets I stared at people and they stared back. I thought maybe longer shorts would have been more appropriate. On the village green a gentleman wearing a stove pipe hat was reading aloud from 'Oliver Twist'. I went past and turned right. (I suppose you could say I twisted and turned.) Round the corner I came upon a pig on a spit. I said hello but being a vegetarian I had no time for idle pork and so pushed onwards and left the village to their Victorian Fete. I ran 'back to the future' and, cheekily pinching my idea, a film of that name, on the theme of time travel, had been released on the 3rd of July, just ten days previously.

Arriving back in Hall Green I was relieved to stop and rehydrate. I looked down at my vest and momentarily thought I'd caught the Plague in my travel back to a less sanitary era. Then it slowly dawned on me that I was actually covered in black flies which had decided that hitching a ride was better than flapping their ridiculously minute wings. They had probably come further than they had anticipated. It seemed to me that they were going to find it extremely hard to get back home on those wings, as I wiped them ever so carelessly and a tad roughly from my clothing.

(Here is a bit of trivia for those soap opera historians out there, all two of you; from 1970, Tanworth was the location for the filming of outdoor scenes depicting the fictional village of Kings Oak in the brilliantly bad series 'Crossroads' [1964-1988]. And, on a worrying family note, Eileen's Nan had turned up with a present for the bride when a wedding ceremony, in one of the episodes, was being filmed in Birmingham.)

Safely back in the present, that night I sat in front of the television with the rest of the family and watched, not 'Crossroads', but 'Live Aid', a concert organised to raise money to relieve famine in Ethiopia. Inspired by the success of the Band Aid's '84 Christmas single, this appeal remarkably raised £40 million. Bob Geldof famously urged, "Don't go to the pub tonight, please stay in and give us your money." He personally took a call from the ruling family of Dubai, who donated £1 million. Mind you, I don't suppose they were planning on going to the pub anyway. Getting out my Sinclair, slim, pocket calculator I worked out that the offering from Dubai's finest was, relative income taken into consideration, the equivalent of me giving 10p. I also may have pressed the wrong function key. 10p may have been an overestimate.

In September, with my fourth Mersey Marathon just around the corner I decided to do two things differently in my preparation. Firstly, in the last week before the race I decided to forgo beer. I know, 'shock-horror'. Secondly and sort of connected, I decided to try 'the diet'. Most people will know about carbo-loading before a marathon. This involves increasing the amount of carbohydrate based food eaten a couple of days before the race to increase energy stores. 'The diet' is a little more complex. Tuesday before a Sunday race a runner tries to eat as little carbohydrate as possible and concentrates on protein. This carbo-depletion continues until Thursday evening when a normal carbo-loading commences. The theory is that when racing over long distances the body will run out of stores of carbohydrates from which to obtain energy. In this situation, a natural reserve of secondary energy called glycogen is tapped into. The idea of 'the diet' is that initially starving the body of carbs panics it into thinking it needs to increase its glycogen stores in preparation for an emergency. Subsequently loading carbohydrates ensures that you not only have a full primary store but also a full secondary glycogen store. As you can see by my Blue Peter nutritionist's badge, I am fully qualified to talk about these matters. All I really know is that by Thursday night I was twitching. Being a carboholic and a cereal killer I struggled to do without. It was definitely harder to give up the food than the beer, although sometimes the two morphed in my mind.

I made it through to Sunday morning without killing anyone but almost killed myself with self-generated stress. My normal pre-race routine was to get my vest out, pin my number to it and put it back in my bag before setting off for the start. For some strange reason after pinning on the number and before putting it away I decided the vest needed an iron. It just shows how the thought of an impending marathon can alter the normal, if limited, workings of a runner's brain. We don't do ironing in our house. We will occasionally iron something we are about to put on, for an interview or a wedding or to be knighted but only if it has more creases than a nonagenarian's face. I had never before been known to iron a running vest. The result was that the iron touched the number which, being a piece of plastic-coated paper, shrivelled instantly to the size of a crumpled railway ticket. With Laura, my daughter, solemnly giving me advice, much to my irritation, I improvised by sticking what was left of the number on the plain back of an old number, completing the bits of the semi obliterated digits with a felt tip pen. I just prayed that the organisers would accept the mongrel number and that the felt tip wouldn't run while I did.

So, what was the result of my dietary experiment? Well, to be honest it is hard to tell. Did I tire in the last few miles because of the fact of that this was my fourth marathon of the year or because the diet didn't work? I managed to record 2:43:24, not a PB but 10 minutes faster than last year's Mersey. I succeeded in coming 34th and received a top 50 T-shirt. So there was some reason for cheer. But the main reason to say cheers was that I could now have a few pints. That was one part of the experiment I wouldn't be repeating.

On the Wednesday after the Mersey Marathon the Liverpool Echo not only contained the marathon results but also reports on how Liverpool city centre had come to a standstill as workers marched in support of the Militant Tendency dominated Labour council, who had refused to set a budget in line with the Conservative government's financial restrictions. All other councils, many of them reluctantly, had fallen in line with the government's demands. In Liverpool the council unions had been asked to vote for an indefinite strike in support but this was rejected in favour of a one day protest. It seemed as if the workforce were telling councillors that they supported them for standing up to the Tories but felt it was time for a compromise.

The situation had descended into farce; more stand-up comedy than standoff politics. The council had done some positive things during their tenure; building homes, improving old dwellings, and investing money in schools, sports facilities and other public projects. However, now they seemed to be more focussed on taking on the government at the expense of care for the council's constituents and workforce. The Conservative government, on the other hand, was determined to get rid of the council whether they had been democratically elected or not. Ridiculous rhetoric flew back and forth. Neil Kinnock, the leader of the Labour Party behaved no better, constantly repeating his condemnation of Militant Tendency instead of concentrating on constructive support for the people of Liverpool. He seemed terrified of losing national votes at the next general election; he knew Liverpool was safe Labour. Too many self-promoting personalities were trying to come up with new ways of insulting each other instead of new ways to solve the problem.

In the Liverpool Echo, Environment Secretary Kenneth Baker claimed that when deputy council leader Derrick Hatton, "appears on radio or TV, the news is bad for Liverpool." From that may we presume that whenever a member of the Conservative Party appeared, the news was good? He also stated that "the only special thing about Liverpool is the irresponsibility of the councillors." And its stand against the Tory government, he might have added. He then went on to contradict himself by saying, "We provide substantial assistance to Liverpool, over and above what other cities get." It would seem then that there was a point in being bolshy after all. Whatever the rights and wrongs of the situation, because of the recalcitrance on all sides, Liverpool was in financial limbo.

At the end of the month, Saturday, September 28th, riots erupted in Brixton after a black woman had been shot accidentally by police. By Tuesday there were riots in Toxteth over the arrest of four black men in connection with an assault. Cars were burnt and the police were banging provocatively on new riot shields. Annoyingly for me, the offie had decided to shut up shop when I popped round for a couple of bottles. In the event, these riots were minor compared to '81 and seemed to calm down quickly. Other parts of London, areas in Birmingham, Coventry, Wolverhampton and Bristol also had their share of unrest. The only common factor in these disturbances was the government's rigid and unsympathetic attitude towards the conditions which had caused them to erupt.

October was a big month in our household as we moved from Liverpool 8 to a small terraced street in Liverpool 15. (The house cost us £19,000 and the building society gave us a 100% endowment mortgage.) We had actually moved into Beatle Land. Just down the hill from our house was the famous Penny Lane. The barber shop in the song was to become my regular scalping post. The move of location also meant different running routes and routines.

As we settled down in our new abode my training continued unabated in spite of jobs to be done. I still managed to fit in another marathon, this time around the shores of Windermere, in the Lake District. I'm not sure why I had decided to enter this race but it must have seemed like a good idea at the time. I can't have been pressurised by anyone because I was flying solo. At that time I was in possession of a full driving licence but was not in possession of a car or even a C5, come to that. We had no need for a car as we cycled and used public transport (or hired a car if we wanted a little more independence). Having no-one to give me a lift on this occasion I borrowed a friend's Mini to get me to the start line.

It was Sunday October 27 and my day started at 5:30 a.m. After breakfast I left Eileen in bed and set off at 6:30 up the M6 arriving in Bowness on Windermere at 8:15, well in time for the start at 10 o'clock. The conditions were ideal for running; dry, overcast and cool, with little wind. The scenery at the start, on the banks of the lake, was stunning. The terrain on the route continued to be stunning but for my legs as well as my eyes. There were no mega climbs but from 13 miles onwards the road was a mad Macadam roller coaster. My progress wasn't aided by the need to make two pit stops, dashing into the woods en route, hoping passing ramblers would mistake me for a bear and local hunters wouldn't. Everything taken into account I was satisfied with a time of 2:44:27. I knew from a long way out that I was not going to PB or break 2:40 so I eased off and saved myself for a sprint finish over the last three yards. I recovered quickly and the sun came out. Sitting by the lake I soaked up the atmosphere, the autumnally enhanced scenery and the warm sunshine. I wished Eileen was there to share it with me and that I had a pint in my hand. With that in mind I jumped back (in truth, eased myself circumspectly) into the car and was home by three o'clock to recount tales of the chase over a couple of beers.

The year came to an end with me having run five marathons, ten half marathons, two 10 milers and four 10 kilometres. In 1985 I had run 3507 miles at an average of 67.5 miles a week and although I would keep up this level of intensity for a few years I would never run more miles in a year.

Another significant incident occurred in this year which, shamefully, I almost overlooked. It was the departure of my oft mentioned and always loved red shorts. We had been through heaven and hell together and they had never let me down but of late they had started to fall down on the job. They had to be laid to rest in that great plastic bag for cleaning cloths in the sky, sorry, shed. To replace them I went for a much more sedate pair. They were canary yellow. I hoped '86 was going to be as bright as the latest shorts.

Chapter 5

1986 The Bad, the Good and the Scilly

Knees are funny things. Some are funnier than others. Visually, they make a comedy of the long and dramatic line of the leg. Practically, however, they are tremendously important. Here is a list of things, not necessarily in order of significance, which I personally believe would be difficult to achieve without the knee.
- Getting into a Sinclair C5 and pedalling it up a hill.
- Picking up confetti off a wet pavement.
- Being knighted by ER indoors.
- Patting a Chihuahua.
- Defecating accurately into a toilet bowl.
- Russian dancing.

Generally, hitting the ground like a felled tree would be a necessary precursor to many activities. All food would have to be served either buffet style or while you reclined on a lectus in the triclinium, like Caesar eating his salad.

I am sure your list of difficulties would differ from mine but the point I'm trying to make is that knees play a pivotal role, functionally and socially. So why, oh why, if they are so damned vital, couldn't they have evolved into a better design? A simple, no frills hinge would have done the job; but no, they have to have a patella, cartilage, menisci, tendons, ligaments, synovial and fibrous membrane, numerous bursae and a whole bunch of other fiddly stuff, which are all just waiting to go wrong and can't be fixed with a squirt of WD40.

Early in February 1986 something went wrong with my knee. From the middle of the month my running diaries were dominated by knee notes which continued until mid-March. I already had my eyes on another Wolverhampton Marathon just after Easter and I was running like an eggless chicken. I had entered the London Marathon for 1986 but had failed to get in through the lottery of normal selection. However, I had discovered that running under two hours and forty minutes gave you automatic entry, as part of the Amateur Athletics Association (AAA) elite national marathon championships. My time in last year's Manchester Piccadilly Marathon had been just short but I believed I could achieve the qualification requirements this year.

January had seen me run 400 miles for the month, the highest monthly total I would ever achieve. It didn't take Hercule Poirot (or Morse) to deduce that there was a link between high mileage and the knee problem. As it was, by now I had developed a genuine fixation on maximising miles and a serious depletion of little grey cells. I believed that any easing off would spell disaster for my progress. The intervention of a chest infection actually helped me at that point. I am not saying it stopped me running but it forced me to run less. I 'only' ran 287 miles in February. My knee had virtually recovered by mid-March but the episode had flagged up a weakness which would eventually catch up with me. At that time I was only interested in preventing rival runners from doing that.

Towards the end of January Whistler drove me to Hell-by-Elysium Helsby where we had, once again, entered the half marathon. As usual, we were both recovering from colds. The rain came down like arrows at Agincourt while we sat in the car park feeling collectively rough and unwilling to de-Polo. Janus, looking down on us with his sad, northern face, didn't like the competition our doleful, steamed-up car facades presented. Being official Roman God of beginnings and transitions he tried to wipe the frowns off our faces by stopping the rain for the start of the race and holding it off for our progress to the end.

Meteorological and health factors taken into consideration I set off at a sensible pace and I reached 10 miles in 57 minutes. With the wind behind me and the course slightly downhill I struck out in the last three miles. What a lovely feeling; running fast and easy is a delight hard to describe. The experience was slightly marred near the end as an attempt to overtake one more person in the last 80 metres brought on a strong impulse to vomit, which I only just successfully resisted. On the plus side I had run a personal best of 1:14:23 and finished 20th which I was delighted with under the circumstances. (Seeing me come in under 75 minutes, the course measurers were yet again sent scurrying on to the route with their tapes and surveyors wheels!)

Whistler had also run well and, after changing, we went into the social club by the finish to rerun the race over a pint of Thwaites bitter; two hours earlier we had been debating whether to get out of the Polo or not. It's a funny old game. Success is in the lap of the gods, (as Sir Clive Sinclair might say).

It seems a particularly human trait to go deliberately and often unnecessarily out of the comfort zones of 'normal' activity and into uncertain situations. On a personal basis I could understand the desire to push physical boundaries, having experienced the pleasure and sense of self-worth this could generate but I could not always relate to it if the risks were too great and the cost of failure too high.

On January 28th the space shuttle Challenger broke apart 73 seconds into its flight. The seven crew members died, including Christa McAuliffe. She was a teacher on board as a result of being selected from 11,000 applicants for the National Aeronautics and Space Administration (NASA) 'Teacher in Space Project', in the United States. It didn't make much sense to me that humans were risking lives and investing so much in attempts to enter alien environments, incapable of sustaining human life, while doing too little to halt the destruction of the only environment that we knew was capable of sustaining it. Billions of dollars were being spent on projects designed to win a relatively futile space race, when the money could have gone towards helping to save the human race.

On April 26th the Chernobyl disaster occurred. When a nuclear power plant in Ukraine blew up, 31 deaths were officially reported as a direct result of the explosion. There is much variation in estimates made of subsequent related deaths caused by exposure to the radiation generated. The Chernobyl Forum Report 2006 commissioned by environmental group Greenpeace asserted that, "the most recently published figures indicate that, in Belarus, Russia and Ukraine alone, the accident could have resulted in an estimated 200,000 additional deaths in the period between 1990 and 2004." This type of statistic is obviously difficult to verify but what is undeniably true is that it was a massive tragedy, the scale of which is still being uncovered.

Humans have a habit of playing with fire and getting burnt. In my view this is fine if it is a personal choice which only puts the pyromaniac in danger but when it implicates thousands of others it seems fatally short-sighted and unjustifiable. Is investing so much money to develop technology around which there is such huge uncertainty for the benefit of humankind? Certainly in the short term, I would say no. I know many would disagree with this view point and protest that unless we 'boldly go where no man or woman has been before' the human race will atrophy. Surely, there needs to be a balance. The view that risk is often necessary to achieve progress may have some truth in it, but it seemed to me that it was also a convenient and too frequently used excuse to justify the threats presented to innocent people by ill-considered or avaricious development. Shouldn't progress benefit all? Technological research rarely appeared to be aimed at those in desperate need. Funding always seemed available to develop advanced weaponry or new consumer gadgets but not always for researching into simple technology to save thousands of lives. Not wanting to feel so pessimistic about progress, I hoped that human ingenuity for solving problems would eventually prevail for the good of everyone. It would have to.

A week or so after the Helsby Half Marathon and four days after my 35th birthday, I found myself enviously observing natural technology. To fit in my running, without having the thought of it hanging over me late each evening, I had taken to running home from work. This was potentially problematic considering that my workplace was in Birkenhead and my home in Liverpool, places which were separated by the wide and wondrous river Mersey. Since I had no intention of practising for an aquathlon, I generally got a train, under the Mersey, from Rock Ferry on the Wirral side to James Street in Liverpool city centre. From there I proceeded to get my run in early, plodding back home via Otterspool Promenade, a recreational green space by the river, created from a former landfill site. It was opened to the public in 1950 and became the site of the '84 International Garden Festival.

Since the turn of the millennium you have been able to run, walk or cycle a traffic-free route the full five miles from the Pier Head in the city, southeastwards to the end of Otterspool promenade, in the southern suburbs. In '86 I still had to trudge a couple of miles down the dock road first, parallel to the river, before I could drop down to the promenade for about two and a half miles and then head up, inshore and home. It was a run of about eight miles in all. I would change before leaving school and carry anything else I needed in a rucksack, which wasn't much as I was allergic to taking work home.

The run never seemed to be the same on two consecutive days. Conditions varied widely and wildly, depending on tide and weather. The eye-filling sweep of water was a constantly changing palette; black, grey, brown, blue, silver and pink being just a few of the hues on offer. The Mersey is at its widest near Ellesmere Port. Here it is about 3 miles from shore to shore. At Otterspool the river is narrower but it is still about a mile across to the Wirral. Being such a broad tidal river could make it behave more like the open sea and the caprice of the wind was always an important factor in deciding what enjoyment, if any, was derived from a run here.

On the day in question a cold southeasterly was blowing against me and intermittent squalls of rain poked the skin on my face. While struggling along, for distraction, I studied the flight of seagulls accompanying me. Unlike mine, their progress seemed effortless. They angled their aerodynamic wings to hold themselves up in the wind before a sudden, slight adjustment saw them slice through an invisible surface to catch a slip stream and accelerate forward. They eyed me beadily and appeared to be smirking. As I ran I wondered if I could master a similar energy saving technique suitable for these conditions. I got some funny looks (from birds and humans) unsuccessfully trying to. Other than tacking into the wind and thereby running twice the distance, I could think of no other method than the usual, battling it head on.

I did, however, come up with a psychological ploy. I decided to chant a mantra to alleviate, hopefully, the depressive effects of this buffeting. "The wind is my friend, the wind is my friend," I repeated as I leant into its velvety violence. For a short while this seemed to work as I forgot my windy woes. My transcendental state soon ended though when I was rudely brought back to this earthly realm, slapped in the mush by a rogue plastic carrier bag travelling in the opposite direction at warp speed. "Bastard," I muttered, wrestling it off my face and curing temporary blindness. The meditative moment had gone and, friend or not, I was glad to part company with that arsehole Aeolus, as I turned north for home.

There were times on the 'Prom' when the wind truly was my friend. Whispering encouragement from the north, it would place a gentle hand on my back to aid my work-weary way along the shore. Other times it was like a boozed-up, so-called mate who frequently but unexpectedly whacked me between the shoulder blades causing me to stagger forward, unbalanced.

Sometimes there was no wind. As the year grew old and days short I would find myself running in still darkness. Once I raced a ship heading for Garston Docks. It was lit up eerily, like the ghost of a pleasure cruiser, no sign of life save a metallic clanking. This plaintive tolling travelled clearly across oil-black water which reflected a rippling sister ship. Occasionally there was no wind and no view, as river fog hung yellow and foul as a smoker's breath. Sounds of the river were audible but from an undetectable source, paranoid and muffled inside a padded cell.

At times the water would be mirror placid, at others unruly and untrammelled. It had been known for crossings of the ferries (not unsubstantial boats) to be cancelled due to dangerous conditions. The river behaved most boisterously when stormy days with big winds combined with high tides. Wild water would fling flotsam and jetsam over the railings at anyone who dared to promenade. Then it was easy to forget this was just a river. It was the quiet dusk days I loved the best. Running through calm air, head turned to watch the spectacle of the distant sandstone ridge slowly pocketing the sun like a thief; the river's lens capturing it red handed.

In January I was working hard with my running and hard at fitting my running in with work. National figures in this month showed that 14.4 % of the workforce was out of work. Obviously, Thatcher's government was not happy with these figures. Even though they were a post-war record, they were determined to push the numbers up even higher in an attempt to make their monetarist policies succeed. In February they saw a great opportunity when the respected and likeable Rupert Murdoch, boss of News International, that noble and trustworthy media organisation, decided to move his newspaper production away from Fleet Street to Wapping and in the process reduce his workforce. Printers (who were about to be thrown on to the scrap heap after years in the industry) objected and went out on strike.

Mr Murdoch claimed his aim was modernisation and efficiency with the use of latest technology. Of course, there is nothing wrong with that, but who was it to benefit? Well, Mr Murdoch for one. He obviously needed to maximise his income to enable him to buy bigger yachts to tow his smaller yachts; and who else? Well the Tories, naturally. They loved a bit of union bashing and were prepared to provide the massive police presence needed to protect Rupe's new premises and those employees who had unselfishly decided to help Mr Murdoch out of this tight spot.

It was probably true that printing practices were outdated and change did need to occur but to totally disregard the contribution and dignity of a whole section of the industry's workforce without sympathetic consultation was not a human solution. Cuddly Mr Murdoch's response was to sack his workers for striking. The Tories rubbed their hands with glee, ticked another union off their list and prepared to bump up the jobless thermometer. There were obvious similarities to the miner's dispute. Murdoch (Mr) and Thatcher (Mrs) were held up as figureheads in a fight for freedom; mainly by Mr M's own truthful newspapers. The unions were "anarchic and archaic." Mrs T and Mr M, the tremendous twosome would lead the uphill march to the pinnacle of progress and liberty in society. The peak would be reached no matter how many ordinary working people they needed to trample over and squash down in the process.

The cosy relationship between the government, the police and News International, obviously formed to protect the rights of individuals and champion the truth in society, continued until recently when, over twenty five years later, a different kind of truth started to emerge.

I was marching my way through the miles in March before my marathon in early April. While training hard I somehow found time to run in several races. The heavy winter mileage was, surprisingly, beginning to bear fruit in the form of extra speed. I ran two PBs; 33.03 for a 10k in Wrexham, North Wales, a time I was never able to better and 1:13:56 in the Ormskirk half-marathon, which I did eventually improve on. I was running well and the obsessive mileage accumulation seemed to be having the desired effect.

Before the Ormskirk run I was still feeling uncertain about my knee. Whistler took me to the race. He was also feeling a bit iffy as he was recovering from a cracked rib after a climbing accident or left hand glove/bollard incident, I forget which. What a sad pair we made, again, sitting in the car whingeing about our injuries and having the usual 'vest or lifer' debate. I had become a hard line anti-lifer since last year's Wolverhampton. He still hankered after thermal comfort even when it was really quite mild (in case you are remotely interested).

At the end of the race I had come through the knee examination well but Whistler had failed the rib test, having got a stitch and performed below expectations. He cried into his pint of shandy as I merrily quaffed an undiluted couple in front of a roaring fire in the Buck i' th' Vine, a lovely 17th century pub in Ormskirk town centre. I believe it got its name because the strength of the ale made drinkers talk with a lisp, but don't quoth me on that.

April was a mad running month for me; a tale of two marathons. How could one be so good and the other so bad even though I ran particularly well in both? The answer to this riddle will be revealed in due course or, you could say, shortly. The first marathon was the Wolverhampton, again. Eileen was away in the Lake District with students from her adult education class. They were on a study weekend, probably studying the ale houses of Cumbria, concentrating on those with names which were difficult to pronounce after an evening's visit. My plan was to go down and stay with her parents in Birmingham on Saturday night and travel to neighbouring Wolverhampton on Sunday morning.

Before this I had some caries to take care of, thankfully not mine. The usual arrangement I had with Laura, my daughter, was for her to stay at my house on Thursday night and then I would take her to school the next day. I would also pick her up on Saturday morning and she would stay Saturday night. So she would be with me approximately two sevenths of the week. This had been the basic pattern since she was about nine months old. During this time I had got used to doing much of the mundane domestic stuff with her from an early age, just a lot less often than her mum. Recently I had noticed that she had a few problems with her teeth and was due a trip to the dentist. Having stayed as usual on Thursday night, on the Friday before the Wolverhampton marathon, it had fallen on me to arrange a fun outing for her to visit the tooth fairy's hit man. It was still the Easter holidays so luckily, no teaching would be missed (lucky for my daughter but not me). I took her to the surgery early and discovered regrettably some teeth would be missed. She needed five extracted, but mercifully only milk teeth, as she was just seven.

Teeth (like knees) are pretty ridiculous objects, sitting in your mouth like mini marble tombstones. They are little things capable of causing big trouble. Would it not have been better if they were fewer in number but made of more robust material and came in just one set which grew with you like the rest of your bones or if, like reptiles and fish, human teeth regenerated as they were worn down or lost? No bridges, crowns or dentures for Peter Piranha. Of all the species, we are supposed to be the clever ones but we have the most stupid teeth. As far as the human body was concerned I thought we needed to go back to the drawing board.

The dentist asked me to take Laura away and come back again at mid-day to have the multi-extractions. Presumably this hiatus was to give her more time to think about her fate and allow blind panic to set in. I felt sorry for her as we entered the waiting room again at noon but soon I was feeling sorry for myself as her exuberance began to give me and the other waiting patients a headache to add to any dental discomfort. Eventually she calmed down but only when they'd given her a general anaesthetic. She smiled as the needle went in. They whipped the teeth out and she was smiling when she woke up. She was smiling but couldn't walk. I carried her out to a taxi and on the journey home she just kept mumbling through smiling, bloodied lips. "Feelth like I've got no teef. Feelth like I've got no teef."

I took her back to her mum's, lay her on a couch and left. Having bought a couple of little treats for her, I went back to see how she was recovering. She bounded down the stairs to greet me almost knocking me off my feet. As she seemed fairly oblivious to pain and discomfort I pencilled her in for a first marathon when she was eighteen.

Paternal duties over for the week, I set off for Birmingham on Saturday. Here I was cosseted by Eileen's mum and dad. I slept well on Saturday night and, over and above the duty of care, I was walked to the bus stop at 7.00 am on Sunday morning by my hosts.

I arrived in Wolverhampton, at the start area, in plenty of time and felt at ease. We were soon on our way. The first two miles were a little fast but then I settled to a comfortable cadence. The snow started falling at three miles but I did no falling at four miles, as I had the previous year. Even in a vest and shorts the cold was not a problem. I was generating enough heat (NB Whistler). I was relaxed enough to joke with the crowd about training for the Moscow Marathon. Ten miles in 58 minutes and I still felt in control. I seemed to be catching people all the time. The miles whizzed by; I didn't even see the 15 mile marker. Some people were running the race as a relay, in pairs, a half-marathon each. At 17 miles a fresh relay man went past me, only four miles into his run. I threw a grappling hook into the back of his shorts; figuratively, of course, otherwise it would have been cheating and potentially dangerous. He pulled me along. 20 miles and I still felt untroubled. Relayman kept saying, "Are you still there?" I just breathed heavily in response which for some reason made him run faster. It appears he was in third place in his race. We passed more people. One runner gasped, "Christ, I thought I was running fast." I tried to think of a witty response about running on water but I was too far ahead of him by the time it was composed.

24 miles and I was still buoyant on the blackstuff and bostiked to Relayman like a barnacle to a boat. 25 miles and tiredness suddenly set in. 25 and a half and my sole mate left me with a late surge and no regrets. I passed two more marathoners and spotted the clock in the finishing straight reading 2:33. I pushed hard and the clock ticked over to 2:34 as my foot contacted the line. Tick, tock, toe, sock, I felt sick. But I felt great at the same time. A few sips of water and the sickness went. I was given a plastic, hooded poncho

and put it on the wrong way round. I grappled weakly with it, like I was fighting off an alien in some bad 1950s sci-fi movie. A lady marshal came to my aid; saved from the monster by my heroine. Suddenly I could see again. It was a miracle! And so was my time. I was delighted. I searched for Whistler, who had also run, having spent the night at his ironic Ironbridge mate's riverside pad. (I had decided not to risk the excitement of spending the night there.) I found him changing in his car. He'd knocked two minutes off his PB but still managed to look underwhelmed. We met another Liverpool running acquaintance, a work colleague of Whistler's. He had improved by nearly 15 minutes; amazing! I got the train back home and persuaded Eileen to go out for a few scoops to help me celebrate my PB, 24th place and a London qualifying time. Any excuse; three actually!

On Monday I sailed through work on a total high. I told a close colleague about my exploits as one of her sons was a keen runner. The next day, in the staff room, she was telling me how impressed her son was with my time when one of the infant teachers overheard us and said, with the innocence of one-who-did-not-understand, "Oh, was that the marathon I heard about on the radio, the one that was too short?" Could it be? Yes it could. I wondered what had happened to the 15 mile marker.

At that moment the bottom fell out of my world and the world nearly fell out of my bottom. Pathetic, I know, as a joke and a feeling, but real nonetheless. A change in the marathon course from the previous year had taken out an earlier awkward section and replaced it at 15 miles with an 800 metre loop off the main road through a housing estate and back on to the highway. The marshal who was meant to direct the lead car and runners on to this loop hadn't turned up for the race and we had all traipsed past, oblivious, missing the section out. We were 734 yards short of the full distance. But short is short, whatever, and all the times were invalid. The highwayman had robbed us.

Billy Wilson the organiser had got his wish from last year. In '85 he didn't like 'so little criticism', in '86 he got it in spades. To be fair, these things happen and it was a shame that it had, after all the hard work put into the organisation. It was usually a smoothly organised and well supported race. What puzzled me was why the driver in the lead car hadn't known the route. It may not have been wise to rely on one marshal to direct runners on to a crucial new part of the course. On the bright side the organisers profited from a brisk trade in voodoo dolls made in the missing marshal's image. I have a photo of myself, finishing triumphantly, with enough reserve energy to raise both arms aloft. You can see the delight and disbelief on my face. I almost feel sorry for myself looking at it.

I was in a similar situation to 1985 post-Wolverhampton, but for different reasons. I had wasted all that hard training. I would have easily achieved the London qualifying time even on a full course. My reaction was also the same as the previous year with the same reservations. I entered the Stratford Marathon again, just 21 days away. Would I recover in time?

The intervening days disappeared like minutes and soon we were heading south to Birmingham again. I had hired a car to make the logistics of the trip a little easier. The newspapers were full of Rambo Ronny Reagan's air attack on Ghadafi's Libya, backed by his B movie, A-team sidekick Mrs T. The fact that this lot were squaring up made the world seem an unsafe place to me. The US reason for the bombing was that Libya was an oppressive regime which supported acts of terrorism. On the day before my marathon, representatives of a state with similar credentials were protected by British police in Stratford. The worst they had to encounter were harsh truths and flour bombs.

The occasion was Shakespeare's birthday celebrations to which, for God knows what reason, South African diplomats had been invited and during which a South African flag was unfurled. Anti-apartheid demonstrators gathered to let their feelings be known. Six were arrested by police who were attempting to protect the liberty of South Africans, well, these particular white ones. The local paper, The Stratford Herald, printed the main speech at the celebratory gathering. John Mortimer, described by the paper as a local barrister/playwright, delivered it. Addressing the Bard as if he was present, Mortimer praised him saying, "You were on the side against tyranny, cruelty and injustice." If that was true and Shakespeare had been there he may well have been arrested too, probably for chanting anti-apartheid slogans in rhymed couplets. At least some Equity members from the Royal Shakespeare Company had boycotted the celebrations.

While all this drama was taking place unbeknownst to us, I was taking Eileen, with her mum and dad, for a drive through the West Midlands' countryside to Coughton (pronounced coat-on) Court; we didn't need our coats on because it was quite mild. By 1986 the Throckmortons, one of the UK's oldest Catholic families, had been in residence at this attractive stately pile for just short of 600 years. I was impressed because we had only lived in our house less than 200 days. I wondered whether they were still paying their mortgage; probably, if it was an endowment.

As we walked down a country lane I suddenly spotted a cardboard box in a ditch. It contained a lovely collection of Victorian bottles. No-one was about so we decided to take a few of the nicer ones. Just at that moment some young children came running out of a nearby house. I thought they were going to voice discontent and shout, "Oi, leave them bleeding bottles alone Mister!" But no, even though they had actually dug them up, they told us we could have them, in fact, they went back into their house and brought us a few more; such nice kids. I was especially pleased with a couple of beautiful beer bottles dating from the late 1800s. I already had a small collection of this kind of container. I have no idea why I was attracted to the genre. Enjoying the walk and finding the bottles kept my mind off the race and prevented my metaphorical bottle from being lost.

Race day; I lay on in bed while Eileen went for a short run with her dad. Once up, I showered, had a cup of ginseng tea but nothing to eat. I felt calm, almost as if I didn't intend to run. I drove Eileen, her mum, her dad and, most importantly, myself to the start of the race and registered. Situated in the open green space by the river, opposite the Royal Shakespeare Theatre, you couldn't wish for a more pleasant start and finish area. As last year, the course was a two-lapper taking in the surrounding countryside and incorporating a half marathon with the full. This arrangement was always potentially confusing and difficult for the full marathoners when trying to establish an even pace.

In cool, still conditions I set off too fast, as usual, dragged along by the half marathoners tearing away. I soon slowed and settled. Pace sorted, I was immediately conscious of how comfortable I felt and how uncomfortable everyone around me appeared. It was getting warmer and we were taking on plenty of water. If at times I felt I was running a little too quickly, I reined myself in to prevent weariness from the Wolverhampton run creeping into my legs.

Approaching the Tramway bridge, at the end of lap one, I prepared myself for the strange feeling of loneliness I had experienced the previous year when all the half marathon runners peeled off to the riverside for their finish. It was a tough psychological moment when you suddenly realised you had to do it all again. I could see the lead car over the bridge, presumably broken down. All the feelings I had expected to experience were then totally superseded by an overwhelming adrenaline rush when I realised that the lead car was fully operational and waiting for me. A prickly tingle flooded my scalp and I felt sick.

The car started to move in front of me and I had to give myself a mental slap on the face. I reasoned with myself to induce some calm and save the energy that I would surely need later on. "They'll soon catch you," I assured myself, "but at least you can say you led at half way." I still couldn't help myself from chasing the car over the next two miles until my boggled brain accepted the fact that it was the car that was supposed to go at my pace not the other way around. By then I had burned off the initial adrenaline deluge. "At least you got to 15 miles in the lead," I congratulated myself. I took a look behind and could see someone about 200 metres back. I promised myself that I wasn't going to twist myself around again and interrupt my stride. I didn't really need to. We were out in the countryside and pockets of spectators were well spaced out, usually at road junctions. This meant that I could hear the applause for the runner behind coming clearly through a rural air, unpolluted by other noise. I tried not to tighten up, staying rhythmic, relentless. A couple of times I felt fear; then I wanted to surrender under the pressure and stop, but this feeling soon passed. At 17 miles I could still hear the clapping. 18, 19 mile markers went by, at 20 I suddenly realised the applause had grown gradually quieter to my ears. I glued my eyes to the

number plate of the time car and forged onwards. I knew there was a hill at 23. I plodded up it. I broke my promise and looked back; no-one in sight. A veteran cyclist came alongside me. "How far back?" I asked. "Nowhere near," he smiled.
I would have jumped on his crossbar and given him a big kiss had it not been for the fact that I was too tired to jump that high and I'm not keen on men with beards.

(Tony P. of Mersey is not strained)

My strength was suddenly renewed by the knowledge that I would have to slow down drastically, stop or be attacked by mad mountaineers, for anybody to catch me in the last three miles. I was pretty sure those scenarios were unlikely (especially the last). One last hill at 24 miles; at the top I could hear noise from loud speakers drifting from the finish area.

Down by the river Eileen and her parents had returned from their saunter through the town-centre shops which had caused them to miss me going past on the first lap. Oblivious to the present situation they nearly had a collective heart attack, like some mass-hysterical, religious cult, when it was announced, over the tannoy, that Tony Peacock was in the lead with a mile to go. Admittedly, it was hysterical that I was leading. They eventually calmed down but then slipped into a state of collective anxiety at the thought of me being caught. I was in a better position. I knew I was odds-on favourite. Coming down the Tramway towards the river I even had time to tidy up my hair a little and wipe the snot from my face before entering the dense corridor of cheering supporters in the home straight. The picture of me finishing shows someone in a state of ecstasy. My eyes are closed and a big fat smile splits my face.

Some people are used to winning and I suppose become a little blasé. It was a unique experience for me that I will never forget. As I came through the finish Shirley Strong, the Los Angeles Olympic 100 metre hurdle silver medallist, put a medal around my neck and said 'well done.' I said, 'thanks'. It was all I could muster. Besides, I suppose it was a bit late to congratulate her in person on her Olympic success. I staggered away to my family, to drink and dress. Later, as Shirley presented me with a Waterford Crystal tankard, she commented, "You look a bit better now."

"Thanks for that Shirl," I replied in my head, "you've got a bit of room for improvement yourself!"

I was also handed a huge trophy by the Lord Mayor who shook my hand. He'd probably shaken the hands of the South African delegation the day before. Had I known that I would have worn my practical joke electrocuting hand-shaker...and cranked up the voltage. I didn't have to worry about these things thankfully as I was the one in a state of shock. The Mayor then took the trophy off me (he needed the help of Strong Shirley because I was reluctant to let go). I was informed that my name would be put on the cup but that I would not be allowed to take it home because it had been returned flat in the post by the previous winner. Looking at the size of it, he had probably needed to adjust its shape to make it fit on the mantelpiece. As it was, in truth, too large for our little house I eventually accepted this. Besides, I joked, it probably wasn't a good idea to give it to someone from Liverpool because it might not come back at all. Tiredness had given me an attack of the stereotypicals. The assembled company laughed with restraint while feeling their wrists to check they still had watches. I checked mine, 2:37:30 a PB and a London qualifying time. Not a bad day's work. A slow time to win in but, as they say, records are about being the fastest, winning is about being the fastest on the day. I was delighted all the faster runners had stayed away. I looked at my watch again and decided it was time to go. I had a stiff-legged drive back to Liverpool to contend with before I could have a celebratory pint or three to match my achievements.

May and June were also months dominated by trophies and body parts. The tenth of May saw the first all Merseyside F.A. Cup Final at Wembley. Liverpool came out winners 3-1 in an exciting game but both sets of fans lined the roads, side by side, to welcome their teams home. The rivalry between the two sets of fans, unlike in many other intra-city or inter-city derby matches, was generally good humoured. Matches between the two had been dubbed the 'friendly derbies'. Some acrimony had arisen in the aftermath of the Heysel disaster when all English clubs were banned from Europe as a blanket punishment. Everton had a strong team at the time and would have qualified for European competitions. On that day though there was a good atmosphere at the homecomings.

In June the World Cup Finals took place in Mexico. Argentina were eventual winners of the Jules Rimet trophy, which had come back in the post from previous winners Italy in reasonable condition. The South Americans had beaten England 2-1 in the quarter finals in controversial circumstances. Diego Maradonna scored both goals. The first goal he scored by using his hand to punch it past the English goalkeeper Peter Shilton. Apparently this is not allowed.

However the referee's eyes were not as sharp as Maradonna's hand was quick and the goal stood. He subsequently described it as being scored by the 'hand of God'. If you ask me he deserved a Jesus boot up his arse for the inability to confess his sins. Four minutes later, err... on the other hand, he deserved to be canonised for scoring a second goal of such beatific and splendiferous finesse. Many were wont to cry foul again and demand that his boots be checked for super glue or an electromagnetic device, so much did the ball appear to stick to his foot in a mazy, ten second, 60 yard run, before he eventually released it over the goal line. England fought back to score a goal through Gary Lineker, who had just finished a season at Everton. Lineker won the Golden Boot for scoring most goals in the competition. At the same time, at home, Derek Hatton, my old football comrade and well known Evertonian, didn't exactly get a golden handshake but was given the big elbow by the Labour Party for being a member of Militant Tendency. Like Gabby Logan (nee Yorath), Gary Lineker went on to be a presenter of the 'Match of The Day' BBC football show. Derek just went on...and on.

Instead of resting after my Shakespearean triumph, I also went on and on in May and June with a mixture of results. I ran in a race on each of the seven weekends after the marathon; Four half marathons, one 15k, one 10k and a five-miler. Two weeks after Stratford I achieved a PB of 1:13:20 in the Liverpool Half Marathon. Four weeks later I got another PB of 1:13:06 and came 8th in the Great North Western Half Marathon in Preston. I also managed to come second in two small local races of five mile and 10k, picking up a trophy on both occasions. The 10k award was about the same size as the Jules Rimet trophy but a little less elegant. To be honest it was an angel topped confusion of MDF and plastic, with layer on layer of bad taste, like a Las Vegas wedding cake.

On May 25th I had wasted the morning, running a bad time, in a badly organised half marathon, in bad conditions in Southport, the seaside town, just north of Liverpool. In the afternoon I ran a far more useful race with about 19.8 million other runners. As you have probably twigged, they weren't all on the start line in Sefton Park at 3.00 p.m. but spread out over 274 cities and other places around the world. London saw 200,000, Barcelona 50,000, Athens 30,000, and

Dublin 20,000. It was estimated that there were about 10,000 runners, joggers and walkers completing the 5k distance around Sefton Park that day. The Race Against Time had been organised by Sport Aid, a spin-off of Band Aid, and aimed to raise money to alleviate famine in East Africa. The response was unprecedented as all the runners around the world set off at 3:00 p.m. GMT to complete a 5k course. It showed what sport and its participants could achieve outside the elite realms of selfish commercialism. It was, and probably still is, the greatest global sporting event ever organised although I was concerned at the time that the earth might be knocked off its axis by all those pounding feet.

I had arranged a mini Race Against Time on the Friday before, at my school. Everyone who wanted, from nursery age upwards, ran a 200 metre lap of the school buildings and donated a minimum of 10p. We made £50 on the day, which for a small school, in a largely poor area was excellent. On the Sunday afternoon, I did the run with Eileen, her dad, her sister, (one of the younger ones) Laura and her mum. Three miles is a long way for the uninitiated and I ended up carrying one of them, a couple of times. Thankfully it was only my daughter.

By the end of June I felt like I was still carrying an invisible relative on my runs. Work and family commitments meant that I was eventually forced to ease off a little, but not before I'd entered another marathon. Encouraged by recent successes I was keen to have a go at running in foreign climes and an exotic location. A great idea but we couldn't afford that sort of summer holiday, so we settled for the Scilly Isles instead. We had also been reassured by the fact that, in these times of conflict and aggressive foreign policies, after 335 years of technically being 'at war', in 1986 the Scilly Islands and the Netherlands had finally signed a peace treaty. The Dutch must have sighed hugely with relief and I could also relax in the knowledge that the race would not be disturbed by the sound of a thousand clogs marching over the hill or by a bombardment of red rounds of Edam.

The Scilly Isles adventure started off with an anti-climax but ended with a storming finish. I wish I could say the same about the marathon race. We had thought about taking our bikes down to

Cornwall on the train where we could get a ferry across to the islands. The fact that there was only about seven miles of road on the largest island (St Mary's) and that a ticket for the helicopter from Penzance was cheaper than the ferry made us plump for the chopper (not Raleigh) and leave the bikes.

The long, long train journey south negotiated successfully, we arrived in Penzance well in time for our departure. We were watching the flight before ours about to leave when suddenly everybody started to disembark. The ground crew then proceeded to put the helicopter back in its hanger and explained that all that day's flights would now be cancelled due to technical difficulties. I was fuming, for about a minute, by which time we had been informed that British Airways, the operators, were going to put us up in a hotel for the night. We were from up north; this was like hitting the jackpot.

At the lovely Smugglers Hotel in New Lyn, we stuffed our faces at dinner, slept as deeply as we could and stuffed our faces at breakfast before a taxi came to pick us up for our flight. I still have the bill from the hotel. It has the date and room number and that's all, except for '£1 for drinks' written at the bottom. (Was there no end to our profligacy?)

The trip across the Celtic sea to the islands, 45 kilometres off Land's End in Cornwall, only took about 20 minutes. I'd never travelled in a helicopter before but it didn't look like the most stable of flying machines to me. The flight did nothing to dispel the initial visual impression. Persistently agitated, we felt like the residual lumps of flour in a sieve. The scenery over the featureless expanse of sea was nowhere near as stimulating. I supposed you could say we arrived shaken but not stirred.

Also at the back of my mind, being repressed for the duration of the flight, was the fact that it was just over three years since a helicopter on the same route had gone down in fog two miles off the Scillies. Out of 26 passengers only six had survived. The logic, with which I was cupboarding this nervous knowledge, was the belief that disasters rarely struck twice in the same place and that more stringent safety measures would surely have been enforced in the aftermath of the tragedy. This may have been why the previous day's flights had been postponed. Besides, the alternative was a two hours and forty minute ferry crossing over some of the most turbulent and unpredictable waters in the British Isles and I wasn't a good sailor.

The helicopter landed on St Mary's, the largest island in this wild and beautiful archipelago. It boasts five inhabited islands and 140 others. The overall population is about 2000 and over 1600 of these live on St Mary's. Hugh Town is the capital of the islands; actually it doesn't have much competition being the only sizeable settlement. We were camping just outside this wannabe conurbation and my first impression was that it was more like a Yorkshire village than a seaside town. It was quietly getting on with its business, surviving mainly on a virtually imperceptible tourist trade. The main entertainment on the island, open 24 hours a day, was the scenery; its rugged coastline indented with sandy coves and cliffs blanketed with wild flowers. At that moment the weather was kind.

The marathon was two days after our arrival and as I stood on the start line I wondered why I was there and not walking barefoot down an empty beach, paddling at the water's edge looking for shells and stones. After recent successes I supposed I saw this as an opportunity to add to them. A marathon with a small field that no-one in their right minds would enter would be easy for someone not in his right mind to win, wouldn't it?

There were maybe 50 people gathered at the start. Some looked like serious runners; some were children there to do the three mile fun run starting at the same time. Amazingly, I spotted someone I knew, a lad I had chatted to at the Wolverhampton Marathon. I was aware he was an accomplished runner and someone who would be there or thereabouts at the end. There was also an entrant wearing exactly the same style vest as me. I joked with him, saying it was like two mothers-in-law wearing identical hats at a wedding. Fortunately for everyone involved I was also wearing a pair of subtle grey shorts after complaints about the distracting glare from my yellow ones; a small quiet race was not a good place to wear loud shorts; some would say there was no good place to wear them.

We set off at a reasonable speed weaving our way through the young fun runners. After the sorting out, we were three; me, my Wolves acquaintance and a young man who was a club runner. He was running his first marathon but had recorded an impressive 72 minutes for a half. Chatting as we ran, he explained that he was in the Scillies, unbeknown to his club mates. The idea was that he would turn up at his club next week and announce that he had run and won a marathon. I had the horrible feeling that the fuse on my petard had been lit and I was about to be well and truly hoisted on't. He had, like me, banked on the fact that he would be the fastest in a small field. He got it right. I got it horribly wrong.

Due to the serious lack of road surface, the race distance was made up of six laps of the island. The young club runner had stopped the rabbit and hared off. As we tried to hang on to him I turned to my friend and said, "I think this is too fast." He replied, "I don't think so." Ten minutes after this confident assertion he'd disappeared behind me and I was left to chase alone. I was within ten yards of our leading leveret with one lap to go. Then suddenly my body gave up. It may have been a tiny signal from the brain offering the beach as an alternative that caused the shutdown but who knows. I could see the leader weakening but I had already totally gone. I got to 23 miles and walked. As I jog/walked the third placed runner went past me. In the last mile the next placed runner came past. I ran the last 400 metres for show and came over the line fourth in 2:49. I was disappointed but philosophical. It wasn't my day. My day had been in Stratford.

We drank in the pub with most of the runners that night. It was hard not to bump into people limping around the island over the next couple of days; it made it all feel quite intimate. The callow winner couldn't believe the post-race muscle agony he was going through. I allowed myself a quiet revenge chuckle. It had been a tough course to run and the atmosphere low-key but great fun. As I recall in my diary; "A Mars bar, a medal and a certificate all for £1." Those really were the days of non-commercial marathons.

When most runners had gone home to the mainland, the next week we took the opportunity to enjoy the attractions of the archipelago in changeable weather. We took a trip to the island of Tresco, one end of which was wild and rugged while the other was home to famous tropical gardens. It was the day after Bank Holiday Monday as, near to the gardens, we stepped on to a pale yellow beach about a mile long. There was only one other person on it, at the other end. This was the height of the holiday season for god sakes. In the following days we also visited the small, idyllic, barely populated islands of St Agnes and St Martins, which were equally tranquil.

After the low point of my race, a high point of our trip was provided by another sort of race. On Friday evening we were taken by launch to Nut Rock, St Martin's, where gig boats, each with a crew of six, had been towed. Gig boats are rowing boats made from Cornish elm, about 30 feet in length and 5 feet in the beam. They were built to withstand heavy seas but also to be fast and stable. The boats, representing the various islands, then raced across open water the three miles back to Hugh Town, St Mary's. It was a great experience accompanying these vessels and watching the crews straining every sinew to gain ascendancy in the lively swells. The spectators were encouraged to adopt and cheer for one of the crews. Having experienced it in marathons I knew how much the supportive shouts would be appreciated by those pushing themselves to exhaustion. The first boat won by just half a length.

Soon it was nearly time to head off home and two nights before our planned departure we were in our usual hostelry, The Mermaid, downing a couple of pints of our usual poison, Wessex Ale. We fell into conversation with some French marine biologists, as you do. They told us that this was the first time they had ever seen a mermaid and also that there was a storm a-coming in. When we awoke the next day the gale had arrived. This reduced our activities to a few sorties out to the shore to watch nature trash the place. We went to the pub again in the evening and heard tales of yachts been thrown about like balsa wood models, even at anchor in the harbour. Wind-nagged and beer-legged, we struggled back to our little, two-person tent. We let the Wessex Ale perform its magic and the still rampaging gale do its worst. The storm had just about blown itself out when we did arise ale-eyed and bed-headed on the morning of our return helicopter flight. Pushing our faces out of the tent we noticed something or, more accurately, the lack of it. There were no other tents or people. The site resembled the aftermath of an American Civil War battle, but without the bodies. Bits of tent littered the grass and ragged scraps of material flapped dejectedly on poles. We decamped with some difficulty, in the still strong wind, and made our way to town to catch the bus for the heliport. Descending the wet and gleaming road we met an old couple coming up, bent against the wind. "Everybody is sheltering in the Methodist Hall," the man breathlessly informed us. His wife nodded breathlessly in accord. I pointed out proudly that far from being refugees, we and our little tent had survived the night unscathed. I didn't mention the part played by the ale.

I was worried that the flight might be cancelled but surprisingly the weather was deemed suitable for flying by now and to be honest, with a following wind, the return seemed smoother than the outward trip. On reflection, although I had failed in my attempt to win the marathon, we had won a victory of sorts over the bullying storm which we later discovered was Hurricane Charlie's coat tails.

The summer's end heralded another Mersey Marathon, my fifth. The usual preparation and expectation were tempered by the feeling that I never ran my best in my home marathon. However I didn't really expect things to go wrong quite so soon. 'Bang' went the gun and 'bang' I hit the floor. Not shot but tripped. I got up, sore arm and leg, and sprinted off to find the perpetrator. I'm not sure what the plan was; swab everyone's shoes and send them off to the CSI lab to check for my DNA?

As if I needed an excuse, the kerfuffle caused me to set off too fast and I was all out of kilter from then on. I dragged myself through the last 6 miles ending with a weary 2:39:09, and 26th place. This was my best time for a Mersey Marathon but well below my personal best. I did however win a T shirt for correctly guessing the time of the eventual winner, Flying Dustman, Ian Corrin. It's a pity I wasn't as successful at running fast times as I was at guessing them.

When the Liverpool Echo published the results of the marathon on October 1st it also reported that enlightened Tory local girl, Edwina Currie had stated that the main factors causing illness in the North were 'ignorance and chips.' This was reassuring coming from a health minister. The fact that Merseyside's mortality rate was 18% above the national average and yet its health authorities were some of the worst funded in the country had obviously escaped her. Knowsley had £129 spent on each person in 1985 whereas in

Hampstead, North London, individuals had £557 spent on them. Had she deliberately chosen to overlook these statistics or was it just 'ignorance?'

Also in Knowsley, it was reported that Derek Hatton had lost his appeal against dismissal from his job for the council. This was 24 hours after the Labour Party conference had confirmed the expulsion of Militant Tendency supporters from the party. Not a good week for Degsy!

My final marathon of the year involved another visit to Windermere. I'd enjoyed the setting and atmosphere so much the previous year that I persuaded Eileen that we could make a mini weekend of it and stay over Saturday night. She entered the 10k which was being held after the marathon's start. We got an early train on Saturday, arriving at about 11 a.m. We made the most of the day by trundling around pretty Bowness in drizzly old weather and then taking the ferry across the still, mist-capped waters of the lake for a walk near Beatrix Potter's old haunt at Hill Top with the lovely National Trust pub, the Tower Bank Arms, adjacent. I felt I had to have at least one beer to support the NT.

Sunday developed into a beautiful, golden autumn day. Having no time for breakfast our guesthouse had made us a packed lunch which we carried to the start. I was determined to take it easy and enjoy this marathon experience. I knew what to expect and wanted to finish in roughly one piece. Setting off in Bowness I enjoyed the scenery in the first half of the race as we ambled northeastwards to Ambleside, turned southwest at the top of Windermere and ran through Hawkshead. We then passed Esthwaite Water and U-turned at the southwest tip of the lake to head northwards again for the last seven, switchback miles. Here my running slowed and I started to suffer into the strong wind. I picked up again after twenty three miles and finished relatively fresh in 13th place, winning a fairly inappropriate bottle of whisky. I managed a time of 2:39:50 just slower than the Mersey but on a much more demanding course. Obviously there was something to be said for restraint but would I listen to what was being said? I think not.

Eileen had thoroughly enjoyed the 10k on a far from easy course and strolled in with a PB of 48:10; brilliant. We sat and soaked up the sun, supping drinks by the lake, watching others finish, before we headed back home. I couldn't think of anywhere else I would rather have been at that time.

By November my training had started to become a little haphazard and I felt I was beginning to lose some enthusiasm for my running; maybe as a result of doing five marathons in one year, again. To keep my mileage up and get the running done during the week I had now taken to running four miles from work to Birkenhead's Hamilton Square Station, travelling just one stop to James Street in Liverpool and then running eight miles home. Those with calculators will be able to work out that this gave me 12 miles. However, it also gave me exhaustion. I was running at a time when my energy levels were naturally low. I could tell this by the way I would almost invariably fall asleep during the one stop train journey under the river. I usually woke, with a start, just in time to get off, wondering where the hell I was and often who I was. Eventually, to counteract the worry of missing my stop, I decided to stand up for the short journey. That way the train grinding to a halt would definitely wake me up if I fell asleep standing, like a horse.

Running this way was all very convenient but it had become a bit dull and left me feeling jaded. Bearing all this in mind I took a big decision in mid-November. I decided to join a running club. Whistler and I had started to drift apart in our running relationship. I was running less and less with him and he seemed to be just generally running less. He may well have been unfaithful and taken to running with someone else when he'd told me he was working late at the office; I don't know. We'd also stopped having meaningful, 'appropriate-clothing-for-the-conditions' discussions. It seemed that this was the beginning of the end of a beautiful relationship. Joining a club would make a cleaner break of it. I never did get to see his glove collection.

There were at least three clubs who trained close to where I lived; Liverpool Harriers, South Liverpool Athletic Club and Penny Lane Striders. So I chose one which trained five miles away. In the words of Eileen's father, 'there was no sense in being awkward and not showing it.' Liverpool Running Club was a relatively new club which met at Walton Park sports centre in the north of Liverpool close to Anfield and Goodison Park, the city's football stadia. I got to know about the club through its head coach and one of its founders, who just happened to be one of Eileen's former students. He was a serious man with a serious moustache and I will call him the Hombre. The Hombre was passionate about his coaching, about the club and about training structure.

On my first night I was introduced to the marathon squad, who eyed me with suspicion. This was a working class club and I could imagine them thinking, "Who does he think he is coming here talking posh (i.e. not Scouse)? The Hombre took me to one side and whispered me a warning. "There are a couple of people you need to watch out for, especially him." He pointed to an equally splendidly moustachioed individual, who shall be known as Rugman. He was the de facto leader of the marathon group and therefore a conduit for the Hombre's particular training schedules for the squad members but he was obviously not one of the coach's favourites. On the first night I was pleased to see that most of the group were round about the same standard as me. The session felt competitive but friendly. I couldn't quite understand the Hombre's reservations about Rugman. Two weeks later it became clear.

The Hombre's style of management was authoritarian with a touch of paternalism. He insisted on rigid adherence to his schedules and an acceptance of his view of running. On the third week I got to the club and met up with my squad. Rugman had the evening's official schedule on a sheet of paper in his hand and was studying it intently. When we had all gathered he carefully folded the paper, until it was small enough to fit into the minute back pocket of his shorts, clapped his hands together and said, "Right lads what do you fancy doing?" We voted democratically to go for an up tempo ten mile run. The Hombre was waiting for us when we returned. He scowled and attempted to give us all a bollocking for our non-adherence to the schedule. He had chosen to throw me in with a rebellious, cantankerous group of ne'er do wells, possibly with the aim of helping to make them toe the line. He had misjudged me. I was going to fit in well.

The first thing the Hombre advised me to do, when I told him about my marathon training, was to reduce my mileage. I did this for about a week. I thought his training regimes were fine for natural runners, sylph-like no-weights who skimmed across mud and sand without leaving an impression. If I reduced my mileage it would mean that I would have to adjust my diet to keep the weight off. Running was a big part of my life but it was also a counterbalance to the other big parts of my life, food and beer. I wanted the best of all worlds. So the relentless pursuit of mileage and the addiction to racing continued.

My final act of running insanity for the year was my daughter's fault. Eileen liked to spend Christmas with her family in Birmingham. I tagged along to watch the fun. This however meant that I missed seeing Laura on Christmas Day. Her mum and I eventually arranged that she could be with me, in Birmingham, on Boxing Day and a few days after. This generally meant that, having hired a car and driven it to Brum, I drove back to Liverpool on Boxing Day morning and brought Laura to Birmingham where, much to her delight, she had a second Christmas Day with presents and fuss off her adopted grandparents and extended family with many aunties. This particular Christmas I had a cunning plan to allow me to get some running in as well as driving over 200 miles. I set off early, drove the hundred odd miles to Speke in Liverpool, jumped out of the car, ran the Speke 10k road race, in 34 minutes, eased myself carefully back into the car, sped off to my daughter's house, picked her up and drove the 100 miles back to Birmingham. It was a shame the motor miles didn't count in my training log. Not content with this, two days later, me, Eileen and her dad were running in the Sparkhill 5 in Birmingham. Believe you me it's an effective way to disperse the Christmas food mass.

This particular approach to the sport marked the difference between me and a really serious runner. They would go easy over Christmas, avoiding overindulgence, so they could do well in races. I would go hard at the running so I could do well in the overindulgence.

And so a bit of a mad end to 1986, a funny old year littered with triumphs and tribulations, PBs and poor performances. 3307 miles run, five marathons, six half marathons, six 10ks and six other races; slightly less mileage than last year but better performances and now a club runner. Had I reached my peak? Would '86 turn out to be my best running year? I was 36 in a month's time, could I still improve? I had just heard that I had been accepted into London 1987, so I had an incentive.

Although I had no way of divining the future, an interesting fact came to my attention which may have held a hidden message relevant to my running in the years ahead. I read this in the local paper at the end of the year; "20% of children out of this country are now born in Wenlock." *Bloody hell,* I thought, *that must push the birth rate up in Shropshire.* Then, on second reading, after rubbing the sleep out of my eyes, I realised it actually reported, "20% of children in this country are born out of wedlock." I had a funny feeling I couldn't describe. Maybe it was one of Billy Wilson's tongue tickles.

Chapter 6

1987 Same Old Tories but a Different Running Story

"A stitch in time may save nine," first wrote Thomas Fuller in his 1732 compilation, pithily entitled, 'Gnomologia, Adagies and Proverbs, Wise Sentences and Witty Sayings, Ancient and Modern, Foreign and British.'

The phrase next cropped up in written form, amended less ambiguously to "a stitch in time saves nine," in 1797 in the journal of astronomer Francis Baily, who described it as that "vulgar proverb" (obviously not too vulgar to prevent old Frankie from using it).

For a runner this phrase made no sense at all. A stitch could never mean any time saving, in fact quite the opposite. A stitch in time could lose nine, often minutes rather than seconds. I had suffered this dreaded affliction frequently, usually in races. I would be zooming along and a stitch would strike, forcing me to slow down or worse stop, to try to get rid of the debilitating pain.

Science had moved on since Francis Baily practised astronomy. The Hubble Telescope, developed in the '80s, was eventually carried into space by the 'Shuttle' in 1990. It would enable astronomers to see billions of light years into space. If Baily had been able to look 200 earth years into the future the Hubble's capability would have amazed him but, being a scientific man, he probably would have been equally astonished by the fact that physicians were no nearer to discovering how to cure 'the side crampie' than the quacks he knew in 1797. In fact, no closer to preventing a stitch or overcoming that other regular and irritating problem confounding your average runner, the common cold. Come on you boffins, stop star gazing and discover something useful!

Theories abounded about why you felt a stitch, what made you get one, what you should do to avoid getting one and how to get rid of one when you got it. All I knew for sure was that a-bounding was out of the question when a stitch came on.

'Experts' said that a stitch pain could be the result of the diaphragm cramping as blood deserted it to go to the limbs when running. Or maybe the discomfort was because of indigestible fluids in the gut, sloshing about and making it tug at ligaments connected to the diaphragm. Or maybe, even, the sensation was caused by a little hairy troll who lived in your belly and poked your insides with a sharp stick in revenge for bouncing him around too much. Which to choose? They all sounded equally plausible to me.

So how did you prevent a stitch? It was suggested that you should always warm up prior to a run and make sure you didn't eat for a couple of hours before. This made sense but didn't explain why my pain could appear eight miles into a marathon when I had been careful to follow all these precautionary guidelines. The stitch theory which really irritated the hell out of me was the claim that people who were unfit got stitches. In 1987 I was running an average of over sixty miles a week and sometimes still getting a stitch? How fit did I have to be? Being fitted up didn't stop the stitching up.

And so, armed with all this 'definitive' knowledge and advice about a side stitch, a side ache, a side cramp, a side crampie, a side sticker or, simply, a stitch (we didn't even have a proper medical name for it) what should you do when you inevitably got one? Again, not surprisingly, advice varied. There were two common suggestions. One recommended the pressing of the painful area with your fingers and gently massaging it. No-one could put their finger on why you got a stitch and in my opinion putting your fingers on it when you did get one didn't clear anything up either.

The second method could actually reduce some of the discomfort when I tried it; unfortunately it also risked an increase in pain. This technique required the stitchee to stop running and bend over several times to ease internal constrictions. This may well have been safe practice on a lonely, long-distance run but in a race with a large number of entrants you risked being swept up by a tsunami of Lycra and subsequently deposited earthwards. Having been forced to use your face as a brake, the stitch you'd tried to relieve would be replaced by the many required to bring your previously gorgeous visage back into some semblance of order. In spite of my thorough research and experimentation I still got stitches.

Shakespeare was attributed with the first written use of the phrase 'in stitches' (as he was with most phrases in the English language). "Laugh yourself into stitches" appeared in 'Twelfth Night' in 1602. Strangely the expression was seemingly not recorded again until the 20th century. (Maybe there was nothing to laugh at for 300 years.) Well, Billy Bard, I can tell you, stitches are actually no laughing matter. In 1985 my records reveal that I had to fight to control one eight miles into your very own Stratford Marathon.

It was true that there were times you could gain some control over the pain without stopping. It depended on the severity of the Troll's attack and the sharpness of his stick. But, even when not totally debilitating, the arrival of a stitch usually had the effect of knocking you out of your rhythm and leaving a residual, irritating and restrictive ache. However, at the end of the day, I suppose running with a stitch was better than walking without one or, worse still, running without a stitch on.

January 1987 was the start of a different kind of racing experience for me. Having joined a club I was suddenly encouraged to partake in the lung bursting, muck fest that is the world of cross country. I had not run cross country since the age of 15 in PE at school. I remember I wasn't too bad at it but hadn't enjoyed the experience. The feeling of dislike stemmed mainly from the fact that the lesson was taken by a teacher who we called Tom 'Bull'. He was aware of his nick-name and thought it derived from his beefy good looks but actually it was because of the bovine excrement that came out of his moronic mouth. He was the type of person who believed he could introduce young boys to a lifetime love of sport and fitness by bawling, 'get a move on you bunch of fairies,' as they struggled to run through mud and driving rain. Standing under his umbrella, thermally swaddled, he would then keep us in the freezing cold, wearing only our vests and shorts, while he proceeded to tell us, in detail, how he excelled at sport, all sport. We never actually saw any concrete evidence to verify his claims.

So this was to be my first cross country PB, not personal best but post-Bull! The occasion was to be the West Lancashire Cross

Country Championships, or the W. Lancs. XC Champs, for short. It was to be held in Sherdley Park. This was a large green space in St Helens, a town famous for glass making, its rugby league team and until recently, its coal mines. It was only 11 miles to the east of Liverpool but it could easily have been on another planet, so different were the speech patterns and culture. I had worked in the town for 18 months as a houseparent in a children's home before going into teaching. The greeting, 'all reet cock' still rings in my ears. This phrase, used by both sexes to address both sexes, as a term of endearment, totally threw me when I first heard it. I thought people who addressed me thus had, at best, misheard my name or, at worst, decided to be extremely familiar with me. It took me all of my 18 months in the town to start to get used to the sound of this salutation.

Moving on, before this section turns into a Cock and Bull story, a week before the race I decided to acquire some appropriate kit. Although pretty standard in the athletics world this equipment was alien to me. Because I had not been interested much in athletics during my teenage years and having come into the sport through road running as an adult, I had never owned any 'spikes'. This may sound like a number of lethal sharp objects but don't worry because what it actually refers to is a set of footwear with lots of lethal sharp objects attached to the sole.

On visiting a local sports shop with Laura, I came out with a pair of Ron Hill Roadster shoes for the blackstuff, a pair of Brooks National XC spikes for the brownstuff and, for Laura, a pair of goggles for the wetstuff. My bank account went from the black to the redstuff. Paraphernalia for running was relatively cheap until buying decent footwear became involved.

On the morning of the race I ran two miles from my house to Broadgreen railway station and jumped on a train heading for St Helens. Happily, it was stationary at the time. Soon I arrived at Sherdley Park, 336 acres of public parkland with grassy knolls, copses, woodland and a lake. It was a freezing cold day and it was immediately obvious that the ground was rock-hard. Many of the experienced XC runners had decided to run in trainers rather than spikes. I had put myself at risk of bankruptcy to get these spiky shoes and there was no way I wasn't going to wear them.

Because of my total lack of familiarity with this sort of event I erred on the side of caution and took it easy. On the flat, my spikes bounced off the rigid surface, clanging like swords in a duel, but on the icy slopes I found myself getting a reasonable grip. The whole experience was totally different to that of running a road race. For a start, on the road, I could usually quickly get into a comfortable rhythm but on the 'country' this was made impossible by inconsistencies in the terrain. The demographic of the entrants was also unfamiliar to me. Cross country was where road met track. There was a smaller field of runners but much more quality in depth. Fast, young, track athletes and top road runners used these winter races to build endurance for the summer season. Lean and light-weight, the speed they took off at (and kept up) was frightening. I was happy to plod along and feel my way, with my sharp feet. I finished in 89th position, tired but not exhausted.

My overall impression of my first XC was that I had enjoyed it but that I wasn't going to be much good at it. I got a lift back home after the race from the youngest member of my club training group. (Most of us were gnarled, old, washed-up footballers in our thirties; he was a fresh faced twenty-something lad who we shall call DJ. I would go on to run many a race with DJ either looking back at him or looking at his back, mainly the latter). The next morning, post XC, my legs deliberately ached in all the wrong places to remind me that they had been forced to do something different.

As I have already intimated, being super fit often made you ill. There was a precarious balancing of the books when deciding how much training would make you fly but not give you flu. In January, inadvisably, I coughed my way through my cross country debut, (cough country) and weekly training. By the time the Helsby Half came around, the day after my 36th birthday, I made the uncharacteristically sensible decision to forgo participation in the event. On the Sunday of the race Whistler rolled up in the Polo, outside my house.

We were still trying to make a go of it, even though he knew I was clubbing it twice a week. He authenticated my cough and went to Helsby on his own. Although I shed a tiny tear as he disappeared round the corner in a cloud of exhaust and fumes from ovine ordure, I was also glad to see him show this independence. He returned after the race, extremely animated, to describe his day without me. He'd got up late, eaten too much breakfast, forgotten his shoes and ran in someone's spare Reeboks. He'd even made his own decision as to what top to wear without a discussion. All this and he had still managed to run a PB in the Helsby Half. I could see he was going to manage without me. I was happy for him but felt that the measurers needed to get back out on that course.

I was full of cold and the papers were full of religion. On the opposite edge of Cheshire to Helsby, on the eastern boundary of the county, is Bollington. It was in this small town that Terry Waites, assistant to the Archbishop of Canterbury was born. He had been sent to Lebanon as an envoy of the Church of England to negotiate for the release of four hostages being held by the Islamic Jihad organisation. His successful intervention in previous hostage situations had made him confident that he could prevail again. Many advised against this latest mission because of the increasingly volatile conditions in the area. Inevitably, on January 20th, he too was taken captive. He would eventually spend 1,763 days in captivity, the first four years in solitary confinement. At no time would he be sure of his survival until he was finally released in 1991. Of his ordeal he said; "I longed for death in the dungeons of Beirut but I am proof you should never give up on life." This was a story of a brave person with faith in humanity and the human spirit.

In February another locally-born person was in the news but for using faith as a weapon to devalue humanity. Edwina Currie, born Edwina Cohen to Jewish parents in South Liverpool, had risen through the Conservative Party's ranks via the Birmingham city council to become an MP and health minister. She was treating us to another of her specious truisms which she only appeared to apply to the lower echelons of society. Her public statement that 'Good Christians don't get Aids,' was disgraceful and stupid in equal measures. From previous experience of her 'ignorance and chips' quote it was obvious that Edwina was not one to bother about factual or statistical evidence to back up her outbursts but a few questions could have been asked about the meaning of her words.

I wondered was she saying that Christian people were immune to the disease as opposed to 'good' people from all other religions or people without religion? What was her definition of 'good'? Did this 'immune' group consist only of those people who had monogamous heterosexual relationships within the bounds of marriage, while worshipping a Christian god? If so, it ruled her out. In her memoirs she admitted to having an extra-marital affair with John Major before he went on to be Conservative prime minister. She almost portrayed this relationship as a carefree romp. If a member of the hoi polloi had behaved like her she probably would have described it as unholy and lascivious, leaving the participants open to infection by STDs, and serve them jolly well right.

This woman seemed happy to make ignorant judgements on the morality and social awareness of those at the base of society's wealth and influence pyramid, but not of those at the top. Disturbing revelations in 2012 supported this view of her 'blind' bias. It was revealed that, Jimmy Saville, DJ, entertainer, celebrity and friend of the great and 'good', had unfettered access to Broadmoor hospital in the 1980s, while Currie was health minister responsible for the country's high security hospitals. In 1988 she would then appoint him as leader of a task force overseeing Broadmoor, after it had been taken over by the Thatcher government, following a series of strikes by staff. Saville assured her that he would sort out the striking staff members by threatening to expose financial irregularities in their expenses claims. "Ataboy", she wrote as a response in her diary. Breaking the unions appeared to be a higher priority than patient safety with this Tory government. Since Saville's death in 2011, over 450 people have come forward claiming to have been abused by him. Police failed to prosecute this man while he was alive despite him being reported by several victims. He had cultivated powerful connections and used his influence in high places to escape justice.

In September 2012, in the Daily Mail newspaper's website, the MailOnline, Currie's latest published diaries were reviewed by journalist Amanda Platell. The title of the article was 'Vain, vulgar- Edwina Currie truly is a vile woman.' I never thought I would ever have occasion to agree with 'The Mail' with its less-than-liberal leanings. It's a pity that these realisations came 25 years too late to stop her holding office.

The first day of March saw my first road race of the year, a 10k, in St Helens again. This was a fairly uneventful event. I ran a relaxed 34 minutes dead. I suppose dead is the most relaxed you can be. Eileen was running too and recorded a personal best of 47:20. I'm not sure what she was putting on her cornflakes, apart from the Glenmorangie, but I wanted some. The week following this race I developed another bad cold which caused me to miss my annual trip to the Ormskirk half marathon. My training was not going well, so much so that, on March 8th, I felt compelled to make an official 'state of the preparation' speech to myself in my diaries. It went like this.

"At this point I must say something about the state of my training. Since January the first, I have had two colds, both lasting well over a week. I have also had a twisted ankle. To be honest I think it's all going from bad to worse, like Labour's prospects in the General Election. I don't think I have had an uninterrupted week. Poor mileage and lack of quality means that I will be running Wolverhampton in four weeks on a 'let's see what happens' basis."

Training was then further disrupted by a week away with the school, at an outdoor activities centre in North Wales. On one hand I enjoyed these breaks because I loved being in the fresh air, being involved in the activities and I didn't have to do any teaching. Added to this, like a lot of my pupils, I wasn't too keen on regular school. The downside was that I disliked being away from Eileen and Laura and not being able to run. It was also exhausting and stressful being with the kids all the waking hours. This trip, however, was one I would have been sad to miss because of one particular experience.

We were planning to sleep in a barn next to Dolwydellan Castle, a solid, stone fortress built in the 13th century by Llywleyn the Great, Prince of Gwynedd and North Wales. As we arrived by mini-bus and although we were well into the month of March, it started to snow heavily. The castle, perched on a rocky outcrop, was almost hidden by the pulsing waves of thick flakes. Putting all our sleeping gear in the barn, we planned to have a ghost story in the small square tower before 'settling' for the night. Under the directions of one of the centre's instructors I secretly went on ahead to the tower and hid up the huge chimney breast by clinging on to the mortared stones. As luck would have it, there was no fire; that would come later. The children were then brought in and the story began. At an appropriate point in the spooky saga I started to make scary noises. "It's Mr Peacock," the children immediately chimed. (Great, they ignored me when I was there but noticed me when I wasn't.)

The story over, one of the instructors beckoned us up the stairs to the top of the tower. "Come and look at this," he urged. Climbing through a trapdoor on to the roof we beheld an amazing sight. The snow had stopped but hanging over the tower was a cloud and we were in it. The static electricity trapped inside this mantle made everyone's hair strands stand on end and caused the tips to glow white like hot needles. The edges of the heavy stone battlements shone out like teeth exposed to ultra violet light in a disco. Thin squiggles of blue-white electricity jumped across the embrasures. There was an incessant, scratchy crackling for the few minutes the phenomenon lasted, like an old gramophone needle stuck at the end of a record. The instructor informed us that this was 'St Elmo's Fire'. I had thought this only occurred on ships. In Greek mythology its appearance was regarded as the embodiment of Castor and Pollux, twins who were the patrons of seamen.

I was astonished. I knew it was a natural, if rare, occurrence but it was as if the Castle was giving off energy left by the ghosts of battles past. The kids seemed blasé. Did they assume, coinciding as it had with the ghost story, that the electric show had just been part of the lame entertainment put on by us or were they just a little freaked out? I slept soundly in the barn that night and dreamed that St Elmo of Dolwydellan would bring a spark back to my running.

Although my training was supposed to be gearing up to the running of my first ever London Marathon in May that year, I had entered the Wolverhampton Marathon again. I couldn't resist! Why I couldn't resist is a mystery. Maybe I wanted to see how badly they could get it wrong this year or what kind of weird physical sensation would afflict organiser, Billy Wilson. It was five weeks until my London Marathon debut and I was full of anticipation. London was such a special place to run, not just because it was the Capital but also because the nature of the course and the atmosphere created by the crowd meant that world records could be broken by the international elite and personal bests set by the rest of us plebs. It didn't really make any sense running a full marathon five weeks before. Yep, it made no sense but it was clear that the planning of my running was notoriously nonsensical. There was no grand scheme, no master plan, I just did it because, well, because it was there.

I decided to try to travel from Liverpool to Wolves and back on race day. It turned out to be a fraught and discommoding journey to get to Wolverhampton by train. Every target set to enable me to arrive at the start ready and relaxed seemed to have been missed. To cap it all an unpleasant sight greeted me when I eventually did reach the line and does every time I look at the picture on the front of the results programme. My diary entry explains and makes no pretence as to my feelings at the time. "Had to hurry to get changed and then dash to the front of the start line. Jimmy Saville was there saying hello to everyone in his usual obnoxious way."

This was not the ideal preparation for running 26 andabit miles and three miles after the start I was already giving myself the option of stopping if I felt like it. Psychologically, this was not a clever race strategy. Somehow I persevered. I drank too much water at the last feed station and started to get a stitch (in time) for the last three miles and had to slow down to control it. I didn't feel like I'd had the right mental attitude from mile one but by some miracle of persistence I finished in the time of 2:40 in 31st place. I felt disappointed for about 15 minutes and then told myself that under the circumstances I had done well and I would be more prepared and 'up for it' in London in five weeks. One positive outcome of this venture was that I had been wearing my club vest and was amazed by the encouragement I got from people calling out the club's name; an unfamiliar but heartening experience.

Of course, no Wolverhampton Marathon would be complete without a weird monologue from Billy Wilson. The contribution to the 1987 results programme was no exception. He wrote;

"The deeper that I get involved, the firmer is my belief that running is probably a new and fresh approach to the world that God intended us to live in for a few short years that we are on this earth.

Politics, greed, envy and sloth are human frailties that have encroached in our lives to our detriment, and running has given many of us the vision to put old 'Satan' and his works behind us."

Next thing you know he'll be organising the Satan Dash 5K so we can show Old Nick a clean pair of heels and holy socks. Sorry Bill, I sort of see where you're coming from but if God had intended us to run he would have given us more appropriate knees. Genuflecting is probably all they're really suitable for.

However, taking up Billy's theme of greed, two sales took place in March and April which I thought illustrated the huge gap between the haves and the have-nots in the world. Aware of the effect of poverty on the lives of some of the kids I taught, I could barely begin to imagine the conditions children in poorer countries had to contend with. Times were hard for many in the world but not for everyone. A year after her death in April 1986, The Duchess of Windsor's jewellery, just her jewellery, sold at auction for £31 million. Wallis Simpson, an American socialite famously became a duchess when she married Edward VIII of England. This union resulted in his abdication. After their marriage they went to live in a mansion, owned by the City of Paris, nestling in the Bois de Boulogne, 20 minutes from the city centre. Realising that this poor couple were obviously cash strapped, the Parisian Authorities decided to lease this mansion to them for a peppercorn rent. The down and out of Paris must have applauded this beneficent gesture! Vive la revolution!

The duchess once famously said that 'you can never be too rich or too thin', but at that time far too many of the world's children were too poor and too thin. The couple continued to live the high-life in Paris, hobnobbing with the aristocrats and fascistocrats of Europe until Edward's death in 1972. Then the duchess's 'too rich' comment came back to haunt her. Her wealth didn't bring her happiness. After Edward died, she led a lonely existence, isolated in her mansion and taken advantage of by those she trusted. This was a sad situation but more tragic to me was that her riches, so impotent in improving the quality of her individual life, were not made available to improve the lives of the desperately poor or disadvantaged. It's a shame the money from the sale of her trinkets wasn't used for deserving causes.

As for those who benefitted from the proceeds of the sale, it is hard to imagine what they had done to deserve them.

I also felt similarly about a sale that had taken place in April. At a Sotheby's art auction, a Van Gogh painting of sunflowers was bought by an anonymous purchaser for a record of over £24 million. I felt this was a travesty on two levels. Firstly, that any individual (or group) had this sort of money to spend on, what was basically for them, a wall adornment, while a fraction of the same sum could have radically improved the precarious lives of thousands; secondly, that this beautiful painting should be covetously hidden away from the rest of the world because of someone's hideous wealth.

This record sale was to be beaten only a few months later when Van Gogh's painting of irises sold for £27 million. He painted this picture in the garden of the Saint-Remy Asylum, where he was a patient in 1889. A few months after painting it he committed suicide aged 37. He died penniless. His paintings are things of beauty and should have been a legacy to the world from a brilliant but troubled artistic mind not commodities for investment.

I had my own record in mind when, May 10th 1987, the big day in the Big Wen finally arrived. Watching the London Marathon had been an inspiration in 1981 but participation had eluded me up until this time. Now was my chance to experience the world's biggest running event. I found myself in Greenwich amongst the swollen flow of runners pouring into the start areas. The atmosphere was something I had never experienced before. Tens of thousands of fellow human beings, their brains electric with nervous energy, built up a colossal, crackling, hair-raising communal charge; Chariots of St Elmo's Fire. It was difficult to keep calm.

I passed long lines of runners waiting for the portaloos; portaqueues. I also needed a portapoo but knew I wouldn't have to queue. I sought out the AAA enclosure for those in the 'elite' Championship Race. As with all elites we were given preferential treatment. There was almost one toilet for each of us inside the cordoned off area and free drinks in a sheltering marquee. While outside a sea of competitors heaved inside offered some tranquillity, however it came at a price; irritating bureaucracy. There seemed to be a division in many sporting bodies between those who wanted to get on and enjoy their sports and those who wanted to make up petty rules to spoil that enjoyment.

Because I was entered in the 'Championship' I had to have my vest inspected. I thought this might be to search for hidden turbo rockets or wings but, no, I was instructed to use my number to cover up the club's name on my vest, the name which in Wolverhampton had encouraged so many supportive comments from the crowd. According to the officials the lettering was too big and didn't conform to International Association of Athletics Federation (IAAF) rules! I cooperated, not wanting to waste precious energy debating what global catastrophes might result from oversized fonts. I left the official tent and sat on the kerb, immediately repositioning my number to reveal my club's name while I watched in awe as the international runners warmed up on the road outside.

At the start we were arranged according to qualifying times. I was in the 500-600 grid. No top ten finish today then! After a few stretches I crossed myself and I was ready. A religious gesture for many competitors, my cruciformality was sensibly secular rather than sanctifying. It was to check that adequate lubrication had been applied to essential areas; eyebrow, lowbrow, nipple, nipple. I'd suffered enough times, on long runs, from jogger's nipple and knobble to know that this was important. Apart from the discomfort caused by the chafing, the triangulated, sanguinary stigmata which resulted could become embarrassingly obvious through thin material.

The greasing of eyebrows may cause a few readers to raise theirs. It was true that this area was not as sensitive to friction as other places previously alluded to but attention to it, for me, was equally important. I was blessed with a thick and lustrous hedgebrow which frequently served as a reservoir for sweat descending from my forehead. When saturated, my thirsty caterpillar would then proceed to piss the gathered brine into mine eyes thus producing temporary blindness and consequently a tendency to veer off course into compromising situations with innocent bystanders. I really wanted to avoid this distraction in this race and so I applied a large amount of Vaseline, for the purpose of diverting the deluge harmlessly around the ocular area. The white petroleum jelly gave the impression that my eyebrows were frost-bitten. Having finished cross-checking that effective unction had been achieved, I was ready for the off.

BOOM! The cannon signalled the 9:30 start. No stuttering here, no being held up by people ahead starting in a leisurely fashion; those in front were not going to hang about. For once, on this the biggest of them, I didn't let the occasion get to me. A sensible six minutes for the first mile downhill. Through the Wen we then wended; Greenwich gone, at the Cutty Sark we embarked on the rest of our odyssey. Here, as it has oft been reported, the crowds were amazing. 10k in 35 minutes, fast but I felt composed. I spotted Eileen on Tower Bridge. I waved and she could see I was doing OK. I passed one of the lead ladies, Paula Fudge at 13 miles; maybe now I was getting a little carried away. Inevitably, at 18 miles, she returned the favour and went past me. Through the Isle of Dogs the relative quiet made me more aware of my increasing fatigue (tiring dogs). 22 miles and under Tower Bridge, I hit the wall. Not the metaphorical excuse type, but one of noise, like you would normally only experience in the last 50 metres of other big races.

In spite of the crowds, I could feel my resolve weakening. I got hold of the psychological scruff of my neck and gave my brain a shake; hard to do while running. It seemed to work. I started to push myself through the tiredness towards the finish, over the infamous carpet, not so magic, on the famous cobbles by The Tower. Uneven surfaces and unsteady legs were not a happy mix. 24 miles gone and I felt drained. Was I paying for a fast middle section in the race or perhaps just the effect of having run over 20 miles at under six minute mile pace? Down The Mall the crowd dragged me onwards. I pushed on past Buckingham Palace and didn't stop to bow; no need, no stitch. 26 miles in 2:34, I had to keep moving; even now it would be easy to stop. I ran under the finish gantry joyously, arms aloft, in 2:35:40, a PB. No time to let it sink in, as stewards gently but firmly pushed me on down the finishing chute. I got my medal. "Well in Liverpool Running Club," said a runner wearing a vest of one of the more established Merseyside athletic clubs; praise indeed. I reciprocated and walked onwards to tables piled with Isostars and Mars Bars. I was over the Moon.

Then on to the double-decker bus which had transported our kit from Blackheath. I sat down wearily on a seat next to my labelled bag, replaying the race inside my head. My reverie was abruptly broken.

"Is your name Peacock?" A voice besides me asked. "Yes, it is." I admitted, "And I am sticking with it, in spite of the piss-taking I have endured over the years." Actually I just said, "Yes", the rest of the sentence had been completed inside my defensive sub-conscious. "So is mine," came the confessional reply. He had run 2 hours and 25 minutes in his first marathon and seemed more excited by the fact that he was sitting next to another Peacock than by his time. I would have changed my name to Rumpelstilstkin in exchange for a time like his. Actually, that is a lie I would defend my name to the death. Actually, that is also a lie.

I'm not sure where that left us, other than on the top of a double-decker bus after the London Marathon, two runners having the same surname, changing into dry clothes with some difficulty, but chatting easily. After all the razzmatazz, our brief and random conversation on the quiet bus added to the vast and contrasting range of experiences that day in London had presented to me. I felt privileged.

I made my way to tree P in Jubilee Gardens, which, before anyone mentally makes the joke I also want to make, was one of many alphabetically nominated arboreal spots for the purpose of meeting family and friends, only. Besides, it would be some time and much liquid intake before that sort of function would return to most. There were but a few portaqueues at the end of a marathon.

Eileen was waiting at the P tree and I tried to put on the old, pretend, 'I've-not-done-well-frown-face' but the 'oh-my-god-I'm-ecstatic-grin-gob' barged it out of the way and took over my countenance divine without me being able to do anything about it. I felt in too ebullient a mood to play the fool. After I had given her a footfall by footfall account of my race, in much quicker time than I had run it and with far fewer breaths, we made our way to Waterloo East tube station.

As I was in the Waterloo queue for a tube ticket, the space-blanketed runner in front of me suddenly found the waiting all too much and unceremoniously threw up. Another person saw this and followed suit. Soon the tiled foyer was echoing with the happy splattering of copycat pukers in this vomitorium and I went through a set of improvised warm-down exercises to avoid sick ricochets. The air filled with the sweet odour of regurgitated Mars Bars.

It had been a great London for me, nearly two minutes faster than Stratford and 333rd, which doesn't sound that brilliant but it's all relative. Be fair, the best runners in the world were there competing, plus 20,000 or more others and I had performed above my seeded starting position. OK, at least give me a bit of credit for managing all the threes.

The performance put me in a buoyant mood for the next couple of weeks which was timely, considering the depressing result the following month. I am referring to running for office not in marathons. The general election saw the end of a long and oppressive term of Tory rule and the beginning of another. Eileen had been out canvassing for the Labour Party while I stayed at home building my own swingometer out of toilet rolls and sticky back plastic; an excellent ploy for all armchair politicos wanting to avoid getting out and actually doing something positive on election nights. Of course, the Tories were obliterated in Liverpool and there were good Labour results in Scotland, Wales and parts of Northern England but not enough to get rid of Thatcher. Most of the voters in the South and Midlands voted to keep her in by a 100 seat majority.

My lack of action didn't help, but much of the blame for the election defeat could be realistically laid at the door of the Labour leadership, who had been so busy trying not to upset voters with radical alternatives to Thatcher that they had forgotten to offer any convincing policies at all. They had done little to oppose this government's ruthless erosion of the employment rights and living conditions of ordinary people. In many ways they got what they deserved but that didn't make the situation any less miserable for those of us who had voted for them.

Eileen and I were lucky to be in secure employment. Life for us carried on much as normal. As the weather got warmer I kept my mileage up over 70 miles weekly, going to the club twice a week, running miles with Eileen and even including some junior miles with Laura. It was in my head that it was an important act of parenthood to teach your offspring to swim and get them interested in physical activity generally. I had been taking Laura to the baths regularly (as had her mum) and, using techniques I had learned on a variety of school courses, was trying to get her to swim a length. She didn't take to it particularly easily and struggled with her confidence. In water, confidence is an important flotation aid. I did not pressure her as she seemed to have a weight of self-expectation pulling her down like a concrete swimsuit.

Seeing me running she had also expressed an interest in joining me, so we had gone out a couple of times together. By the end of that summer she had managed to swim her length and run three miles without stopping. Eileen and I also went on bike rides with her on clement weather weekends. I almost felt like it was 'job done'. I certainly didn't want to push her any further. In my mind, laying the foundation for a lifetime of enjoyment in sport was more important than pushing kids too hard or too early into competition. I just wanted her to develop an enjoyment for activities, generated from her own volition, without any ulterior ambition; no Bull.

The swimming lessons also had a practical purpose. Eileen and I had decided, because we were now settled in our new home and both in steady jobs, we would use our positive credit rating to spend some money on a decent foreign holiday with Eileen's family and take Laura with us. It fell on me to organise this. We needed to find somewhere reasonably cheap which would take me, Eileen, Laura, Eileen's parents, eldest sister, the sister's husband and their two daughters. The travel agent found a three-story house which would hold the nine of us on the top two floors. It was on the island of Spetses, just off the southern shores of the Greek Peloponnese. Apparently the house was detached, overlooked a bay and the owners lived on the ground floor. It seemed like a bargain and I paid for it with the usual certainty that I wouldn't really know what I was actually paying for till I got there. Laura was excited as she had developed a close relationship with Eileen's nieces over the years and they were all about the same age. We had been on short staycations together and got on well but this would be unknown territory in more ways than one.

Ignorance was bliss-tering as we left for Athens on the night of Sunday, July 26th. We were unaware that this was published by Reuters the day before;

"More than 100 people have died in a heat wave in Greece in the last five days, hospital sources said today.

Temperatures have remained above 107 degrees Fahrenheit and the weather service said the heat would last at least until Sunday.

Hundreds of people have been hospitalized and the Health Ministry put all hospitals in Athens, including military hospitals, on round-the-clock alert."

Whilst the UK was having a mediocre summer in 1987, the Greeks were experiencing a fierce heat-wave which went on to claim over one thousand lives during July 1987. The Greek government announced a state of emergency on the 26th. By the time we arrived the temperature had peaked at 111 degrees Fahrenheit. I'd got all the threes in London and now I was getting all the ones in Athens.

Because of our flight times we arrived at 3 o'clock in the morning but getting off the plane was still like having hot cotton wool stuffed into your airways. You could see the look of panic on peoples' faces as they disembarked. We then had to endure a five hour journey south from Athens along the Peloponnese, in a clapped-out Mercedes coach with no air-conditioning. The bus had been overbooked, as well as overcooked, which meant our three girls had to share a double seat for the entire journey. In Greek mythology, Pelops was the son of Tantalus. As a child, he was killed by his father to be served up as a meal for the gods. I think our kids must have thought that we were roasting them till tender for the same purpose. They spent most of the journey kneeling on the floor with heads on the seat, like they were praying to the Greek gods to be spared from the heat and from being meat. They missed all the dramatic scenery as we crossed the Corinthian Canal and spluttered southwards through the mountains. Somehow we all avoided being char-grilled in the charabanc and the gods were not served with or by us. We arrived at Kosta beach and boarded small boats to make the short journey across to the island. The light sea breezes here made it a little, but not much, cooler.

Spetses was virtually free of motorised traffic and normally the main form of public transport in the town was a fleet of ornate horse-drawn carriages. At the time of our arrival it had been deemed too hot for the horses to work. They stood be-hatted in the shade, motionless save the fly-phobic flicking of their tails. A mini-bus was provided to take us to our accommodation. This was in the old part of town. It was a house with big balconies, overlooking a bay, from which we could watch traditional boat building going on in the daytime and astonishing sunsets at dusk. The first thing Laura did when we arrived was throw up. The heat had finally got to her.

Pine clad and rocky, with small secluded beaches, Spetses is an island famous for being the location of the John Fowles novel 'The Magus'. It is 25.5 square km and has a perimeter of about 24km. Most of the 4000 population live in Spetses Town which spreads out for 4 km along one side of the island. It proved to be a gorgeous place to holiday but considering the ridiculous temperature, undulating nature of the terrain and unpredictable condition of the bye-ways, you would have to be really foolhardy or slightly demented to run there; I qualified on both counts. I managed to run every day but one. Admittedly most of these were five miles or less but I did also manage a six, eight and 15 miler. I tried to be sensible (for me). Managing these conditions relatively safely generally entailed getting up just after six, before the really sapping heat kicked in. The shorter runs were through the town on the flattish coastal area but the longer sorties meant going further inwards and upwards.

On Wednesday of the first week we were all going to the other side of the island to Anargyri beach. With most people taking a water taxi round the coast, I decided to try to find the track which went to the top of the island and over to the beach, a distance of about five miles. As it transpired and I perspired, I couldn't find the track and so had to follow the coast road, a distance of about eight miles. Apart from the amazing views and the crushing heat, my abiding memory of that run was being passed by the local bus, which was driven by a Rastafarian playing Bob Marley tapes. As the vintage vehicle carefully manoeuvred around me on the dusty, narrow road, some wag on a back seat stuck a hand, wrapped around a beer bottle, out of the open window, offering the drink like a carrot to a donkey. I knew I would be partaking myself once I reached the beach so I saw the funny side; hee-haw.

Coping well with the heat, hilly terrain and loose road surface I arrived at Anargyri just before the water taxi pulled in. This meant I could grab a few early beach brollies and find a prime spot before the rest arrived. The sensation of plunging into the pellucid, placid, turquoise sea was greatly enhanced by running beforehand, as was the taste of a cold Amstel.

The next day I found the elusive central path and ran to the top of the island. A lung-bursting climb rewarded me with a 360 degree view; on one side the red-tiled, white-walled houses in the town overlooked harbours where traditional craft and modern yachts rubbed hulls; on the other the pine-green, thyme-perfumed mountains descended to little bays, sparkling sapphires in the island's lee. Coming back down was tricky and demanding because of the gradient and untrustworthy topsoil. As I cautiously descended local young goats mocked me, 'baaa,' but it was worth tolerating Billy the Kid's bullying in return for my visual feast.

The long run I had in my mind I saved till the last week of the holiday. I decided I wanted to try to circumnavigate the 24 km of the island. I'd only seen one other runner since arriving. That was in the second week, when the temperatures had changed from insanely hot to slightly eccentric hot. At least I wasn't the only mad one. This runner I'd spotted five times. It hadn't been difficult because she was running next to me. Eileen had overcome her intense dislike of high temperature jogs and accompanied me on a few leg-stretchers. On the morning of my epic voyage we left at 6:30 and she ran 15 minutes with me before retracing her steps. I ploughed on through the thick, sticky, static air, water bottle in hand.

About halfway through my round trip the road turned into a rocky track which soared then dipped with every cove it encountered whilst also twisting and turning to follow the contours of the hillside it clung to. I almost became accustomed to the sumptuous views of sea and sky, two-tone blue welded together at the horizon. As I reached the most westerly point of the 'road' it climbed and climbed and didn't seem to have any intention of coming down. To my relief, as I turned to head eastward again it reneged and started a descent. The uncouth surface was beginning to take its toll on my legs and, by association, the rest of me. My flagging spirits were revived when the smooth metalled road suddenly and unexpectedly reappeared like a tarred rope dragging me homewards. Reaching the town centre at Dappia I knew I was almost there. Soon I was staggering through the gate of our villa, finishing in one hour 55 minutes, pleased with the achievement. I certainly enjoyed breakfast after the luxury of a shower. I say luxury because, having no significant natural water source, the island relied on daily supplies delivered by ship from the mainland. The huge storage tanks had run dry on several occasions during our stay. A constant water supply is one of the many things we in the UK tend to take for granted.

The holiday hadn't only been about running. We'd all had an amazing time in spite of the merciless heat, which gradually eased. We'd enjoyed each other's company and the kids had loved it. Laura's confidence in the water dramatically improved. Countless visits to the swimming baths at home had paid off. As well as being together, we had also managed to do what we each wanted in a group setting. Taking turns to be with the kids meant individuals had time for themselves; in my case that meant getting my runs in.

The truth is that maintaining any sort of running routine while on a family holiday can be quite difficult and may cause friction, with or without Vaseline. It has to be done cleverly to appear to be considerate. (Many would say, "Why bother running you idiot. Just relax and enjoy yourself!" In my (weak) defence I would reply that running was now part of relaxing and having a happy time, for me. As with getting out on the road at Christmas, it made the usual excesses of a beach holiday all the more enjoyable. It was also a cheap form of transport.)

Having thought about this problem while lying on the beach, I devised a few possible training sessions which could fit in with a group holiday without rocking the boat. This is especially important if you are on a cruise. For those with any interest here are my suggestions.

If staying in a hotel, parts of your accommodation can be adapted for training sessions. Running up staircases inside tall buildings, has become an acceptable alternative to hill training but be aware that it has been known for holidaymakers to be lodged in unfinished residences. If you tear up the internal stairs of the hotel to the top floor only to suddenly find it isn't there, the session will come to an abrupt and messy end. (NB, the Tower of Pisa is not recommended for this type of session.)

If your hotel has revolving front doors, try staying inside them for some speed work. Increase your cadence until you become but a blur in the eyes of bystanders. When your legs can no longer match the velocity of the doors, you will be catapulted across the lobby's marble floor, scattering friends, family and staff like nine pins. At this point the session will have the additional benefit of giving you the experience of hitting the wall (non-metaphorical).

The beach is also a suitable place for some sly holiday repetitions (not to be confused with sly holiday reps). If with a big group of family or friends show uncharacteristic generosity and offer to buy everyone an ice cream. Buy them one at a time. Sprint hard over the hot sands to the ice cream vendor and jog back carefully, cornet in hand, to recover. Repeat this until the requisite number of purchases has been made. This session has an added advantage. On your recovery jogs, imagine that it is not a Mr Yipee Supersoft Cone you are holding but the Olympic torch; this acts as a boost for morale. If you are beside the seaside in Britain, also try this; wearing your skimpiest swimsuit, jog gently down the beach towards the sea and plunge into the murky depths. I can guarantee that you will smash your PB for the distance back to your towel when you discover how cold the water is. In my experience, although invigorating, this session tends to be (like your speedos) brief. A similar result can be achieved abroad, in warmer but shark-infested waters. However, in this scenario, take the precaution of getting a friend to agree to enter three-legged races with you in the future.

Another possibly beneficial training run abroad is a more stimulating version of hare and hounds but needs to be planned with some caution. Find the beach most popular with the locals. Make some loud derogatory comments about the local football team, main religion or national leader and then run like hell. It will provide healthy competition, but only if you are faster than the armed mob in pursuit.

Spare time when travelling to and from your holiday destination can also be used to catch up with your mileage. The airport is an ideal place for a long run. Your flight will be delayed and you will be able to spend an eternity dashing around trying to find someone who can give you some information. The deck of a ship can also provide a smooth flat area to run on but not during a storm. On these occasions although the slippery, rolling surface will build up your leg strength for trail running, you may be forced to do some unplanned triathlon training.

To end on a word of caution; never jog on an aircraft! Running up and down the aisle may well help combat D.V.T but it scares the living S.H.I.T. out of the other passengers, especially if your tracksuit resembles, in anyway, a pilot's uniform. (I would also just like to add that anybody attempting any of these sessions does so at their own risk.)

Soon after we had returned from our holidays when thoughts of running in the significant, natural environment of Spetses were beginning to fade in my memory, I became aware of a seemingly, insignificant natural event which led me to consider the future of our relationship with nature.

In June 1987 the Dusky Seaside Sparrow, a small, unspectacular bird, became extinct. The demise of the species was essentially caused by two big influential American organisations.

The story starts in marshlands, on the Southern Florida Atlantic Coast, where the bird's natural habitat was to be found. First categorised as a species in 1873, the number of breeding pairs were reduced from 2,000 to 600 in the 1940s after DDT, sprayed on the marshes to control mosquitoes, had entered their food chain. By 1963 the area had become dominated by the Kennedy Space Center (previously Cape Canaveral) and mosquitoes were still irritating the humans. Apparently, having learnt nothing from their previous decimation of the bird's population, the authorities flooded the marshes to get rid of the mosquitoes and, oops, also the Dusky Seaside Sparrow.

Some breeding pairs had fortuitously survived in marshes higher up the nearby St John's River. It would be natural to think that an awareness of the need to care for this now threatened species of bird would have developed; think again. The authorities proceeded to drain the marshes around the river in order to build a highway to join The Kennedy Space Center to Disneyland Florida. Pollution and pesticides eventually took their toll and by 1979 only 6 birds were known to exist, all males; the last time a female had been spotted was in 1975. In a pathetic and obviously futile attempt to shut the cage door after the birds had flown, the remaining Duskys were rounded up and brought to Disneyland where, in a 'wild life' sanctuary, they saw out the rest of their days, all expenses paid.

It was, apparently, one thing to spend millions on making children's cartoons depicting cute talking animals, or on technology to make amazing discoveries on sophisticated space missions but another to spend a little time and thought to save a tiny sparrow from extinction. Is this a template for progress? I hope not. The bird did not just become extinct; it was pursued to extinction because other things, human inconveniences, were deemed more important. For the 'Dusky', Disneyland was the last resort.

Earlier in 1987 an agreement had been reached between Disney and the French government to build Disneyland Paris. The last 'Dusky', aware of its possible fate, amazingly found the strength to fly bravely across the Atlantic. Having experienced all kinds of trials and tribulations, it finally arrived in France, at death's door, to warn the other bird species (who all spoke English with a French accent) about the treatment to expect when Disneyland was built. Then Dusky Dave miraculously recovered, miraculously found a mate and settled down to raise a family, save the species and live happily ever after. Hooray! Oh no, sorry, that was the cartoon version.

The Dusky Seaside Sparrow can actually still be seen in Liverpool. It is depicted in a copy of one of the greatest natural history books ever published, owned by the City Library. In 1861, Joseph Shipley, an American who had Liverpool business connections, was invited to the opening of the city's newly built library. He was unable to attend but sent a generous cheque for £1,000. In a shrewd investment, librarians used £168 of the donation to buy a copy of the four-volume Birds of America by John James Audubon, from a London book dealer. The book is often hailed as one of the most beautiful books ever printed. A set of the books sold at auction in London in 2010 for £6.5 million.

Liverpool's Central Library is situated on William Brown Street, now referred to as the Cultural Quarter, because of its collection of public buildings with their variety of architectural styles. The library, the World Museum, the Walker Art Gallery, St George's Hall and the Empire Theatre are clustered there. The conjoined museum and library are housed in a Grade II listed building. Built in the classical style with a huge portico entrance supported by six Corinthian columns, 400,000 people attended its opening in 1860. The building was hit and badly damaged by German bombs in the Blitz of 1941 but the elegant façade survived. Many of the museums artefacts had already been moved to safer storage before the bombing but Audubon's book was still on the site when a 500lb bomb destroyed 150,000 volumes in the library. The precious book, however, had been stored in vaults and was rescued by a vigilant museum employee who prevented it from being damaged by water from fire fighters' hoses. Many books which survived the bombs were destroyed this way. The library underwent a major £50 million refurbishment in 2012 and was reopened in 2013. Audubon's book, with its Dusky Seaside Sparrow captured inside, is on permanent display.

After the freedom of summer I always felt captured and caged by September. It was a funny month. For many school children it heralded the awkward beginning of a fresh term after the carefree holidays and much the same for teachers. On my calendar it was also the start of the traditional run up to the Mersey Marathon. The 1987 event was to be my sixth. This time I decided to get sponsored for running it. Money raised would go to Alder Hey children's hospital. I always felt embarrassed to ask people for money because I usually ended up asking the same people and let's face it running a marathon was no longer a great challenge for me. I just let people know I would accept donations and left it at that.

In Liverpool before the marathon we were reminded of past events, which many would have preferred to forget, as 25 Liverpool

FC fans were indicted to stand trial for crimes committed at the Heysel stadium disaster two years earlier. It was Britain's biggest mass extradition. At the time a Belgium newspaper published an article with the unhelpful Sun-like English headline, "Welcome in Belgium, Red Animals." It stated that the men had let down their club, their city and their country. The extradition warrants had been signed a year earlier but proceedings had been held up by lawyers of the accused, who feared they wouldn't receive a fair trial in Belgium; a reasonable view judging by the newspaper headlines. After a five month trial, 14 of the 25 were found guilty of voluntary manslaughter. Seven were given three year prison sentences and the rest three year suspended sentences.

As for the Mersey Marathon I have to say that the best result for me was raising £50 for Alder Hey hospital because the race itself was, as usual, a non-event. I ran 2:40:07 and finished in 28th place which was respectable but, of course, way off my 'London' time. New to me was the experience of running with my club mates for large parts of the race. At 20 miles, four of us were still together, me, Rugman, DJ and another of our squad, Grimm the Elder. Grimm the E. went on to be the first of our club home with a brilliant 2:36:14. I was second and DJ came in third after we'd had a little battle in the last couple of miles. Rugman had 'piles' of trouble in the final six and walked most of them. A positive result was that the positions of Grimm, me and DJ gave us 2nd team prize.

Sunday, October 18th saw me and about 200 other brave souls take part in a Run for Peace and Freedom in Sefton Park in high winds and rain. We were lucky. 'The Great Storm' had torn its way across the South-East of England. 23 people were killed in weather related incidents, thousands of homes were flooded and without electricity, thousands of trees were blown down, blocking roads, crushing cars and crashing through roofs. For once the North/South divide had benefited the North as we experienced far less severe conditions. I only got a real sense of the damage done when I visited my younger sister in Leatherhead, Surrey about a year later. The number of huge trees still lying scattered in the wooded areas around the town was staggering.

We had a bit of wind and rain but not enough to stop us running. I finished in 5th place in the race but got the third place award because two vets, who finished in front of me, received their own category trophies. It was a bit of a weird achievement being given a trophy for being defeated by two old fellas. As I had jogged around before the race I exchanged nods with a couple of familiar faces making an appearance after a time away from the limelight. Derek Hatton and Tony Mulhearn, disbarred and surcharged Militant councillors, were running; getting a bit of fresh air after all the hot air.

On October 25th I was guaranteed a PB in a race. No, I didn't intend to bribe the timekeepers or use performance enhancing drugs. The guarantee lay in the fact that I had never run the distance before. I thought it would be interesting to run a 20-miler. When I say I wouldn't be using performance drugs, I tell a bit of a lie. I was fed up with the singularly boring carbohydrate bleed and load diet which I had been using regularly before marathon races. This required a lot of discipline and self-restraint with food and drink. You can see my problem. My marathon performances had varied greatly using this monk-like pre-race approach. For this twenty mile run, I decided I could risk some experimentation. My plan was to follow a beer diet. I would drink a 'small' daily quota of ale from the Tuesday before the race. As chance would have it, I managed to stick to my plan doggedly and woke up on the Sunday race morning feeling in high spirits.

DJ drove me to Winsford in Cheshire where the race would take place. The course turned out to be a multi-lap, hilly, countryside route, which judging by my Stratford performances seemed to be a type that suited me. I breezed the course and finished 9th in front of DJ who was in 11th. My time was 1:56:57, which meant I had been running at 5:50 mile pace. 'That'll do me', was my reaction. I would have to try the beer diet more often. The drive home was quiet. DJ somehow managed to be quieter than Whistler had ever been. I don't think he liked finishing behind this old fella.

November saw the end of free eye tests and the start of acid house raves. I don't think the two were connected. The charging for eye tests was just another measure brought in by the Conservative government to gradually erode the services provided by the NHS, in the name of economic austerity. However they still had money in their 'empty' coffers to build Type 22 frigates for £162 million each. On October 7th my school had been invited to watch the launch of one of these vessels, H.M.S. Campbeltown, at Cammell Lairds shipbuilders. We were offered this opportunity as one of the closest primary schools to the yard. Before the decline in ship building, almost every family in the area would have had someone working for 'Lairds' and the firm's sports and social club was over the road from our school.

    I enjoyed the spectacle of the ship ploughing majestically into the Mersey and seeing the obvious pride of the shipbuilders in a job well done but I'm not sure I saw the point. In 1983 I'd bought Elvis Costello's album 'Punch the Clock'. The lyrics to the track 'Shipbuilding' resonated:

It's all we're skilled in
We will be shipbuilding
With all the will in the world
Diving for dear life
When we could be diving for pearls.

    Singer-songwriter Elvis Costello (Declan McManus) had lived in Birkenhead in his late teens when his Liverpool-born mother had decided to return home to Merseyside from London in 1971. In 2008 he was awarded an honorary degree of Doctor of Music by The University of Liverpool. HMS Campbeltown was decommissioned in 2011.

```
                                              N°  .0532
       CAMMELL LAIRD SHIPBUILDERS LTD
                                         BIRKENHEAD

              Launch of
           HMS CAMPBELTOWN
      on Wednesday 7th October 1987 at 11.35 am

   ADMIT ONE TO SHIPYARD      FOR CONDITIONS
   NOT BEFORE 10.45 am        SEE BACK
   GREEN LANE GATE ENTRANCE ONLY
```

(We could be diving for pearls)

Although not all runners possessed the saintly qualities Billy Wilson alluded to in the 1987 Wolverhampton Marathon results booklet, they were generally a good natured bunch. As in all walks of life, however, there were exceptions. On November 16th I was up in Preston yet again, running a ten miler (unsurprisingly named the Preston 10). I'd run in a cross country the day before and I had a cold, yet again. It was a perfect day for running with little wind and a light drizzle. There was a high quality field and I was feeling my way into the race when at two miles some idiot came barging past me, Rambo style (he may well have been auditioning for Rambo III to be filmed in 1988). I told him to behave himself. He replied with sign language. I then told him to be careful not to have a dope test because it would confirm he was one. All this acerbic wit was a bit wasted as it was addressed to the back of a rapidly disappearing running vest. I managed to finish in 55:35 which amazingly only put me in 77th place. Who were all these fast buggers?

November was a sad month. The 'Irish Problem' at heart also a 'British Problem' wasn't going away. In Enniskillen 11 people were killed by an IRA bomb at a remembrance parade. Ten of the victims were civilians. The bombing, sanctioned by the IRA Fermanagh local brigade command, horrified many republicans and was seen as a monumental 'error' which would merely strengthen their opponents and weaken their cause. This turned out to be true as the IRA's political wing, Sinn Féin, lost support. It was to be 14 years in 2001 before their electoral backing returned to its 1985 level. Gerry Adams, Sinn Féin leader, apologised for the bombing on behalf of the republican movement in 1997.

Ten days after Enniskillen, 31 people died as the result of a fire in Kings Cross tube station. The combination of antique wooden escalators, an accumulation of debris beneath them and a carelessly discarded match caused the fire to start. Inadequate awareness of fire control and safety procedures combined with the lethal results of the newly discovered 'trench effect' helped the small fire turn into an inferno. By 1989 smoking had been banned on the Underground and all wooden escalators replaced.

Spending on research to improve safety on public transport often seemed to be a response to disasters and not investment in an attempt to prevent them. After the Zeebrugge disaster in March, when the ferry MS Herald of Free Enterprise had capsized off the Belgian coast killing 193 passengers and crew, individuals were blamed for negligence but they had been working in an environment where safety issues and safeguards did not appear to be of paramount concern.

A depressing November moved into December. The Pogues and Kirsty MacColl were singing 'A Fairy Tale of New York' and the boys of the NYPD choir were singing 'Galway Bay'. Not the most upbeat of Christmas Songs but somehow appropriate for the time.

Nike, the sports shoe manufacturers, launched the first Air Max running shoe. The shoe would go on to capture a huge chunk of the athletic and fashion market. The end of another athletic 12 months was also closing in for me. By December 17th I had run 10 thousand miles in less than three years. I was still performing reasonably well. On the 6th I ran in the Liverpool Road Runners half marathon and was only six seconds off a PB with 1:13:12 and on the 27th I recorded a PB for five miles with 26:42. I had raced in one 5k, one five-miler, eight 10ks, three ten-milers, six half marathons, one twenty-miler and three marathons. I had run 3301 miles in 1987. The highlight of the year had definitely been the London Marathon. The thought of running another 3000 miles next year suddenly became daunting. I was overcome with fatigue just considering it. My odd reaction was to start to wish time away, imagining myself as an old man of 60 only having to run a few miles a week for fun. Although the compulsion to carry on was strong I wasn't sure that I could keep this intensity up or that I even wanted to.

Chapter 7

1988 Cross Country, Cross Words

It had been over a year since I joined the club. My position in the marathon training group was secure and I had got to know the other members well. Although originally from a different part of the country, living in a different part of town and, being a teacher, from a different, professional (ha!) line of work, I felt more at home with this mixture of characters than I had done in any other sports team. On a practical level it was important that we got on reasonably well because we often spent two mid-week evenings and many Saturdays and Sunday mornings, training and racing together but there was more to it than that. We seemed to have bonded through the bounding.

The squad was potentially a large group, some would flit in and out, odd ones suddenly appeared then disappeared immediately, but there was a solid core, of which I now counted myself as one. There was Rugman, so called (by me) because of his hirsute carapace. He was strong-willed and determined, with an abrasive manner. A dark and brooding exterior hid a sensitive side which always caught you by surprise. He had a tough physical job 'on the hod' for a building firm. I don't know how he found the energy to run (this was true of a lot of club members) having tired his body with physical work before even coming to training. You would have thought that being a pen-pusher would give me an energy edge, but it never appeared to. Rugman, although not the oldest, was the unofficial (god) father figure of the group and, like naughty kids, the rest of us would occasionally wind him up. Renowned for his tightly coiled spring we took care not to overwind him.

DJ (his initials were M.C.) was the youngest of the group though not strictly supposed to be in it. Coach Hombre had put him in a 'middle distance' squad with a schedule of less endurance and more speed work but he always gravitated to us. I'm not sure what the attraction was. He was a proper runner not having arrived as a football has-been. Initially it was hard to make out what he was thinking because he tended to speak only if spoken to. After I really got to know him better it got no easier. What was obvious was his thoughtfulness; he was always willing to drive us to races and it was virtually impossible to get him to accept a share of the cost.

The Bard was Rugman's mate and was the 'character' of our group. He was always acting up and playing the fool. That is not why I have given him this theatrical name. I dubbed him thus because he told me that he had been kicked out of a lot of drinking establishments as a young man. The Bard had spent time at a Royal Institute for Wayward Youths and you could occasionally see the flashes of a quick temper which may have got him into trouble. He laughed long and hard at his own jokes and would punish you with a punch on the arm or a squeeze of a tender body part if you didn't join in the celebration of his wit. He may sound awful from this description but he really was a lovely fella, as well as being a nutter. If you were a friend he would do you a favour and expect nothing in return and was the sort of bloke you would prefer to have on your side. He also worked on the 'buildings', for the council, as a foreman bricklayer. In spite of his rough render he was a thinker.

Testerman was a core member of the group but not always there. He worked away as some sort of engineer on various sites which I think were to do with oil production or storage. As you can see, when he came back from wherever, doing whatever, I figured he wouldn't want to talk about work so I never really found out about it. Many of these lads knew each other, or, at least, of each other, from playing footie and or living in the north of Liverpool. Rugman told me that Testerman had weighed in at about sixteen stone before he started running; now he was like a skeleton which is why I gave him this pseudonym, last will and Testerman. He was quietly spoken and unassumingly friendly with the same 'strange' streak of generosity as the others.

The Brothers Grimm sometimes came to the club together although the Elder was more prominent in our group. They weren't grim; in fact at times they were really funny. I gave them their moniker because they were brothers from North Liverpool and as we all know it's grim up North. They had another brother who also ran but he couldn't be classified as a 'Grimm' because he now lived on the Wirral. Although funny, Grimm the Elder was extremely serious about his running and did much of his training alone, 'secret training' as it was ironically described by other squad members. The truth was we all tended to be coy about the training we did outside club nights. We deliberately played down the mileage we were accumulating in the lead up to marathons. Runners typically liked to keep their cards close to their flat narrow chests and were always cagey about form and race prospects. Training was <u>never</u> going well. It was always wise to get your excuses in early. This was understandable as pride came before a fall, or a wall. Grimm the E. was, however, the most clandestine of us all; ultra-enigmatic and also ultra-aggressive in races.

Apart from these leading actors, there were many other players at the club, too numerous to describe fully. There was the Ducker, a docker whose true personality was hard to pin down. I learnt never to recount an experience or story in front of him because he always had a better one, on exactly the same subject. Some of them may even have been true. There was Eyefull, a quiet young lad, who was taller than the Ducker's tales and anyone else in the club, mainly because the rest of us were hobbits (something to do with the northern diet, Edwina). We had Miami Twice (paying homage to a popular US crime drama at that time) two flash lads, who had a local market stall which sold (ahem...) 'designer' sports goods and fashion wear. We had Donnys and Ronnys, Bennys and Kennys, Billys and Willys; also a variety of Micks, Macs, Paddys and Wacks. There were also a few Thelmas and Louises but not so many; the female side of the club would grow later. All these names are fictional. The characters may or may not be fictional; that's for them to decide.

In spite of starting the running year with less enthusiasm than previously, I had a busy January. This was mainly due to cross country commitments. Having a relatively small and inexperienced membership, the club didn't have many candidates to pick from to form their cross country teams, so I generally got in. I didn't consider myself particularly fast over shorter distances or off road but I was always happy to turn up for the club and give it a go.

On the 9th of the month the Northern XC Championships were being held in County Durham, across the Pennines. Middlesbrough, where I was born, was close by the venue so I decided to hire a car and combine the race with a visit to stay at the house where my grandmother (a midwife) had delivered me 37 years before. My dad was away working on the North Sea oilrigs; he'd left his job as an electrician at British Steel many years earlier to take on more lucrative, but less secure, contract work. My stepmother was at home and played host to Eileen, Laura and me over the weekend.

It was always a perplexing experience to return to the place which had been home for the first 20 years of my life. My mother had died in my first term of university and my dad had soon married a younger woman with four kids under the age of eleven. There had been no room to return to live in this house, after university, even if I had wanted to. It was a place which held few really happy memories but also few really sad ones except those of my mum's death. I was neither particularly emotional about the place nor comfortable in it. It no longer felt like my home and I had no recollection of it having been really homely. My abiding memories of the '50s and '60s were of a cold house with threadbare furnishings, shortage of money, mum always being at work and dad always being away, working shifts or abroad on long contracts.

At the time my mum died I was a self-absorbed young person who decided to sever geographical ties with my birthplace and to some extent emotional ties (what few there were) to my dad, who had decided to make a new life. The lack of a committed fulcrum for our family caused its disintegration. My two sisters, brother and I went our own ways, crossing paths at times but never again converging fully as a complete group; dad didn't exactly encourage us to.

My younger sister and I kept in touch regularly; she was my only constant blood family connection through the eighties although I had been adopted by Eileen's clan. I went back to Middlesbrough at most once a year. It had become more of a duty than pleasure. For myself, I wasn't particularly disappointed that my dad was absent during our visit but I did like to give Laura a chance to see her grandfather occasionally, in spite of his generally muted enthusiasm and consequently mine.

Having stayed in the 'Boro' on Friday night we set off for the foot races in Chester-le-Street. Here I met up with the boys from the 'Pool' and we had a laugh about the toughness of the terrain; course humour. It was four laps of rough, hilly parkland, with a couple of knee-deep mud-traps.

I ran the race feeling unpressured and actually enjoyed it. The situation which caused most amusement for our group was watching and cheering other runners who were forced to stop in the centre of a particularly bad quagmire in order to grope around in the depths of the dun detritus to retrieve their shoes which had been gobbled up by the clag monster; mine had stayed afoot. All in all I was satisfied with my performance and happy to be outdoors, on a nice day, in light spirits, with my friends and close family. What more could I ask for?

My birthday came around as it always tended to at this time of year. Yippee, this year it was on a Sunday. And what special treat was waiting for me on my birthday weekend? On the Saturday DJ drove me to a cross country race in Sherdley Park, St Helens. I liked to spoil myself. Actually, considering the conditions, I was more likely to soil myself. It was a freezing day with horizontal sleet. Entering the car park we knew it was going to be a tough one. The area was clogged with droves of concerned parents carrying blue-lipped, tearful, shivering sons, back from a junior race, to the sanctuary of their vehicles; they looked like a miniature army fleeing the battlefield.

Icy water covered the course. As I warmed up, my feet froze as soon as the liquid chill seeped through my shoes. We were to do one small lap and three large laps, about seven miles in all. Many people seemed to lose interest and dropped out after the first lap as the appalling conditions became more apparent. Of those who remained, the proper runners skimmed the surface but I was sucked down at each step. On the three large laps there was the added attraction of an impromptu pond, about 15 metres across, where water, topped with a skim of mushy ice, had gathered in a dip in the ground. Having ploughed through the knee-high water the first time round, we found out that the pond deepened each lap as the earth on the bottom was eroded by the clawing of spikes. By the last lap, a titanic effort, mythological not nautical, was required to cross the pond. By now we were almost waist deep in freezing slush and the cold reached places you really wished it hadn't. Everyone who finished agreed it was a great course. I got home to thaw out my bits and looked forward to my birthday when I would be taking it totally easy and….. running the Helsby Half Marathon. Come on, what did you expect, sanity?

DJ called at 9:00 am. I was allowed out to play. We went on to pick up another runner, who lived nearby who was a work colleague of Whistler's and occasionally ran with me. I shall call him the Prof, not only because he properly was one but also because he properly looked like one. He had a beard that covered virtually every spare inch of space on his face. He wore round glasses and communicated in a way which always seemed to leave a philosophical proposition dangling in the air. He would often smile enigmatically. When he did this, his beard would move like there was a squirrel in the undergrowth.

Because it was my birthday I started the race at a celebratory rather than serious pace. DJ was way ahead. However, my laid-back approach, like the Co-op, paid dividends. I started to move easily through the field of runners. Into the last three miles I suddenly spotted DJ in the distance and the gap between us was shrinking. He was struggling. Near to the finish he became aware of my close proximity and because it was my 'special' day he slowed down further, to allow me to catch up. Yards from the finish I got within touching distance of him but not wanting to be touched he put on the afterburners and left me for dead. Happy Burnday! Hey, I would have done the same to him, the bastard! Although we all got on well individually in our training group and as a team, the competitive edge was always there, especially in races but it was never malicious. Fair play to DJ though, he then took me to a nearby pub and I was bought several frothy pints of Boddington's bitter and spent the rest of that afternoon at home on the settee in a pleasant, mildly catatonic state.

I wasn't the only person celebrating that month. Margaret Thatcher patted herself on the back (who else would?) for becoming the longest serving prime minister of the 20th century. Some said good old Maggie, others told the truth. Those 8 years and 244 days had seemed like an eternity.

The Thatcher government's longevity and continued support made them even bolder in their erosion of public services to suit private ends. They pointed to falling unemployment and a property boom as evidence of economic recovery and the success of their policies. On the face of it this claim may have seemed to contain an element of truth but a closer look at the facts revealed the divided nation they had created. Figures released that year showed that the house price boom had boosted wealth in London by £39 billion over the previous four years but in the North West and Scotland over the same period there had been an £18 billion slump. In spite of lower unemployment, even in London it was estimated 50% of men and 80% of women were earning less than the lowest sum needed to buy the cheapest houses. Ordinary people were not part of this wealth bonanza. In February nurses were forced to go on strike to try to persuade the government to improve their pathetic pay rates. The Tories seemed oblivious to the suffering caused by their policies. (In 2013, this all sounds familiar.)

Some people would regard cross country running as self-inflicted suffering and they would be right. As in most running activities, the pleasure came from it all being over. The 'National Championship' was the final fixture in the cross country season (as the Cup Final at Wembley used to be for football). This race was an all-male affair, the women having their own separate event until the first joint championship in 1995 after the amalgamation of the male and female organisations in 1992.

The National XC Championship or 'The National', as it was commonly called, should not to be confused with the 'Grand National', although in 1988 there were many similarities. This year's race was held at Newark in Nottinghamshire, at the Showground. 230 teams and 2136 runners assembled on a fresh Saturday morning late in February. The ground was dead flat and frozen hard at the start but where the course wandered off into surrounding farm fields birds pecked vainly for sustenance on the ploughed and rutted earth.

Like horses we were saddled err... with using animal stalls to get changed in. Fresh hay, exuding that distinctive farmyard smell of sweetness on the verge of decay, had been spread on the floor. Although tempted to linger in this five star accommodation we were soon lined up at the start, in our teams. A maximum of nine runners was allowed in each team and the first six would count in the scoring for the team competition. The fastest runner on each team stood at the head of a single-file queue of his team mates, supposedly arranged in approximate order of speed. This meant that the front of the starting line, for the sake of fairness, had a row of 230 runners on it. That was a wide start; at least a 100 metres in width in fact! This was not a problem at the beginning of the race because it consisted of a charge across the broad stretch of the Newark Showground's sward.

The noise of the starting gun was soon followed by a low growl of distant thunder even though the sky was cloudless blue. The noise came from over two thousand pairs of feet hammering the firm turf. The volume of sound was surprising and not dissimilar to hearing the Grand National up close. The temperature at the centre of this rampaging horde was also amazing; human steam and body heat defied the atmospheric conditions, creating a mobile sauna. After a few minutes of running we came to a sudden concertinaing. Everyone's hands, (except the leaders') went out on to the backs of those in front to prevent a stumbling spiky pile-up, like a bunch of hedgehogs in a tumble drier. We ground to a halt as the 100 metre wide start was decanted, through a 10 metre gap, into the fields. Runners patiently trickled through the gate like grains of sand in an egg timer. On reaching the other side running was easier, but not much, as the race struggled to sort itself out.

The iron hard corrugated ground caused runners to sprain ankles. I managed to tweak mine in the first mile but, because of the slow speed I was travelling, it wasn't the serious type of twist I had been prone to since my footballing days. This would have stopped me in my tracks and left me all but immobile for weeks. After running the first of three laps in single file, spaces began to appear and I began to enjoy myself, picking off runners and improving my position. Feeling strong at the end I managed to overtake more than ten people in the home straight. I was then able to lay claim to being the 787th fastest male cross country runner in England, that year, and our team was the 123rd best. In spite of appearances created by the large numbers, these were actually commendable achievements...honestly. (Totally truthfully, the fact that many bigger clubs had a host of talented runners, faster than me, who would not have even made their teams, made it a flattering personal result.)

At the finish, in a shed, concrete animal pens had been lined with black polythene. These converted constructions were then filled with hot water, brought in by tankers. This was then cooled down by the fire brigade, pumping cold water in from two engines. These were the amazing ad hoc, post-race, washing facilities and hundreds of sweaty, muddy bodies, presumably all runners, piled into the monstrous, makeshift baths. The hot water had a sweet smell which, I discovered, was because it had been brought in from the British Sugar Corporation's refineries nearby. I was glad the fire engines hadn't been called out on an emergency otherwise we would have emerged from the pens not only smelling like sugar beet but also looking the colour of beetroot.

The next weekend back in Liverpool (a city built, to a significant extent, with profits made from West Indian slave-grown sugar) I found myself being entertained by Peruvian sailors. I think a little background information may be necessary to explain these circumstances because I can assure you it wasn't something I usually went in for. To start the explanation we need to go for a walk up Hope Street in Liverpool. Come along don't dawdle!

This half-mile byway is generally famous for the fact that it runs between the city's two cathedrals; the towering, sandstone, gothic Anglican and the sixties, concrete and glass, space-module-shaped Catholic Metropolitan, or 'Paddy's Wigwam' as it is affectionately known. Many other fine and famous buildings also look out on to the thoroughfare between these two. Travelling from the Anglican Cathedral you will first pass what was once the Mechanics Institute. In the 1800s, public lectures were frequently given here by well-known speakers. Charles Dickens once spoke on 'Hard Times with

Motorcycle Maintenance'. OK, so it's true he gave a lecture there but I don't know what the subject was.

Mechanics Institutes were generally set up by philanthropic industrialists to provide technical education for working men. Astute business men had realised that they would ultimately benefit from a skilled and knowledgeable workforce. The first were set up in Edinburgh in 1821 and Glasgow in 1823, quickly followed by the first in England, in Liverpool, also in 1823. The organisation moved into the building on Hope Street when its construction was complete in 1837. The College of Art was added in 1882. These buildings subsequently housed the Liverpool Institute High School for Boys and the Art College; two places of education famous for Beatle connections, Paul McCartney and George Harrison having attended the former and John Lennon the latter; less interestingly Derek Hatton also went to the Institute or 'the Inny'. Closed in 1985, the school's buildings later became the home of Paul McCartney's Liverpool Institute of Performing Arts (LIPA) which opened in 1996.

Moving further down the street on the right we come to Blackburne House, which was once a country mansion, built by John Blackburne, Mayor of Liverpool in 1788. It became Blackburne House Girls School. This school was closed in 1986 but not before Edwina Currie managed to get some kind of strange education there. It is now the Women's Technology and Education Centre.

Venturing onwards to where Hope Street crosses Hardman Street to the right we see the Art Deco splendour of the Philharmonic Concert Hall, built in 1936 to replace the original 1849 building which was destroyed by fire in 1933; to the left is a white building which was built as a 1932 extension of a school for the blind which had been opened in 1850. Looking across Hardman Street, on the corner we see the Art Nouveau, architectural potpourri of the Philharmonic Hotel, completed at the beginning of the twentieth century. This famous pub has an equally ornate interior and the most fanciful urinals I have ever encountered; a pleasure on the eye but not the nostril. Many a misdirected piss has been caused by an appreciative inspection of the decorative tile work. These male toilets have also received more inquisitive female visitors than any other in the country (I'm guessing).

At the northern end of the street, near to the Catholic cathedral is the Everyman Theatre; opened in 1964 and closed for reconstruction in 2011. The theatre company was responsible for spawning acting talent like Julie Walters, Bernard Hill, Jonathan Pryce, Pete Postlethwaite, Antony Sher, Bill Nighy, Barbara Dickson, Matthew Kelly and Cathy Tyson, to name but a few. Originally built as Hope Hall, a dissenter's chapel, in 1837, it became a concert hall in 1853, then a cinema 1912 before becoming a theatre. In the '80s, it was not only a great place to watch gritty, modern theatre but the bar was one of the few interesting places where a gritty, after-hours drink (the glass washers were a bit lax) could be enjoyed in the good old 'double-up-quick-its-last-orders' days. I went there, once or thrice. Eileen had the claim to fame of stumbling down the original rickety basement bar steps (before she'd had a drink she says) and being caught by a combination of Matthew Kelly and Julie Walters. Mama Mia, she saw stars in her eyes! Just before its closure for rebuilding in 2011 it was also the venue for another auspicious and grand occasion. I was actually surprised by my 60th surprise birthday party in the basement function room; a great night to say goodbye to the old building and hello to my bus pass.

Hope Street has now been rebranded 'The Hope Street Quarter' and in 2012 was voted 'Britain's Best Street' by the Academy of Urbanism and by golly they know their British streets. But stop! We have come too far. Now I want you to travel backwards in time and space with me (take care, no moonwalking or hoverboarding) towards the corner of Hardman Street, and the School for the Blind. Here I will stretch out further this spurious and ever elusive link to South American mariners.

A certain Edward Rushton was born in 1756 and became apprenticed to a firm that traded with the West Indies. He soon became an experienced sailor and, by the age of 17, a second mate. He worked the slave ships and encountered their horrors first hand. He tried to help the captive human cargo of these vessels by sneaking food and drink below decks. His contact with the slaves caused him to be charged with mutiny and to contract ophthalmia, a contagious eye disease, which was rife on the slavers. He went blind in one eye, developed a cataract over the other and was discharged from the navy.

Unable to sail, he returned to Liverpool and started to write poetry and radical political tracts against slavery and poverty. When he eventually became financially comfortable, from book selling, he turned his attention to putting his money to good use. He established the Liverpool School for the Indigent Blind on London Road. After a school in Paris, this was only the second educational institute for the blind in the world and the first to be founded by a blind person. The school was moved to the new Hope Street site in 1851 where it stayed until 1957.

And the Peruvian connection? Hang on I'm getting there. After 1957 the building, with its original, yellowing, Bath stone front aspect and the 1932 white, Portland stone Hope Street extension, was occupied by the Merseyside Police as their headquarters. The police then left as money was somehow found for brand new premises shortly after the 1981 riots. The building was subsequently established as the Merseyside Trade Union, Community and Unemployed Resource Centre (MTUCURC) in 1983. When this organisation moved into the space they found that the place had been somewhat trashed by the previous lawful tenants. National Front posters adorned some of the former police office walls and surveillance information about trade union activists had been left, to be found. These seemingly puerile acts of provocation indicated that there were elements in the police force that clearly held bigoted and paranoid attitudes. This behaviour could only have been reinforced by policies of some of their superiors and political masters at that time.

Over the next few years, MTUCRUC, or the Unemployed Centre as it was known for short, became a great facility and a hub of activity for the city's fight against the government's elitist and divisive policies. Along with a nursery, print room, offices and function areas it also had a music venue and recording studio. The music facilities were set up and managed with the help of donations from, among others, Pete Townsend, Elvis Costello, Paul McCartney, Yoko Ono, Phil Collins, Jogging Joe Strummer, Depeche Mode, Ringo Starr, Suggs of Madness, Peter Gabriel, New Order, Paul Weller and The Royal Liverpool Philharmonic Orchestra. 'The Picket' (as the rehearsal space, recording studios and music venue became known) started to promote unheralded musical talent in the city and continued to do so for twenty years. (Today 'the Picket' continues to be a spawning ground for local musicians at a dockland venue where it reluctantly moved after the Trade Union Centre and all its facilities were forced to close in 2003 due to lack of funding.)

'The Centre', as MTURUC was even more shortly known, also had a bar called 'The Flying Picket', after which the music venue was named. Eileen had somehow been roped into being lay secretary of the Management Committee of 'the Centre' and spent many of her evenings in endless meetings there and I spent many of my evenings in the bar waiting for her to eventually emerge from a smoke-filled room into an equally smoke-filled bar. If there was a cause worth fighting for then people in 'The Centre' would be helping to fight it and if there was a pint worth drinking to help 'The Centre's' finances I would be in 'The Flying Picket' drinking it. And at this point we have thankfully walked forward and backwards enough to reach the sailors from Peru and their entertainment.

In February 1988, 29 Peruvian seamen had been stranded in Merseyside for three and a half months. Their ship had been seized by the Admiralty Marshall because of debts owed by the Peruvian Steamship Company. Ship arrest in this country was a relatively easy procedure and only involved lodging an application accompanied by supportive witness statements with the Admiralty Marshall. It did not involve any hearing; fairly straightforward considering the size of a ship. However the little matter of the welfare of the sailors on board didn't appear to be part of this easy bureaucratic procedure. The Peruvians were receiving no wages, had no recreational facilities and had no prospect of getting home to their families, who were reliant on their wages. In Peru, at that time, it was normal for an employer to pay the school fees of employees' children but this benefit had also been withdrawn for these seamen's families. As usual the people who were suffering most were not to blame. So, finally, there I was in the Flying Picket, attending a 'social' organised by 'the Centre' and the Liverpool Dockworkers to raise money to help these sailors through their worrying time. We were served up South American ballad singing of the worst order, especially by the ship's cook.

Although the cause was good, the music was bad and I couldn't help but wince through the chef's performance, hoping his cooking was better than his crooning.

SUPPORT
THE 29 PERUVIAN SEAMEN!
SOCIAL!
SURPRISE ENTERTAINMENT!
TRADE UNION CENTRE,
HARDMAN STREET,
8.00 TILL LATE,
SAT. 27 FEBRUARY.

£2waged/ £1unwaged

29 PERUVIAN SEAMEN STRANDED ON MERSEYSIDE FOR THE PAST 3½ MONTHS, REQUIRE OUR URGENT SUPPORT. THEIR SHIP HAS BEEN SIEZED BY THE ADMIRALTY MARSHAL BECAUSE OF DEBTS OWED BY THE PERUVIAN STEAMSHIP COMPANY, AND THEY, AS THEIR FELLOW EMPLOYEES OF THE COMPANY, ARE NOW ON STRIKE WITHOUT FINANCIAL SUPPORT. Full Details overpage.

(A long walk up Hope Street for a good cause but bad music)

1988 was also the year that another spectacular bureaucratic exile began. The case of Merhan Karimi Nasseri started when he was allegedly expelled from Iran, minus passport, for protesting against the Shah's government. While in Belgium he was granted refugee status by the United Nations High Commission for Refugees and given permission to reside in any European country. He decided to settle in Great Britain, claiming that one of his parents was British. In 1988 en route to the UK via France it appeared that his briefcase containing all his refugee papers was stolen. Undaunted, he boarded a plane from Paris to London. Predictably he was turned back at London for not presenting a passport and returned to Paris. Here he was arrested but then quickly released, having not committed a crime, except perhaps that of posing as a human being but having no papers to prove it. It was then he started his 18 year residency at Terminal 1 of Charles De Gaulle Airport, luggage by his side. He spent his time reading, writing a diary and studying economics.

His story was the subject of many documentaries, an autobiography and eventually a film, 'Terminal Man' by Steven Spielberg. It is reputed that Spielberg paid Nasseri $200,-300,000 for the rights to his life story but the resulting film, starring Tom Hanks, was fictional and bore only a superficial resemblance to Nasseri's experience. Presuming he had received this pay-out it would have made him the richest homeless person on the planet but he didn't appear to be interested in money. His 18 year wait for a plane came to an end when he was hospitalised in 2006 and his sitting area dismantled. On recovery he was eventually transferred to a homeless shelter in Paris.

There is no doubt about the veracity of his odd and extended stint of statelessness but Nasseri's original account of how it came about is now thought to have been largely a construct of his own imagination. Information eventually emerged to indicate that his exile was at least partially self-imposed. It seems he did have a family to go to and was never actually expelled from the country of his birth. Although a French court had decreed that he could stay in the terminal but could not step on French soil there were a couple of occasions when he was offered the possibility of going elsewhere. At some stage he stopped protesting and appeared to have decided that 'terminal life' suited him. Some would have found the interminable routine he adopted soul destroying. In some ways however it was easy to see how an existence which was completely devoid of responsibility and commitment could become attractive to a man of fragile mind struggling with the pressures of life in the outside world. The strangest thing about this case, in my opinion, was not so much that Nasseri had acted in this way, because we all act in funny ways, but that the authorities didn't act. He was basically abandoned, reliant on unofficial kindnesses, like our Peruvian sailors. The human factor within bureaucratic systems was not paramount, in fact, in these examples it was apparently irrelevant.

The case also had a resonance for me, causing a light bulb to flicker at the back of my mind again. Nasseri had been brought up in the town of Masjed Suleiman, the birth place of the Iranian oil industry, near to the Persian Gulf. Here his father had worked as a physician for the Anglo-Iranian Oil Company. Around the time he claimed to have been tortured by Savak (the Sha's secret police) and politically exiled (in 1974) I had spent a month in Iran, mainly in Ahvaz. This was the oil town just south of Masjed where my elder sister and brother were both employed as teachers by the oil company and where my sister had married an Iranian. During my stay 'Savak' was a word on everyone's lips, usually followed by a Shhh! There was certainly an atmosphere of paranoia as everyone suspected everyone else of being secret police informers.

In the late '70s, soon after my brother's return to the UK, my sister and brother-in-law also fled Iran with their two sons to escape the regime of the Ayatollah Khomeini after the fall of the Shah in the Iranian Revolution of 1979. This was the sister who now lived with her exiled husband in Wolverhampton and whom I had not seen for a decade.

No visas or refugee papers were needed as I left the Republic of Merseyside late in March 1988 to cross into West Lancashire. An informer had told the authorities in the 'not famous for much' neat little market town of Ormskirk that I was back to do the half marathon after last year's absence. On my arrival I expected the flags to be out on the church steeple or maybe the tower. They had the choice. Disappointingly they chose neither.

DJ drove and we parked near the town hall next to the car of eventual winner Dave Wilson of Liverpool Pembroke Running Club. We cleverly deduced that it was his car because his name was emblazoned on the side of it. That was the closest we would get to him that day. The race was memorable from my perspective in that I could easily have been cited for being illegally paced, by vigilant AAA informers with no large fonts to challenge.

It was an extremely wet and windy day. At about five miles from the start we turned into the unfriendly wind, so I tucked in with two other runners. We took turns to give each other protection from the gale, an arrangement which is part of the unwritten code of conduct for road runners. This worked well as we were gaining on people in front of us. In spite of nearly being left behind by my two gutsy, gusty amigos at eight miles, I clung on and felt strong again at 11 miles. This time I decided to push on and surprisingly one of our trio weakened and became detached. The other was more adhesive. Suddenly, a man on a bike overtook us. At this stage I was taking all the buffeting from the wind and not wanting to look an iron gift horse in the mouth I tucked in behind the cyclist. I heard the runner behind me curse, as my sudden surge to lock on to the bike left him struggling. If I had been acquainted with this bike bloke or if I had slip-streamed him all the way to the finish, or worse still, clung on to his seat, I suppose my actions might have been deemed unsporting and illegal. The truth was we hadn't been introduced and I had absolutely no intention of grabbing his seat or any other rear protrusion. I was however prepared to luxuriate in his lee as long as was necessary. It turned out to be a short respite as we soon hit a hill and I found myself almost kicking his mudguard. I drew up alongside him and said, "Can't you go any faster?" Abridged, I think the breathless, blue barrage of expletives he uttered roughly translated as 'no' and so I carried on past him over the hill before storming down to the finish. I came 8th with 73 minutes and 30 seconds, a time I was chuffed with considering the conditions. So, retrospectively, I'd like to say thanks to the blue bile-cyclist. DJ had finished way behind me and consequently had a cob on. Not in a pub mood, he took me straight home. I'm surprised he didn't make me run behind the car.

My next race had me making an assessment of my chances in the 1988 London Marathon based mainly on the thinking of a man whose brain had been turned to blancmange as a result of it being repeatedly bounced around his skull. The Stafford 20 miler on March 24th was going to be a pointer to predict my form for London, of course not accounting for the total unpredictability of the Magical Mystery Detour which is the last sixandabit miles of any marathon.

I ran a reasonable race, going off a little too fast and slowing a little too much at the end, but nothing disastrous. For me, 1:54:35 was a satisfactory time and a pace which could get me under two and a half hours in a marathon. These were my woefully naïve and blindly optimistic observations written in my diary after the race while wearing rose-tinted spectacles and eating a bowl of cherries.

"Do I really think I can get under 2:30? Well I'd rather have a go at it than run even pace and finish with 2:35. So be it! I don't fear the distance. It's always worth having a go."

Why was I such an idiot? How many times had I told myself that even pace was the key? How many times had I come to grief when I had ignored my own advice? What was it about running that gave me the logic of an amoeba?

Human beings always have the capacity for logic but hatred and fear can all rob us of this gift. A sad and depressing chain of events occurred in March. On March 6th the SAS shot and killed three unarmed IRA members in Gibraltar. On the 16th, at the funeral of the dead from Gibraltar, in Milltown cemetery, West Belfast, Michael Stone of the Ulster Freedom Fighters killed three of the mourners and injured sixty in a grenade and pistol attack. On the 19th at the funeral of a victim of Milltown, two British army corporals, in plain clothes, were dragged from their cars and killed after driving into the procession and discharging their weapons. Just over a month later, in May, three off-duty British servicemen were shot dead by the IRA in Germany. Eleven pointless deaths, these words of Martin Luther King went some way to expressing how I felt;

"Through violence you may murder the liar, but you cannot murder the lie, nor establish the truth. Through violence you may murder the hater, but you do not murder hate. In fact, violence merely increases hate. Returning violence for violence multiplies violence, adding deeper darkness to a night already devoid of stars. Darkness cannot drive out darkness; only light can do that. Hate cannot drive out hate; only love can do that."

The sense of injustice and depth of hatred felt within the republican community in Ireland never seemed to be fully gauged or understood by British governments which seemed to opt for repression before discussion. Hard-liners on all sides were prepared to take the easier option of vengeance. This was never going to lead to any solution, short or long term.

April 1st this year coincided with Good Friday and Eileen and I travelled down to Birmingham to stay with her mum and dad. On Easter Sunday I had an encouraging pre-London jaunt when I finished 2nd in a 10k race in Canon Hill Park, with a time of 33:53. Eileen and her dad also ran. We all enjoyed the atmosphere of the event which was organised by an Asian community group. That night I celebrated with a few pints of Courage Directors at Eileen's mum and dad's local, The Baldwin, in Hall Green. The combination of Directors bitter and a delusional runner's high had me again imagining all sorts of heroic results for my London run; this time it was either Dutch Courage or a classic case of April fool.

Sad to say, after running in such an enjoyable multicultural event in Birmingham my actual un-heroic performance in London may have had the effect of putting community relations back a few years. The warning signs were there when I arrived at Blackheath on race day and again availed myself of the preferential toilets in the AAA elite athletes' tent. It wasn't the earthenware moving experience I was accustomed to. Usually several visits occurred to jettison excess weight, like a dirigible dumping sandbags to gain height. This did not happen. Maybe I had carbo-overloaded and my system had backed up. I had certainly enthusiastically stuffed myself silly with anything vaguely edible since Friday.

As there were no AAA regulations on size, weight or shape of stools deposited in their special toilets I was allowed to proceed unhindered to the start. I put my clothes on the baggage bus and met up with Rugman and Grimm the Elder. Soon the race started and I ran 5:40 for the first mile, much faster than last year but I felt OK. I spotted Coach Hombre at the Cutty Sark glowering at me from behind his moustache and barking instructions. Then I gave my now customary wave to Eileen at Tower Bridge (if two occasions can be classified as a custom). I reached thirteen miles in one hour and fourteen minutes which was good but my gut felt uncomfortable, which was bad. The inevitable happened.

Running and urgent bowel signals just don't go together. There are a variety of ways to deal with this problem. The civilised way is to discreetly locate a toilet and do the necessary. For top runners this is not always an option as too much time would be wasted. So, another alternative is to be uncivilised and to quote Paul McCartney, 'do it in the road.' Pride comes well down the list of a runner's deadly sins. There had been high profile examples of this approach, some of which were televised. In the 1985 London Marathon Welshman Steve Jones was vying for first place with Charlie 'itchy feet' Spedding, winner of the '84 London and Olympic marathon bronze medallist. With about five or six miles to go and having a healthy lead over the rest of the field the cameras caught the pair having a little chat. Some minutes later the aerial camera followed their progress to an underpass which they entered neck and neck and at which point they disappeared from view as camera signals were disrupted. At the other side of the underpass Spedding emerged with a 30 metres lead over Jones. Eventually the Welsh runner caught up and won the race. Apparently, in the nicest possible way, they had been talking crap. The conversation between them had consisted of Jones explaining to Spedding that he needed to go and asking for advice; not on how to but where to. The ever formal and meticulously prepared Spedding told him that shortly they would be coming to an underpass where Jones could do his business privately, out of camera shot. This he did before getting down to the business of snatching first place from Charlie, who vowed never to allow anyone to be privy to his emergency privy preparations again.

I also remember watching the great Norwegian runner, Greta Waitz, being a little less coy than tough man Steve Jones in another televised race. She just did it 'en courant' and her husband later handed her a wet sponge to allow her to restore her legs to a state which vaguely resembled sanitary, while she ran. I suppose dropping a load while running meant that those spectators who witnessed the act would be a safe distance behind you by the time the horror of the situation or olfactory ramifications kicked in.

I myself had occasionally needed to transfer an urgent package 'al fresco' in training, but on these occasions a quick dash into any convenient bushy thicket usually did the trick. Only twice had it happened in a race; once, as I've already alluded to, in the Windermere Marathon but also in a smaller race in Freshfields, a sandy strand on the Sefton Coast, near Liverpool. Here I was able to veer off into sand dunes discreetly. The main problem on that occasion had been the lack of any material, other than sand, to tidy myself up with afterwards. This resulted in friction smoke and a sound, not unlike that from maracas, being emitted from my big end as sandy cheeks rubbed together in the last couple of miles.

This occasion was different; London - so many people, so little privacy. Things got more and more urgent and the toilets, supposedly placed at regular intervals en route, were not placed for my convenience. Desperate and not wanting to do a 'Greta', I slipped from the course and into a council estate where it quickly became quiet. Away from the hullabaloo of the race I found space for a possibleloo; a secluded corner next to an electricity sub-station. Checking again that there was no-one about I dropped my shorts and quickly relieved myself. I was soon readjusting my attire in readiness to return to the race. I was also congratulating myself on finding a place for this private time. Then I made the mistake of looking upwards.

There, above, on a second floor balcony of nearby flats, looking down at me, aghast, was a whole family of Sikhs. They were out to watch the marathon but saw much more than they had anticipated. The looks on their faces, a mixture of horror, disbelief and disgust, meant the best I could do was scuttle away shamefaced and get back to the run. I imagined that my performance reinforced their views that Anglo-Saxons were an unhygienic and primitive race and should go back to where they came from. I had no defence.

I continued with less stomach but also less heart. In spite of my earlier efforts I still felt uncomfortable and had to dash off course again. This time I was lucky to find a building site with a wooden toilet shed. It was warm inside this little hut which, incongruously, had pretty flowery wallpaper. I had a powerful desire to stay there, for ever.

Eventually I re-joined the race and struggled on, still managing to reach 20 miles in less than two hours but not without beginning to suffer. Grimm the Elder went past me at 23 miles. I was badly dehydrated from the running and the trots. Coming up The Mall I got stomach cramps. I had to stop two or three times in the last mile. To my surprise even after all the stopping and dropping I finished in exactly two hours and forty minutes. I was still desperately disappointed. I had been wooed by my own over-ambition and jilted by reality. Grimm the Elder had pushed on to get an excellent 2:36, running one minute and 20 seconds a mile faster than me in the last three miles. His secret training had obviously worked.

Rugman had a bad race and DJ had an awful one, being beaten by Grimm the Younger, who ran a PB. Testerman had also been running. He selflessly ran with a club mate to help him get under three hours for the first time. Afterwards the gloom gradually lifted as we all got together for a quick pint and had a laugh, recounting our tales of pos, woes, and (in the case of the Brothers Grimm) heroes. The race taught me a lesson. I was determined to be less ambitious and realised that, if I was to improve at all, I should aim to improve by seconds not minutes. Wise thoughts indeed but would they be converted into action, would head learn to rule heart?

While we are on the subject of taking a step backwards in community relationships, May 1988 was the month of the enactment of Section 28 of the Local Government Act which stated that a local authority;

"...shall not intentionally promote homosexuality or publish material with the intention of promoting homosexuality" or "promote the teaching in any maintained school of the acceptability of homosexuality as a pretended family relationship."

It was as if being gay was a new fashion or fad and that advertising it would persuade more people to take it up. And what the hell was a 'pretended family relationship'? This was a description that could have been applied to a large number of heterosexual families.

Section 28 was repealed in Scotland in 2000 and in the rest of the UK in 2003 and although no-one was ever prosecuted under this provision it caused many lesbian, gay and bi-sexual support groups in schools and colleges to be closed down for fear of falling foul of the law. At the time of the repeal, a survey in 300 secondary schools by gay rights group, Stonewall, found that;

"82% of teachers were aware of verbal incidents linked to homophobia and 26% knew of physical attacks. Only 6% of schools had anti-bullying policies designed to combat homophobia."

At the same time the mental health charity Mind also reported that two in three gay people were likely to have mental health problems believed to be primarily due to homophobia. This could only have been reinforced by Section 28.

Of course, the repeal of the act did not bring the end to prejudice but it removed a barrier preventing it from being challenged. In 2012, Bob Blackman, 'enlightened' Tory MP for Harrow East, was still calling for section 28 to be brought back. I think an appropriate response to this would be the slogan of a Stonewall advertising campaign. Bob, 'some people are gay, get over it.'

Back in Liverpool in May 1988 Prince Charles was in town to reopen the Albert Dock which had been named after his great-great-great grandfather Prince Albert who had originally opened the docks in 1846. Built from cast iron, brick and stone, with no structural wood, it was the first non-combustible warehouse system in the world. It was also revolutionary in that it had a docking system which loaded goods straight from warehouse to vessel and vice versa. Two years after the original opening the first hydraulic cranes in the world were introduced there. The docks finally closed in 1972 and redevelopment started nine years later. The 1988 version contained the first Tate Art Gallery outside London. On Thursday, June 2nd, school half-term, the dock received a visit from another prestigious guest... me. Eileen and I took a break from painting (mainly wall-papering actually) in our house to go to the Tate and look at the paintings.

Having returned home from a hard day (why is it so tiring shuffling around and staring) at the art gallery, that evening I went to Warrington, with DJ, to run a half marathon. This industrial town is

16 miles east of Liverpool and famous for textiles, chemicals, brewing, tanning and steel, particularly wire. The town's renowned rugby league team was once called 'the Wire' before the game's administrators decided to go all modern and market the sport like American football. Most of the teams were rebranded by 1996 for the first 'Super League' season. Warrington were renamed 'the Wolves.' I didn't get it. There was already a football team with that name and the Wire was much more original and appropriate.

But by 1988 Warrington had already started getting all contemporary. The town had been well and truly put on the map as a cultural trendsetter when the first IKEA in the UK was opened on the edge of town. For a while, attention was diverted from the rugby team's flat back line to IKEA's flat-pack pine. (Apologies for that, but you rarely get the chance for self-assembly furniture/rugby themed puns.)

As textiles were another of Warrington's 'famous fors,' it was quite appropriate that the race I had entered should turn into a bizarre fabric dominated experience. The month before this race, our running club's committee had decided to change the team vest from plain blue mesh, with a diagonal white stripe and a Liver Bird print, to a thicker, acrylic material, in blue and white hoops. The new vest had caused rumblings in the marathon squad because of the fabric's heaviness when wet and its lack of breathability. The fact that there had been little consultation with members over the choice of different kit had also proved contentious. This background information is pertinent to help garner some understanding of the goings on in this race and the repercussions.

As we set off in a field of several hundred, DJ and I were surprised to find ourselves near the front with another runner and a few metres behind the leading two. (The unusual Thursday night start had obviously made many fast runners stay at home!) As the race progressed the leading two went further away and we three behind settled into a comfortable rhythm. It turned out that the third person in our trotting triumvirate was none other than Terry Lonergan, purveyor of running goods. He owned 'The Complete Runner' shop based in Ilkley, Yorkshire and had begun the Fastrax brand in the early 1980s. Terry had donated Fastrax vouchers as prizes for the race. Not only was he a decent runner, he also proved to be a persuasive salesman. As we ran along, I tell no lie, he gave us a sales pitch. He took one look at our vests and rolled his eyes. He scoffed at the thick material and referred us to his aerated, lightweight vest. He could see ours were already heavy, saturated with sweat and claimed he could hear the chafing. "Feel that," he said inviting us (thankfully) towards his vest. "It's dry as a bone." And feel it we did, as we were processing through the streets of Warrington, and behold it was dry. It was another miracle. I was going to ask him what temperature he washed it at to retain such vibrant colours but I was too out of breath. He had upped the pace. I almost expected him to follow up his demonstration by whipping a business card out of a secret pocket in his shorts but instead he finished by saying, "See me after the race and I'll see if I can do you a deal for your club."

Business concluded he concentrated on the race. He kept trying to pull away from us but we worked to pull him back. At ten miles he'd opened up a ten metres gap. I could feel DJ wasn't responding so I gave chase alone in the last three miles. I caught up with the bugger three times but he just kept putting in little spurts to create a gap and knacker me. I knew he was toying with me really, just doing enough, but I wasn't going to give up. With about 800 metres to go I caught him again but he timed his finishing sprint to perfection taking 3rd place and leaving me in 4th, four seconds behind. I reckon it was because his vest was lighter!

The good news was that he had dragged me along to an unexpected PB of 1:12:56! Under 73 minutes at last! I'd waited two years to improve my half marathon time. The bad news was that Terry decided to accept the third place prize from himself, leaving me with nothing. It got a little awkward at the presentation ceremony when he tried to shake hands with himself while giving himself an envelope with one of his own vouchers inside.

So Terry left for Ikley with 3rd prize and an order for vests, after DJ, who had finished 20 seconds behind me, had discussed terms with him. Those vests would work wonders for our perspiration but damaged club member's interrelations. Dry as a bone of contention.

Soon after I'd got under 73 (minutes), Nelson Mandela remarkably reached over 70 (years), in spite of being imprisoned by the apartheid regime in South Africa for 25 of those. A growing global campaign pressing for his release was particularly strong in the UK. To bring attention to his plight a musical event was arranged at Wembley Stadium. It was broadcast in 47 countries to an underestimated audience of 600 million. Now, that's what I call raising awareness. The Fox Television network heavily edited the political aspects of the concert. Needless to say the broadcast was also banned in South Africa although many got to see it illegally. Now that's what I call censorship.

The day after the concert on June 12th I ran another marathon. Having restricted myself to only one that year so far, I decided that I needed to remind myself what an excruciating/exhilarating experience running the 26 mile distance provided. I must have subconsciously decided that, because I had done so many now, I needed to try to make this one even harder by taking on a variety of extra challenges, some of which were beyond my control and some which, indubitably, were not.

I picked the hottest day of the year to drive north to partake in the Blackpool Marathon. Much of the course followed the white, concreted, un-shaded linearity of the promenade; not my fault. Having parked up near to the start which was by the Blackpool Tower I got changed in a leisurely fashion. Not wanting to stand around in the heat too long I left it as late as possible before I walked casually to the start area with Eileen and Laura, who had come along to sunbathe, holidaymake and laugh at the mad runners. The problem was that when we reached the Tower I discovered that the start wasn't there, it was another mile further on. I had misread the race instructions; yes, my fault. I left Eileen and Laura and started to jog up the prom in the right direction. Checking my watch anxiously the jog got faster, then faster. As the time for the 'off' drew closer the jog grew into a canter, then a gallop and then a sprint as I finally spotted the start line and the starter with his gun raised. Seeing me approaching in a flustered and panicky manner he relaxed his itchy trigger finger. I ducked under the starting tape and turned around. Almost simultaneously the gun was fired and I returned from whence

I had come, thoroughly warmed up. In spite of the calamitous run up, the heat and the strong hot off shore breeze, which provided no respite, miraculously I felt OK.

As the race progressed, although in control, I noticed that I was gradually slowing down. At twenty miles I decided that to get under two hours forty minutes I would have to kill myself. Not literally, of course, but running in hot weather you never knew. I shocked myself by making a conscious decision to slow down further for the last six miles; uncharacteristically sensible of me. This wasn't a day for quick times and my decision would hopefully allow for a quicker recovery in the weeks that followed. It also allowed me to banter with bemused spectators near the finish about the need for alcoholic refreshment.

(Finishing first with Laura a distant last. Competitive? Me?)

I finished in 2:45:50, which was no disgrace and, although I say so myself, enabled me to be the best looking person in the finish area, if you know what I mean. Some people seemed to have aged 20 years, having pushed themselves in the heat. To be fair they may have usually looked like that. Rugman, DJ and the Bard had all dropped out. Testerman had struggled in with a near personal worse of three hours twenty minutes. I, on the other hand, felt fine even though I had actually run over 27 miles. To prove it I took Laura to the fair. She particularly liked the huge undulated slide called the Astroglide; so did I. Getting to the top of the slide required climbing a long set of stairs. We went on it eight times. My thighs survived but my Gluteus Maximi were mashed from bouncing down the corrugations. Astroglide my arse!

The observant amongst you will have noticed I mentioned that I had 'driven' north to Blackpool. I had learned to drive when I was 29. I was now 37 and had finally succumbed to buying a car. Several factors had persuaded me. Firstly, I was conscious of the fact that, since I'd started running, when going to races, I'd had to rely heavily on the goodwill of others to get me there. Now I could repay some of that kindness. It also made it quicker to get home from work, which was a big plus. It would give me more time to run from home. As you can tell by my choice of vehicle I was not a fan of the Top Gear programme which Jeremy Clarkson had (unfortunately) just started to present in 1987. I bought a new Nissan Micra. The main reasons for my choice were that I had heard they were reliable and Nissan, desperate to get a foothold in the market, were offering interest free, no deposit finance over three years. It was an offer I couldn't refuse in spite of the loss of green brownie points.

On the Tuesday after Blackpool I was back training with the marathon squad. We were doing speed work on our track. Where we trained was similar to the Iffley Road track, in Oxford, where Roger Bannister had recorded the first sub-four minute mile in 1954. The difference was that by 1988 ours hadn't been upgraded. Weeds grew through the cinders where there were no shards of glass or dog turds and it didn't appear to have been levelled since the year of Roger's record. It was more like a lava field than a running facility and when wet the surface turned into a sticky morass as if someone had dumped waste plum jam on it from the nearby Hartley's factory

We did four times 400m hard with 400 metres jog between. My post-Astroglide 'glutes' weren't really up to the hard running but it was the politics not the athletics which were causing me to wince. It irritates me when I hear people say that they are not interested in politics. Politics is an unavoidable part of life. People rarely have exactly the same viewpoints on everyday issues unless they have been brainwashed. Therefore, to coexist in society, we are constantly coming together with our different viewpoints, at different levels, on all sorts of matters, mundane or crucial, to try to work out tolerable compromises. That is politics.

Compromise can generally be reached but not always. Conflict can especially arise when views already established by an existing hierarchy are suddenly challenged. There are many important and calamitous examples of this in history but my example is a conflict over material for vests at a running club. When challenged, a classic reaction by those who wield power is often to discredit the opposition. Rugman had an argument with Coach Hombre over our unofficial, lightweight, breathable, FASTRAX club vests. It was moustaches at dawn (dusk actually).

For our club's coach, I believe it went deeper than vests; we had got under his skin. The Hombre seemed to have been working on a list of grievances with our squad because if his rant was spontaneous I was impressed. He told Rugman; we were uncoachable, we didn't stick to schedules, we were moaners, we gave the coaches abuse, we had done nothing for the club and we didn't exist as a squad. If Powerpoint had been invented he could have shot us down using bullet points. It was an astonishing tirade and, to be honest, mostly true. It was not, however, all a bollocks of our squad's making. Yes, we were uncoachable, but mainly because we didn't actually have an official coach. This said, we probably would have given him or her verbal abuse if we'd had one; this sort of addresses accusation four also. We did stick to schedules but only if we were in the mood and they were nicely written. Yes, we were moaners but all runners were moaners. So we did accept some 'mea culpas' for the first four barbs, but it was the last two statements which I, personally, took most exception to and wanted to seek exculpation from

It was the fact that we had formed such a cohesive unit which I suppose made us a threat to those whose organisational paradigm of the club was pyramid shaped. We were perceived as the enemy within and yet strangely we were the same people who ran in as many cross country and road races as we could to represent the club and spread its name. (I thought back to last year's London marathon and the congratulations of the runner from the established Liverpool athletics club as an example.)

So outraged was I by the accusations of lack of devotion and squadliness that the inner artist was dragged out of me. In the knowledge that the club's summer dance was to take place on the following Saturday, I produced badges for the marathon squad on Laura's badge making machine. They read; 'The Uncoachables.' These works of art proved to be a talking point, for those who could decipher them.

The badges' message was a play on the words, 'The Untouchables,' the name of a film released in 1987. It was about US Agent Elliot Ness's campaign to bring mobster Al Capone to justice; it starred Kevin Costner, Robert De Niro and Sean Connery. Even excluding Sean Connery's moustache, there were so many obvious parallels between 'The Uncoachables' and 'The Untouchables' situations. For some reason, only I could see them. Those who could read my badges may have missed the nuances of the text but they appreciated my colouring in. I think the squad only wore them to humour me.

(Badge of dishonour)

The club politics simmered throughout that humid summer night. I employed my usual tactics in these politically tense situations and I danced the night away with Eileen. I did hear that the Hombre had subsequently resigned. I hoped it wasn't over the poor quality of my badges.

July and August were traditionally quiet months for road running. The majority of races, particularly marathons, took place in spring and autumn, theoretically to avoid the heat of the summer (yeah, very funny). I had a couple of racing experiences in July which proved I had reasonable residual fitness and a capacity for improvement. On July 17th, as part of a PE teachers canoeing course, I travelled to West Kirby on the northwest tip of the Wirral peninsula. Here I was to meet the rest of the course members and paddle to nearby Hilbre Island. It was really windy and apparently so was everyone to do with the course, including the instructors, because I was the only pillock who turned up on the rain strafed shoreline. Having no canoe, I decided to abandon the project. Eileen had taken Laura out so when I got home I was determined not to waste the day. I remembered there was a series of races taking place in Garston, South Liverpool, close to the Mersey, just north of Speke (now John Lennon) airport.

I quickly made my way there, arriving five minutes before the start of the three mile 'Up the Shore Race', and just managed to register. I was running to the start when the race began, as I had in Blackpool but this time I was going in the right direction. Having caught the tail-end of the small field of runners I was still in about 15th place after half a mile. I pegged away and surprisingly managed to catch and pass twelve overenthusiasticrats to finish in 3rd place. Pleased with this little jaunt I ambitiously entered for the eight mile 'Devils Gallop' half an hour after. This would be the first and last time I would experience running hard back-to-back races. It was more like a training session devised by the Marquis de Sade than sensible racing.

The 'Devils Gallop' was aptly named because it consisted of four miles on the road followed by four on the Mersey shoreline. The last four mile stretch was like a diabolical obstacle course. Building bricks, broken bottles, slimy mud pools, slippery condoms and a whole host of fascinating yet unsettling nautical refuse (aided by an infernally strong headwind) lay in wait to impede our progress. Towards the end of the route, understandably, I began to tire and again Grimm the Elder went past me. Not wanting a repeat of London I clung on and managed to summon up enough energy to repass him in the last few metres to finish 7th. DJ had been two places ahead in 5th but neither of my club comrades had been stupid enough to do the three miler as well. So I basked in my stupidity in our group post-race analysis.

DJ nearly always beat me in short races. It seemed I could only get near him in distances of 13 miles and over. Confirming this hypothesis and my suspicion that I was better than many at hot weather racing, in early August, on a scorching Sunday, I beat DJ in a half marathon in Newton le Willows.

A little market town about 15 miles from Liverpool, Newton had a big part to play in the birth of the railways. It was one of the main early railway towns until the likes of Crewe and Derby overtook it in size and importance. The town's station still has five platforms. It was also famous for being adjacent to the site of the very first railway accident.

It was 1830 and the day of the opening of the Liverpool to Manchester Railway, the world's first twin-track inter-city passenger railway in which all the trains were timetabled and ticketed. Trains full of dignitaries, en route from Edge Hill in Liverpool to Manchester, stopped at Parkside, near Newton le Willows, to take on water. MP for Liverpool, William Huskisson, alighted from his carriage having decided to use the water break as an opportunity to break the ice and make his peace with Prime Minister, the Duke of Wellington, who he had been politically at odds with for two years. When he reached the Duke's carriage he forgot the first rule of politics and didn't watch his back. Distracted by having to lick Wellington's shiny boots, he failed to notice a locomotive heading towards him like a rocket (because it was the Rocket) along the adjacent track. He panicked. Unlike the rest of his entourage who sensibly stepped back from the line he tried to jump forwards, on board the Duke's carriage. It is said that as he grasped the carriage door it swung open. No-one is sure how the door came to open (are they Duke?) but it caused Huskisson to fall backwards on to the parallel track. His legs were crushed under the locomotive's wheels and he subsequently died of his injuries. There is a story that he wasn't allowed into the Duke's carriage because his ticket had the wrong time on it; this story was made up by me.

Parkside was also famous for being home to the last coal mine to close in the Lancashire coalfield after the 1984 Miner's Strike. Incidentally and irrelevantly, while at Hull University, I was told by a Scouse friend that, in Liverpool, 'getting-off-at-Edge-ill' was a euphemism for coitus interruptus because Edge Hill was the last station before the terminus at Liverpool Lime Street. I'd laughed even though I didn't know what interruptus meant or for that matter coitus.

In the Newton le Willows race DJ set off like a train. He was a hundred yards ahead of me after four miles but the heat started to take its toll and his boiler began to overheat. I worked up steam gradually. Chugging along I caught him and another runner at seven miles. My sudden appearance gave him a second wind as he uncoupled from his previous partner and hitched up with me. We began passing people again, some of whom, admittedly, had started to walk. We ran together until 12 miles in the demanding conditions. I could see he was suffering and I did a bit of soul searching. *Should I nurse him to the finish?* I asked myself. As the remembrance of my Helsby 'birthday' race came into my mind, the answer, *should I hell,* joined it. So I pushed the pace harder and harder until he wilted and I finished twenty seconds ahead. I felt ambivalent; a teenyweenyweeny bit ashamed but also mightily pleased (chuff-chuffed). Afterwards, the words of the 1987 number one hit by Newton le Willows born Rick Astley, 'Never Gonna Give You Up' tormented me for days. Nothing to do with DJ, I just didn't like the bloody song.

On August 30th, we took Laura and two of her friends to Alton Towers as part of her 10th birthday present. We had a lovely time. These simple facts were to complicate my life fundamentally, in a positive way.

September and Mersey Marathon time had rolled around again. Two weeks before the race I did my last long Sunday run with the lads from the club. We ran north from Walton, past the jail, out towards the sand dunes of Formby. On the way back we passed Aintree Race Course, the home of the Grand National. It was

10'oclock in the morning and people were queueing outside. Not for the geegees or even for the Beegees but for an EmJay concert taking place that evening. A few more were expected, 125,000 in all. This was the last date of the European leg of Michael Jackson's 'Bad' tour. I wondered how many would have turned up if it had been good. He wasn't expected on stage until 9:00 p.m. so it would be a long wait for the fans. It was reported that over 1500 were injured that night. Most of injuries were self-inflicted, minor bruises as a result of poorly executed moonwalking and overenthusiastic crutch grabbing, I believe. I am surprised how many times Master Jackson has made it on to these pages because I didn't really understand the phenomenon or like the music but, clearly, a few others did.

Legs and arms like rubber bands and feet moving unpredictably; not Michael dancing but me finishing my 7th Mersey Marathon. I may even have also been cradling my privates to prevent my undercarriage from descending any further. Would you believe it, I'd had another disappointing run. Unlike in London, Grimm the Elder had decided to pass me a little earlier in the race. I'd set off at a pace that would have got me home in two hours and thirty. Even though at the back of my mind and the front, to be honest, I knew I wasn't in that kind of form (and probably never, ever, ever, would be) I pushed on heedlessly and chickenheadlessly. I thought I was running fast but at about seven miles, on Duke Street, just beyond the Anglican Cathedral and China Town, a blue and white striped mirage, like a tea-cup on legs, eased up beside me before making me eat his dust. Grimm Sr and I had a brief but nuance laden conversation.

"Howyer feelin' To'?" said he. (Translation: you look like you've gone off too fast and you'll be crawling at the end.)

"OK," I replied, (Translation: I've gone off too fast again and I'll be crawling at the end.) It took me several paces to get enough breath to continue.

"How are you?" I gasped. (Translation: you look a lot better than I feel, you bastard.)

"Terrible," he responded, (Translation: I feel a lot better than you look, you idiot, and I am going to show you how a marathon should be run.)

I tried to pull off a casual grin but only ended up looking like Jack Nicholson in 'The Shining'. It must have scared him off because that was the last I saw of him until the end of the race when he was receiving his prize for first over-40 veteran, having run an amazing 2:36 again. I got to half way in an impressive one hour and 15 minutes but my body was already beginning to fear for its future. With four miles to go, I only had enough fuel left for about four minutes. I slowed radically to spread the energy out. I almost walked at 25 miles but kept going and shuffled over the line in two hours and forty two minutes. I had run the second 13 miles nearly a minute a mile slower than the first 13; a perfect example of how not to run an even paced race.

And what of the rest of the squad who were running? Testerman almost caught me on the line coming in seventeen seconds behind me and most of the squad ran under three hours. Many achieved PBs, so the conditions were no excuse for my below-par performance. Grimm the younger was just seven seconds over the three hours. His non-Grimm Wirral brother ran well, finishing with 2 hours 53 minutes. If there had been a tri-sibling team prize they would have won it easily.

Waiting for a successful marathon performance is like waiting for a bus, you never really know when one will come along. But unlike in the oft quoted bus joke it is rare that three come along at once, especially if you try to run too many in a year.

Fully aware of this, I had still decided that it would be a good idea to run another marathon in October. To be fair the urge was prompted not only by my addiction to the distance but also by the desire to complete a race overseas (with apologies to the Scilly Isles). I had booked Eileen and myself a week's holiday, at half-term, in Split, in the country then known as Yugoslavia.

Our trip would incorporate my running of the Second Split People's Marathon. The course was the route which had been approved for the European Athletics Championships in 1990. It was to start and finish on the main promenade in front of the Roman Palace, former summer residence of the Roman Emperor, Diocletian. All arrangements had been taken care of by a firm called

'Sportsman's Travel' so all we (including the sportswomen) had to do was turn up at the airport and maybe do a bit of running later.

Before this prestigious event took place another minor get-together was being held in Seoul, Korea; the Games of the XXIV Olympiad. It turned out to be a bit of a first place flop for the Great Britain athletics team, who failed to win a gold medal, although to be fair, six silvers and two bronze were won in track and field. This constituted one third of the UK's team's total medal haul of 24. These were the first Olympic Games to hold a 10,000 metres women's event. The distance was previously thought to present a far too arduous challenge for the poor delicate creatures. Scotland's Liz McColgan took the silver for Great Britain. The team eventually finished 12th in the overall medals table behind the likes of Bulgaria, Romania, Hungary, France and Italy to name but five. Yugoslavia had finished 16th in the table with three golds and twelve overall, a quarter of their medals had been won in shooting events!

I had received reams of information before the Split event and was flicking through it as we waited in Manchester Airport. It struck me that the Yugoslav language did little to make places sound inviting. The precise timetable announced;

Friday 21st - Arrival of foreign competitors and accommodation at 'Lav' Hotel.

I had been unfortunate enough to stay in accommodation at home and abroad which resembled a lav but this was my first time in a place that actually went by that name.

Saturday 22nd 11 a.m. Reception given by the Sports Association of Split at the 'Gripe' Sports Centre.

It was well known that sports people in general and runners in particular were moaners (take note Hombre) but it was a bit blatant to name a sports facility after their bad habits.

Our flight from Manchester did not actually arrive in Split until Saturday at 8:30 pm so we were too late to go to Gripe and be received officially. Nor was there a great deal of time for acclimatisation. My main worry had been about the standard of the accommodation with its off-putting nomenclature. I need not have worried. Although still considered a communist state, Yugoslavia catered well for foreign visitors, probably because tourism was such a big part of its national income. Travelling by coach from the airport we arrived at a huge hotel with an indoor swimming pool, shops, tennis courts and several bars and restaurants. Incredible facilities, considering the price we had paid. It was pristinely kept and in a prime position right on the water's edge, with its own beach. Yugoslav competitors were staying at another hotel, I'm not sure why.

Having had my worries about the accommodation allayed, I quickly found something else to angst about. We were informed that there were only 70 odd entrants in the full marathon and half of those were from Great Britain. The same was true of the accompanying half-marathon. It was going to be lonely out there. I didn't have enough time to dwell on and nurture my concerns. The race took place the next morning.

As usual, I woke up thinking, why have I got myself into this? Split looked like a lovely place to visit, why did I need the pressure of running a marathon? I'd smuggled my own Weetabix past customs, thinking they might try to force me to eat raw goat's meat for breakfast but the restaurant table groaned with the weight of every food you could have wished for. This facility would be made full use of in the latter part of our stay but for now I exercised the restraint I only reserved for race mornings. We were bussed into Split for the 'off' at 10:30 a.m.

The start area was busy with entertainments and promenading spectators or spectating promenaders. When the half and the full marathons set off together there was a mad, mass sprint by the Yugoslav contingent, trying to get into the pictures being taken by local press photographers. There seemed to be about a hundred people ahead of me after a couple of minutes but I managed to maintain a sensible pace. Being even more sensible, Trevor Hawes, the eventual winner, didn't pass me until well into the first mile. After this I was joined by Charlie, a restaurateur from Chester. It was his first marathon and he had been aiming to run under two hours forty minutes but had revised that to two hours forty-five when the day dawned warm and sunny.

We ran together until about nine miles but I started to feel uncomfortable and urged him to go on alone. I'd had enough bad marathon experiences over the year and I wanted to try to enjoy this one, if at all possible. I put all thoughts of a quick time out of my head. The pressure off, I immediately felt better and started to take in the scenery. The course went through several small, quaint but slightly ramshackle villages where all the locals were out. They were generous in their animated support, shouting encouragement. At least I think that's what they were shouting. Small children ran alongside me for short distances, chatting and laughing. I talked back to them in my best Serbo-Croat. This produced more laughing; my phrase book may well have been out of date. Considering the country was going through turbulent times, this race was probably a welcome distraction for the locals, especially with foreign idiots like me talking gibberish while running in the sun.

I knew I wasn't running my hardest but I felt this might enable me to muster a stronger finish. The miles slipped by, a sure sign I was running within myself. At 15 miles I noticed Charlie Chester restaurateur in the distance and he was getting bigger. He had overcooked his goose and had no stomach left for the second course. I passed him.

By now we had done a U-turn and were retracing our steps on the route. Close to the town centre we took a sudden detour into the pine-wooded peninsula on the outskirts of Split known as the Marjan. It was a beautiful area, fragrant and shaded, but it was also bereft of encouraging supporters and contained a two mile hill. I spotted a Yugoslav runner ahead and worked to catch up. This done, I tucked in behind him for a short while, waiting until we reached a drinks stop before making a move to pass him on the big hill. He had no energy to respond. Alone again, I worked up the incline and enjoyed the eerie tranquillity of the forest scenery. Reaching the highest point of this rocky outcrop we turned back towards the town with a few miles to go. I was tired now but in decent shape and the road declined in my favour. I caught one more person, a young Turk, and passed him.

The last half mile was a strange experience as runners were expected to weave their way along a crowded prom. No one deliberately got in the way but you could see that they were reluctant to adjust the course of their habitual Sunday stroll for the sake of a few mad running dogs (mainly Englishmen) out in the midday sun. Approaching the finish banner, dramatic classical music was booming out of speakers. It coincidentally came to a final crescendo as I crossed the line. I felt obliged to act in a way befitting the musical accompaniment and so mustered the deepest bow I was physically capable of (flamboyant on the blackstuff). Although bending over energetically at the end of a marathon is not a recommended warming down procedure it was certainly a crowd pleaser. An extra cheer and ripple of applause erupted from those watching as they waited to see if I could regain an upright position. My time of 2:49:50 was nowhere near my best but I felt happy and even better knowing that I was now going to enjoy a holiday.

5-7 p.m.   Award of diplomas to all participants and the cocktail party, Lav Hotel.

After I had become vertical again, Eileen and I had a couple of beers and then I had a soak in the bath. Later we came down for the awards ceremony in the hotel. I'd never been to a cocktail party before and was looking forward to the occasion. I was a bit disappointed to find out it involved a lot of people standing around drinking. I'd done that before. There were no international jetsetters present although there may well have been a few foreign spies and a smattering of secret police.

They read out all the results. To my surprise I had come 10th behind four other Brits, four Yugoslavs and one Czech. I strolled casually on to the stage, to disguise the limp, and the Mayor of Split was on hand to present me with a variety of goodies, including a 1990 European Championships T-shirt and a barometer which I would use to test the atmosphere in the bar that night. I was glad I had made the effort of wearing my liquorice allsorts bow tie for the occasion. I met the young Turkish man I had just prevented from getting into tenth position and the prizes. He was gracious in defeat and gave me a coaster from his home town, Gumuldur near Izmir. I responded by giving him a cloth Liverpool Running Club badge, complete with Liver Bird. I hoped the Liver Bird and Turkey would get on OK.

One amazing or dismaying result, whichever way you want to look at it, was that a nine year old girl, Marjana Letica, who was a bit of a local celebrity, had been allowed to run in the marathon and finished in three hours and fifty six minutes. In the UK you are generally supposed to be at least over 15 to run in a 10k race, never mind 26 miles. I wonder where she is now and whether her knees are still with her.

(Lickety-Split, finishing through the persistent promenaders)

    The rest of the holiday was a pleasant mixture of sightseeing and occasional running. The highlight was a 70 minute hydrofoil trip taking us to Havar, considered by some to be one of the most beautiful islands in the world and a tourist destination since the late 19th Century. Whereas the people on the mainland seemed fraught with concerns about the volatile political and economic situation, Havar folk were laid back and welcoming. The island was a verdant patchwork of olive trees, vineyards and lavender fields, fragrant and fascinating with nature gently rubbing up against ancient sites and artists' haunts. We had a day of eating, sitting, swimming and bimbling in the old town under a vast lapis lazuli sky. At about 5pm as the autumn sun was setting, we caught the hydrofoil back and it conveniently docked at the hotel.

    The next day, in town, we tried to spend our money on souvenirs but it was quite difficult because things were so cheap for us. We ended up bartering stallholders up to get rid of fistfuls of notes. The coins were virtually worthless and it was common to see people drop them on to the floor rather than have the inconvenience of carrying them.

There seemed to be an anger and frustration simmering in town but it wasn't directed at us few tourists, that is, not until the last night of our stay. There were few Yugoslavs in the hotel, in fact few people at all, apart from runners who had come to do the races. There was definitely an 'end of the season' feel to the place and many facilities were closed down because there was no demand for them. A small but perfectly formed group of runners, including Eileen and me, did make full use of the disco. It stayed open till twelve o'clock each night for drinks and dancing. On the final night we gathered for a last hurrah. Unusually, there were also three local men in the room. They appeared drunk and wild-eyed. There was trouble in the air.

Amongst us there was a small group of young lads from London, inexperienced runners who had come to do the half-marathon for a laugh. They were cheeky chappies but we'd got to know them and they turned out to be lovely fellas and harmless. One of their number was black and the Yugoslavs in the disco seemed to take exception to his colour. His mates took exception to their exception, as did the rest of us. There was a bit of a Croatian standoff before one of the locals took a couple of swings at the Londoners and, just when mayhem threatened to ensue, a huge bouncer, built like a shipping container, appeared from nowhere and threw a piston powered right hand over the black lad's shoulder knocking the most aggressive local troublemaker spark out. His felled body arced backwards to a horizontal position before eventually sliding gently to a halt, shoe heels squeaking, on the polished disco floor.

There was a shocked hiatus and then, in what seemed like seconds, the offending locals were whisked away, the blood mopped from the floor and the music cranked up. It was a sad way to end a great holiday but gave me an indication that all was not well in this country. Although I have no evidence that the bouncer and the drunks came from different sides of a political, ethnic or religious divide, this brutal intervention smacked (literally) of a bit more than just doing a job.

After these uncivilised proceedings in Split at the end of October I found myself present at civil proceedings finalising a split in early

November. Laura's mum and I were officially divorced. After nine years of separation this was hardly a trauma for anyone but it was good to tidy up loose ends. It was very straight forward and took little time. The presiding judge actually made a point of commending us for our mature and sensible approach to the separation, maintenance matters and access arrangements. He was probably made up that he would be getting an extra hour for lunch while still being paid plenty to put his name to a document which proved we were no longer married when we hadn't been for nine years anyway. I also resented being called mature and sensible by a judge.

December was a month of disasters. On the 12th, 35 people were killed and over 100 injured as several trains crashed at Clapham railway station because of faulty signal wiring. On the 21st, 270 people died in the little Scottish border town of Lockerbie when a bomb exploded on Pan Am flight 103, causing it to crash on the town. 259 died on board and 11 on the ground from the falling debris. These disasters are firmly fixed in my memory. I suppose it is an indication of how events close to home have more resonance and perhaps how occurrences elsewhere are reported differently by the media that the Bangladesh cyclone at the beginning of the month and the Armenian earthquake, on the 7th, were less memorable for me. Horrifically, an estimated 25000 people died and 500,000 were made homeless in Armenia and 1300 were killed in Bangladesh and 500,000 were also thought to have lost their homes. The scale of these disasters cause exact figures to give way to rounded up or down estimates. Individual deaths get lost in the immense loss of life.

It seems trivial to start talking about running again after relating these shocking statistics but trivia is what binds our lives together. Our interests, our little obsessions are the things that make us who we are and can make us happy. It was times like these, when so many had their lives taken away, which made me reflect on how lucky I was to be able to continue with the trivia of my life.

My love of running had not waned through this year but my marathon performances had. After so much expectation generated by the previous year's personal best, in London, I had failed to get under two hours forty minutes, never mind reach anywhere near, a pie in the sky, two hours thirty. On the bright side I still achieved personal bests in the half marathon and five miles distances; a glimmer of hope for future improvement.

I had run 30 races in 1988, four marathons, eight half marathons and 18 other assorted events over a variety of distances and surfaces. Up until the 31st of October I had run 2882 miles. Although I was still enjoying my running, at some stage, I stopped enjoying the habit of recording of it. After my return from Split I stopped keeping a log. I have no record of how many miles I ran till the end of the year nor do I have any idea why I stopped writing down my mileage. Could it be that I had decided to take a less intense approach to the sport?

Many runners claim that it is essential to record training so that you can look back to see what sessions you were doing when you were running well, perhaps in the hope that replicating these work outs will reproduce better performances. Of course you have to do some training to run well but a combination of many different types of training can produce the same results. In fact, it was now my belief that jadedness from repetition was often what caused bad performances and that the best way to avoid this was to vary your training as much as possible, avoiding repeating seemingly successful patterns. Maybe this approach had now allowed me to break away from rigid record keeping (something, incidentally, I was hopeless at in a professional capacity) and just run and train as and when I saw fit (a philosophy which also happened to closely resemble my approach to the world of work). Besides, for me, it wasn't essentially about the training it was about the races. I knew I raced too much but I loved the experience and the high. Training was a necessary evil to help me enjoy the racing more. I had lost interest in the clocking up of high weekly mileage and obsessively recording it but not in the act of running itself

The year ended on a bright note for me and many others when our friend Edwina Currie re-emerged to be involved in another 'ignorance and chips' debate but this time her ignorance meant she'd 'had her chips' with eggs. Her misinformed statement "most of the egg production in this country, sadly, is now affected with salmonella" caused outrage in the farming community and she was, at last, forced to resign as health minister. It was one thing for her to insult the working classes or Aids sufferers but farmers were mainly Tory supporters so she had to go, forced to cluck off to the back benches; cock-a-doodle-doo.

Chapter 8

1989 Barriers and Walls, Grief and Joy

It is a big mistake to tell marathon runners that they look well. This simple compliment will cause a look of panic to spread across their faces. Like deer desperate for an escape route in a forest fire, their darting eyes will seek the nearest exit to the open road and the extra lonely miles required to banish the accursed appearance of wellness. To be at their peak they need to look sick; sunken cheeks, hollow eyes with dark rings, limbs with less meat than a veggie burger. That is a proper runner's look. Health doesn't come into it. An involvement in running marathons is unhealthy; physically, mentally, socially and too many other alleys to go into. If not deluded by a good performance you are made melancholic by a bad one. If not suffering depression from under-training you are incurring injuries from over-training and all the time pernicious little microbes are just waiting for the opportunity to waltz around your seriously compromised immune system. Health takes up at least 97.5% of a runner's conversation and of that 99% is about ailments, injuries and bits falling off. The other 1% is about good health, usually with reference to another, rival runner. Mention of personal healthiness is taboo and will only bring pestilence and plague upon the mentioner.

I accidentally attended a Merseyside Regional Health Authority Health Fair at the beginning of 1989. It was no secret that people in parts of the North-West had more health problems than those in most places 'down south;' Edwina Currie had already enlightened us on this subject. Health campaigns to address this inequality would often spring up but most of them were little more than window dressing. A lot of money was spent on collecting government health statistics to tell us northerners how unhealthy we were but governments themselves stopped short of dealing with the real causes.

And so it goes on. A study of life expectancy in 2012 showed results from all parts of the country. I have 'randomly' selected two

areas, Kensington in Liverpool and Kensington in London and compared the figures. The results are quite 'surprising';
Life expectancy in years; Kensington in London: women 89, men 84; Kensington in Liverpool: women 79, men 74.

Even more 'surprising' is the fact that life expectancy in that corner of London is getting higher at a quicker rate than in its Liverpool namesake. I just can't work out why there is such a discrepancy. After all, we live in the same country. Goodness me, the places even have the same name.

So, back in January 1989 I had gone to pick up Laura from where her mum was working. This was at the Health Fair, on a stall that offered a set of tests you could volunteer to take to prove how wrecked you were after bingeing through Christmas and the New Year. Laura volunteered me. We could not leave until I had taken the four tests on body fat, flexibility, grip strength and stamina. I knew it was going to be a mistake.

In each test, your score placed you in one of five different categories. Poor, below minimum, minimum, good or excellent for grip strength and flexibility; poor, below average, average, good and excellent for stamina; and a little more controversially, for body fat, obese, above average, average, ideal and slim. The words chosen to describe the two extremes of body fat (both potentially dangerous conditions) were judgementally loaded, making a very low weight score seem more acceptable and almost desirable. You can't imagine too many people being stigmatised by someone shouting across the street at them, "Eh you, you're slim!" Surely 'underweight' would have been a more accurate term to use. Describing an infant in this way usually flags up the possibility of a problem.

I had my own problems with this grading. Having gone through the embarrassment of having my flesh squeezed between a pair of callipers in four places (only, thankfully) on my torso (only, more thankfully), in front of my daughter and anybody else who was passing, only to be classified as 'ideal' left me disappointed. I was a marathon runner. I wanted slim or even skeletal, if a special, extra category had been added.

I had never been slim (apart from after my visit to Iran in the '70s when I had dysentery for most of the month I was there). My footballing weight had been between 12 and 12 ½ stone (76-79 kilo) but on the day of the Health Fair after seven years and many miles of running I weighed in at 67 kilos (10 ½ stone). After a pre-race carbo bleed-out I had been known to drop to just over 10 stone. I had run countless hard miles to get to that weight and I was only given an 'ideal'. That was far too healthy; I was gutted.

My flexibility came out as 'good' which was a little surprising because my hamstrings were tighter than a Victorian corset; so tight that if challenged to pick up a hundred pound note off the pavement, without bending my knees, I would have struggled. My stamina came out as excellent and, after the body fat debacle, I would have thrown myself in the Mersey if it hadn't.

That left the grip strength, which came out as below minimum; a little embarrassing but not particularly surprising. Bulky upper body and arm muscle is not a necessity for long distance runners; it is surplus weight. The sport is known for its bulging eyeballs not biceps. I remember listening to a commentary before the start of the London Marathon. Brendan Foster, former Olympic 5,000 metres bronze medallist (UK's only medal in track and field in the 1976 Montreal Olympics) was commenting on the weather. It was ideal for marathon running; dull and cool with no wind. He said that the elite runners would have woken up, looked at the weather through their hotel windows and done cartwheels of joy. "Well, not literally," he corrected himself, "because their arms wouldn't be strong enough."

Brendan himself had developed as a great middle-distance runner in the '70s. He was whippet thin until he retired from running. He obviously decided that the pursuit of his lucrative promoter's career left no time to maintain any fitness, because he then developed a great middle. I left the Health Fair feeling below par. The results had left me pondering. One thing was certain; I needed to get a grip.

Also losing its grip in 1989 was the Soviet Union. It would be a year of great political change around the world but not, regrettably, in this country where in March, Maggie, Maggie, Maggie, out, out, outdid all other prime ministers in the 20th Century by reaching 10 years in office. Hip, Hip, Go away!

In January, over the pond, a change took place but nothing changed. Maggie's mate, the highly 'astute' Ronnie Reagan, who never had a grip, handed over the keys (once he'd remembered where he'd put them) to the head office of the most powerful country in the world. George W. Bush became the next President of the USA. God Bless America, God save us all! Why wasn't dope testing compulsory in political contests?

So it was 'same old, same old' in Washington during the first month of the year, but not so in the capital of dubious fast half marathon times and suspicious chemical odours, Helsby in Cheshire. The organisers had decided to reverse the direction of the course at the request of the police. Perhaps the bobbies on duty were bored with watching runners go round in the same direction year after year. Parts of the course were also altered. Course measurers rushed from every corner of the known world of West Cheshire and the route was certified as accurate and don't ever let anyone persuade you otherwise.

On a mild, sunny, still day in January, doing an impersonation of May, two days before my 38th birthday, I smashed my half marathon personal best by over a minute, running 71minutes and 44 seconds. I was amazed. DJ also excelled, recording a stunning sub 70 minute time and coming in 11th in a high class field. As usual, questions were asked about the validity of the course and the organisers felt compelled to drag out the, by now seriously pissed-off, course measurers yet again to verify its accuracy. So it must have been right. Please tell me it was right! Personally I think it may have been something in the air that day which helped my performance. It's fortunate we weren't tested for chemical stimulants because I don't think the testing lab would have been impressed by my fluorescent yellow sample. God knows what we had inhaled. Whatever the reason for my time I was never able to replicate or better it over the distance (and I wasn't going to ingest bottled Helsby air to try to do so).

In February Ayatollah Khomeini supreme leader of Iran put a two million pound bounty on the head of Salman Rushdie for writing 'The Satanic Verses'. Rushdie survived, which is remarkable; a coconut based chocolate confection of that weight would have fatally crushed most people. Making light of this situation does not take away the dismay I felt at the fact that anybody could think that they had a moral right to order the killing of another human being because they felt their beliefs were being mocked. Mockery should not be a capital offence. Surely holding on to your ideas firmly yet peaceably, in the face of mockery and worse, is a true indication of strong faith and belief. Martin Luther King and Ghandi managed to conduct their successful campaigns this way.

Back in Walton, Merseyside, the Hombre had long since ridden off into the sunset but Liverpool Running Club had managed to survive. The non-existent, uncoachable, do-nowt-for-the-club, recently renamed, high-pressure marathon squad had a successful month in March, representing the club. In the Ormskirk (what's left to say about the place) half-marathon we claimed first team prize. DJ was 6th and Rugman, performing like a flying carpet, was 8th beating me into 9th. Testerman came in 17th to complete our team's counters. The same combination snatched the team prize in the Anglesey 30k at the end of the month, almost in the same order except I was on fire and finished in front of the Rug, as opposed to finishing on a rug in front of the fire, which would have required much less effort.

Anglesey proved to be an interesting place to run. It is the largest Welsh island, connected to the mainland by two bridges. The Britannia Bridge was designed by Robert Stephenson and originally opened in 1850 to carry rail traffic. In 1970 it was destroyed by fire, rebuilt and reopened in 1980 to carry road and rail traffic. The Menai Suspension Bridge was designed by Thomas Telford in 1826. Both span the narrow Menai straits. In spite of these bridges and the fact that Holyhead, the main town on the island, is a main ferry port for boats to Dublin, Anglesey is a remote and sparsely populated place. Rugged, largely barren and open, it is host to much wild weather but on a climatically benign day its remoteness can be sublime. We were lucky as the weather was kind for our race.

Anglesey has some of the oldest rocks in the world dating from the pre-Cambrian period and, running along its winding, open roads, I did feel disconnected from the present day. Curious sheep were the only spectators as the course gently undulated and the ungulates slowly ruminated. En route we were offered views of the giant muscles of the Snowdonia range and the bony finger of the Llyn peninsula pointing across the Atlantic at distant Florida. In the early 19th century many inhabitants of Anglesey and the Llyn had followed that geological fingerpost to America, impelled to leave home by high prices, low wages and the enclosure of Common Land. The ghosts of those forced from this land left a sense of past sadness, lifting like mist from the peaty heather and tingeing the beauty of the island with melancholy.

On Merseyside, the sadness of loss and the bitter pill of injustice were also to become the lasting legacy of an event on April 15th 1989. At the Hillsborough stadium in Sheffield, Yorkshire, during an FA Cup semi-final game between Liverpool F.C. and Nottingham Forest F.C. a disaster occurred. The game was stopped after six minutes as people entering the overcrowded Leppings Lane stand were caught in a crush. The result was 96 fatalities and hundreds of other lives destroyed as a result of being at the event or close to those involved. Sadness and psychological damage were compounded by the inaction and reaction of the authorities and scurrilous reporting by some newspapers, in particular the Sun, which lay all the blame for the disaster at the door of the supporters. The Sun had accused Liverpool fans of a litany of heinous behaviours from attacking and urinating on policemen to stealing from dead and injured bodies. They had no proof but that didn't seem to matter. The police version of the events vindicated their own actions while condemning the fans. Before any investigation had taken place, there followed a scrambling of miscreants wanting to jump on the anti-Liverpool bandwagon, including representatives of the government. Vilifying people from Liverpool was obviously seen as a convenient and easy way to avoid identifying real responsibility.

It was again like an echo of the Miner's Strike. The South Yorkshire Police, the Sun newspaper and representatives of the Tory government closing ranks to portray ordinary people, trying to live their lives, as monsters.

The Liverpool haters depicted the Scouse mentality as one riddled with self-pity and paranoia. But courage and dogged determination in the face of injustice would be a more accurate description of the attributes which led to, after over twenty years, the setting up of an Independent Hillsborough Panel. It concluded, in September 2012, that no Liverpool fans were responsible for the deaths in Sheffield, 23 years previously. It was revealed that 164 witness statements had been altered by the police to deflect the blame on to the fans. Multiple failures by emergency services and public bodies had exacerbated the disaster and experts on the panel estimated that 41 lives out of 96 could have been saved if injured fans had received prompt medical attention.

After the Independent Panel's report, relatives of the deceased and other fans at the game received apologies from David Cameron (the prime minister), David Crompton (the chief constable of South Yorkshire Police), David Bernstein (Football Association chairman) and Kelvin McKenzie (editor of the Sun in 1989) for their organisations' respective roles in the cover up; so much for Scouse paranoia. On December 19th 2012, to the delight of the Hillsborough families and friends, a new inquest was granted in the High Court, to challenge the original inquest's verdict of accidental death. It was a day many on Merseyside, including myself, thought would never arrive.

Back in 1989, in the month following the disaster, Gerry Marsden rereleased his hit 'Ferry Cross the Mersey' to raise money for those affected. The Christians, Holly Johnson and Paul McCartney also featured on this version, which was the UK's top selling single for three weeks.

On April 23rd the week following 'Hillsborough' I ran my third London Marathon in a time of 2:42:20. The time was neither here nor there but a just reward for what was a lack lustre performance. The mood in our club was inevitably and appropriately sombre. Anfield, Liverpool FC's ground, was a short jog from our base in Walton. Most people at the club knew someone affected by the disaster. Our running club's trip to the 'London' was overshadowed by the previous week's events.

In line with my usual response to a disappointing performance I entered another marathon which took place just three weeks after the London. I didn't realise that, when I travelled across the country to Derby to take part in the Ramathon, I would also be entering the heady world of almost-but-not-really professional athletics.

The simple facts of the race were that I ran quite well on my tired old legs, recorded a surprising 2:38:22 and achieved an even more surprising 6th place. The prize list was generous. In those naïve days before the full-on commercialism which now taints athletics just as much as other sports, cash prizes were not supposed to be awarded unless they came in the form of a subvention. This described money which was lodged with the British Amateur Athletic Board (BAAB) in a trust fund which could be drawn on by prize winners for 'athletic expenses.' A training grant of £100 was sent by Derby city council to my trust fund. This was the first and last time any money went through this account which was set up for the sole purpose (apologies for this rare unintentional pun) of transferring the prize money to me.

I had to make up some request to prove the money would be used, in some way, to enhance my training. I may have claimed expenses for seventy-five tubs of Vaseline, I can't quite remember. The cheque went south from Derby to the BAAB HQ in Francis Street, SW1 and then, like greased lightning, back up north to Liverpool for the purchase of desperately needed lubrication. In truth, it was more likely to have been spent on a different sort of 'lubrication' to ensure that I stayed well oiled. What a palaver, old school, but quite endearing really. I certainly wasn't complaining. A bonus added to the joy of running.

It was certainly a far cry from the mercenary antics associated with some top runner's these days. I recently had a conversation with a friend who happened to be involved in organising the Birmingham Half Marathon, which since 2008 has grown into a high profile international event. He told me that a top female distance runner had once promised to appear in the event but withdrew at the last minute. The official reason given was injury. The rumoured real reason deserved less sympathy. Not satisfied with the chance of winning the generous first prize with bonuses for records broken, it is claimed that her manager also demanded exorbitant appearance money for her. When his demands weren't met she was suddenly withdrawn from the race with an equally sudden injury. Apparently it wasn't the first time she had 'cried' off in a big race!

Meanwhile Jill and Jack jogger put their hands in their pockets to pay inflated prices to enter this type of race while often also raising money for charity. Most sports are democratic at grass roots level, running is more than most, and it's a shame that some of the top athletes bring it into disrepute with their big heads and small minds. As often seems to be the case, as soon as money comes into the equation democratic structures suddenly develop economic elites.

Democracy is a word used to describe many different hues of politics. It was a word much bandied about in 1989. Democracy, describing the right to take part in free elections, had been denied to Eastern European countries for many years. In May a sliver of light squeezed through the Iron Curtain separating Eastern and Western Europe when the government of Hungary removed 150 miles of barbed wire from their border with Austria. Political changes meant that Hungarians would soon be allowed to have a say in the running of their own country. Removing a physical barrier preventing them from leaving was a signal to show that they had more reason to stay.

One of the problems with 'democracy' is that it means different things to different people. Freely elected governments, once in power, often act in undemocratic ways, failing to protect the rights of large sections of the electorate. In June the Conservative government condoned the arrest of 250 people at Stonehenge. Their crime was the desire to celebrate the summer solstice peaceably. In the same month the racist British National Party were allowed to march freely through Dewsbury, an area with a high number of Asian residents. This march resulted in riots. At Stonehenge solstice celebrators were arrested whereas, in Dewsbury, fascists were given police protection. Why was one demonstration of views stopped and the other not? Which was most democratic?

In Liverpool, in July, dockers had rights snatched away from them. The National Docks Labour Scheme (NDLS) was scrapped. Introduced by a Labour government in 1947, the scheme was intended to end the scourge of casual labour by giving dockers the legal right to minimum holidays, sick pay and pensions. Thatcherites wanted to go back to the good old days of maximum profit for employers with minimum protection for the employees. The dockworkers went on strike in protest but the dispute didn't last beyond August, except in Liverpool. Here the strike continued with workers refusing to give up union rights in return for compensation. Again this was not a struggle for more money but one to protect decent working conditions. By the end of the dispute over half the workforce had been sacked and only 500 jobs remained. The Employment Secretary, Norman Fowler, described the NDLS as an 'anachronism'. I suppose it was in Thatcher's brave new monetarist world where democracy meant the removal of obstacles impeding a minority's pursuit of individual wealth. It was also a blatant attempt to continue the de-unionisation of the UK workforce and ensure the erosion of workers' rights.

In the wider world, political balances were also shifting, not always with positive results. At the same time as Chinese students were massacred in Tiananmen Square for demanding more freedom, the Solidarity Party won the first free elections in Poland after years of a one party state. Some totalitarian regimes were toppling, some were viciously clinging on. For me, the photographic images of students confronting tanks in China echoed those I had pinned to the wall of my university bedroom in 1970; black and white images capturing Prague's youth bravely facing invading Soviet tanks in Wenceslas Square in 1968.

An event in another influential Asian country this year would result in the emergence of a new human sub-species in developed countries. Homo Virtualus is distinguishable by its pale skin, hunched shoulders, shortened neck, glazed eyes, big thumbs and the increasing inability to read, pay attention to simple tasks or move energetically for more than a few seconds at a time. Its habitat is, typically, enclosed man-made spaces devoid of natural light or clean air. The Nintendo Game Boy was released in Japan in April and the USA in August 1989. Before Game Boy Colour's release in late 1998, the Game Boy alone had sold 64.42 million units worldwide. In Asia, Japan was increasing its world influence through commerce. China would eventually see this as an example to follow.

Back in Merseyside for some unknown reason I had voluntarily taken it upon myself to have some contact with my work life, outside school hours. Maybe it was a fear that the world might be taken over by limbless, speechless, white-eyed Gameboids that provoked my uncharacteristic decision to invite some pupils from school to get some exercise by joining me on a series of evening runs.

The Wirral Seaside Runs had started in 1985 and consisted of low-key, mid-week, monthly runs from late spring to early autumn. Having already taken part individually in these events on a few occasions I thought it might be a fun way to get young ones into the fresh air and a not-too-competitive exercise environment. It was ideal for children, a three mile route, devoid of traffic, flat and virtually idiot-proof in terms of navigation.

The run started adjacent to Leasowe lighthouse which was built in 1763 by Liverpool Corporation's Docks Committee and is the oldest brick-built lighthouse in Britain. According to local folklore, its foundations were built on bales of cotton from a nearby shipwreck. (There is no material evidence to substantiate this claim.) The lighthouse was operational until 14 July 1908, 'manned' by Mrs Williams, the only known female lighthouse keeper at that time. On closure it became a tea-room for a short while but then was unused for a much longer period. Eventually, it became a base for the ranger service of the North Wirral Coastal Path in 1989.

The point to point course of the 'Sea-side Run' followed a small road two hundred metres southwards past the lighthouse before it U-turned and ran dead straight, northeasterly, along the knuckles of the Wirral fist, until reaching King's Parade in New Brighton. The run was along the sea embankment for almost its entirety. The plan was for me to meet the children, brought by parents, at the race start. Here I would try to keep some semblance of order, which is easier said than done with 25 hyperactive ten-year-olds in a crowd of 200. At the gun I would charge off ahead and leave them to it; simple.

Some might have suggested unkindly that the real aim of me getting away quickly was to absolve myself from any mayhem that might occur behind me. They would have been correct but the official explanation was that getting to the finish first meant that I would be able to see all the kids complete the run safely, counting them in to make sure no-one had fallen into the sea. (This would have been highly unlikely because the water was usually about a mile away across the sands, but you never knew with my kids.) The fact was, by the time they got into their running, hyperactivity quickly dissolved into oxygen debt and they were too knackered to do anything but stagger in an approximate straight line. They actually seemed quite glad to see my face and hear my shouts of encouragement at the end. This wasn't normally the case in other scenarios.

After one race, official written complaints were included on the results sheet claiming that some children *"were not respecting other runners at the start, being encouraged to push themselves too hard and were not being accompanied on the run."* I wasn't sure whether this was a snipe at my charges, who I was nominally in charge of and who errr... had been charging, if you see what I mean. There were other schools and children at the runs and a couple of factors made me suspect that (amazingly) the problems were probably not of our making. Firstly, I knew that most of my kids wouldn't push themselves too hard, unless there was money or chocolate involved. I'd been trying all year. The fact that the race started on a narrow track with two hundred people meant there was bound to be a bit of coming together in the rush to get some space. Knowing my lot, this burst of energy would only have been of limited capacity, approximately one lungful. I also had the third complaint covered in that of all the schools present I was one of the few teachers running and, although I wasn't accompanying all 25 children individually, I was technically with them all, omnipresent, in spirit, if not in body.

My suspicions were happily confirmed when the results sheet of the next race on July 19th had the following added to the thanks and 'credit dues' at the bottom of the page.

"Congratulations to the Dell Primary- well supervised – a credit to their school and teachers, plus a personal best for "Sir" individual entry Mr Peacock."

I don't know what we had done right and I did wonder whether money or chocolate had changed hands. It might have helped that I had taken the extra precaution of roping in our deputy head to run and watch out for dubious tactics (which he was an expert in) lower down the field. All in all I was delighted that day, especially with my PB!

In 2013 the seaside runs were still going strong in their 29th season and many runners still used them as a short sharp workout, as

I used to. When I wasn't accompanying children I found that a convenient way to get some speed work into my running would be to leave my car at the lighthouse, run the race and then jog back to the start, clocking about six miles altogether. The course's geographical position made it prone to widely varying climatic conditions. With a strong sou'wester you could hope for a fast time and an easy run but a hell of a tough jog back. Grinding out the race into a stiff northeasterly wind would mean your jog back would be almost as fast as your race time. In the rare summer heat, the lack of shade and the reflective white concrete surface made it a sweaty, mouth parching experience which made me regret the lighthouse was no longer a tearoom. It was always an interesting place to run but at its best late and early in the season when runners were often treated to the sight of the beach ball sun bobbing on the Irish Sea.

And in August it was over that sea that Eileen and I did travel with her mum and dad to visit all her father's family in Dublin. On my arrival I was surprised to find that, having been informed of my general interest in sport, the relatives had arranged for me to watch the All-Ireland Hurling semi-finals at Croke Park in Dublin. Hurling is a fifteen-a-side team game of Gaelic origin which requires players to hit a small ball (sliotar) with a stick (hurley or camán) through the opponents' upright H-shaped posts. One point is awarded for a shot over the horizontal bar and three for a shot into the netted goal under the bar which is guarded by the goalkeeper. This uniquely Irish game is administrated by the Gaelic Athletic Association (GAA). Other sports organised by the association included Camogie (a women's version of hurling), Gaelic football, handball and rounders. The GAA also promoted Irish music and dance and the Gaelic language. In 2012 the association claimed to have over a million members worldwide.

Tickets for these semi-final games were not easy to come by but the process was facilitated by the fact that the Eileen's family had long and close associations with Croke Park. Eileen's grandfather had been a groundsman there for many years and her uncle and cousin still worked at the ground on match days. The ticket came gratis but with strict instructions. While the Irish relatives were finishing off their match day duties and before I joined them in the stands, I was to be left on the terraces, alone. Here, I was told, I must stay and stand silently. I perhaps need to give some more historical background to explain these strange instructions.

The GAA was formed in 1884 and became closely associated with the nationalist cause. The British saw it as, little more than, a training organisation for republican soldiers and banned it in 1918, although games continued to be played after this ban. In 1920, after political violence had taken place elsewhere in Dublin, as a reprisal, the British forces entered Croke Park during a Gaelic football match between Tipperary and Dublin. They fired indiscriminately into the crowd. Fourteen people were killed including Michael Hogan a Tipperary football player. One of the stands in the ground was subsequently named after him. Historically, Gaelic games, including hurling, became a symbol of defiance in the face of oppression and an expression of nationhood and culture whilst being under foreign rule.

The All Ireland finals are a competition between all the counties of Ireland including the six still in the UK. The staging of this semi-final round was quite alien to me. I was to watch three games; one junior game and two senior semi-finals. Start time was at 12:30 pm and finish at about 5:30 p.m. The supporters of all the teams involved were in the stadium at the same time, without any segregation (something which would never have happened in an English football match). One of the semi-finals that day was extra-unusual in that it was between Antrim and Offaly. For the first time since 1946, Antrim had the chance to reach the final and a big and vociferous following had come to Dublin from the North.

Considering the extremely volatile political situation in the northern counties, Eileen's relatives were worried that if I got in with a bunch of supporters from Antrim and they found out that I was a 'Brit' I would be in physical danger. Although sceptical, I did as I was told and played mute no matter how much members of the friendly crowd tried to engage me. I did at one stage consider putting on a French accent but felt that it might have been a bit of a strain. Besides it would be just my luck to stand next to a fluent French speaker from Ballymena. As it turned out, being quiet wasn't too hard a task as I am not normally a big talker. This is sometimes referred to as being 'a miserable taciturn bastard'. However, while never feeling under any threat, I did affect a lot of nodding and faux smiling. My fellow spectators must have taken pity on me as some kind of eejit. I think I may well have felt more threatened had I ended up at the 'wrong' end of an English football ground in the '80s. Later I joined Eileen's cousin and uncle in the stands for the last game and watched Antrim reach their first final for 43 years. There was much joy.

I had been mesmerised watching these contests. The skill of the players carrying and hitting the small ball and the sheer physicality of the games beggared belief. In 2010 it became compulsory for all players to wear helmets with face guards. In 1989 a few wore helmets but more didn't. As I watched, one player had his head sliced open accidentally by an opponent's stick. After a brief respite he returned to the field of play with an already leaking scarlet turban.

During the summer months struggles for national independence around the world were being fought and reacted to in different ways. An amazingly effective and peaceful demonstration for freedom from foreign rule occurred at the end of the month. Organised by nationalist movements in the Soviet Baltic states, a human chain of approximately two million people was formed, stretching over 600 kilometres through Lithuania, Latvia and Estonia. I was surprised they could muster enough people to complete the task and envisaged people at the back running to the front to keep the chain unbroken. However, manage it they did and the Baltic Way (or Baltic Chain) demonstrated to the world the solidarity of the three would-be independent countries in their fight against illegal Soviet occupation. Within six months Lithuania became the first of the republics of the Soviet Union to declare independence.

In September, back in England, in the 20th year since the deployment of UK troops in Northern Ireland, the IRA continued its violent campaign for Irish independence with the bombing of Deal Barracks in Kent. This resulted in the death of 11 young Marine bandsmen. A month after this four Irishmen, who had been convicted and jailed for life for the bombing of pubs in Guilford in 1975, were released after serving 14 years. Their convictions were quashed by the Court of Appeal, following an extensive enquiry into the original police investigation.

Condemnation of the Deal bombings was naturally widespread but the Government's response was not to seek a resolution to the problems which had initially prompted the IRA's bombing campaign. Instead it continued to encourage a climate of hate in which to be Irish seemed enough proof to accuse someone of terrorism. Irish people had been demonised by certain politicians and sections of the press in this country. This inflexible response had only served to drive moderate nationalists closer to the hard-liners and push a peaceful solution to the conflict further away.

On my return from Ireland I tried vainly to catch up on my training for the September Mersey Marathon; this was to be my 8th Mersey. It was a special event this year as it had also been chosen to be the trials for the Commonwealth Games being held in New Zealand in 1990. The first two to finish would be immediately selected. I only missed out by 29 places with a time of 2:42:54. So close. Or maybe not so close, considering the first 10 had run under two hours thirty and Carl Thackeray, the winner, recorded 2:14:19. As you would expect this year's race had attracted a high-class field. Rugman had continued his good form and beat me with 2:39:29. I had the solace of beating the older Grimm by four minutes.

My excuse for yet another below par performance was that I had just come back from a week in North Wales with the school again. An excessive portion of the trip had been spent in freezing cold water. If I wasn't tipping out of a canoe on a lake I was submerged in a stream during a gorge walk. In those olden days of outdoor pursuit centres, money was not available to provide individual wetsuits for students, so a towel and change of clothes was the most advanced kit recommended for these activities. We generally came back dripping wet and shivery from our pursuits outdoors. In the cool, early autumn weather I found that my 'ideal' body fat meant that I had to work hard to keep warm. The following cautionary tale demonstrates the havoc that even the most benign looking Welsh water could play with the human body.

We were staying at Oaklands Outdoor Education Centre, owned and run by Wirral borough council. This was a converted Victorian country villa perched on a hillside in the Conwy valley between LLanwryst and Betws-y-Coed. The Victorians who built the house were obviously fans of Spartan, ascetic activities having excavated a swimming hole in the grounds, which was fed by mountain streams. On one of the days of our stay, as we returned to the centre after a rock climbing/abseiling session where we had managed to keep comparatively dry, one boy asked me if he could jump into the swimming hole, as we were passing it by (presumably in a bid to rid himself of his unusual state of dryness). Initially I refused knowing what the outcome would be. He continued to badger so, to shut him up, I eventually agreed, on the condition that he wore a buoyancy jacket, of course. He accepted my conditions reluctantly, protesting that he was a good swimmer, which he was.

He jumped in flamboyantly with flambuoyancy. As soon as he hit the water, the cocky look immediately disappeared from his face, as did the blood. The shock of the cold took all his breath, energy and pride away and it required a great deal of comic thrashing to cover the couple of metres back to the edge of the pond. We all laughed but, not wanting to be accused of child cruelty, I felt obliged to submit myself to the same trial. I was mentally prepared for the effect but nothing can physically prepare you for that feeling. I imagine it was what it was like being hit by a taser. You are momentarily paralysed as the lines of communication between brain and body break down. I suppose I had the advantage of having experienced a similar sensation in some of my marathons or after a few pints (or both). A couple of other kids followed me in but most sensibly eschewed the pleasure. No one spent more time in the water than it took to struggle to the edge of the pond. It would have been dangerous to stay in any longer. On reflection this may not have originally been a swimming hole but instead a place to throw wayward children who wanted to be heard too much as well as seen. The Victorians had some good ideas.

Along with hypothermia and hyper schoolkids, another cause of serious energy depletion for me was being entrusted to make a video of this trip. The fatigue was not caused by the pressures of directorial or artistic duties but because the bloody camera weighed a bloody ton. It was not of the modern hand-held variety but more shoulder-held; like carrying a sack of coal. All this malarkey was hardly an ideal run up to a marathon. After my 8th Mersey race I made sure everyone at the club knew about my far from suitable preparations, especially Rugman.

On October 17th 1989, lots of people hit the wall. They hit it again and again until it crumbled. Then they took bits of it home to remind them of what life had been like when it had loomed over them. The Berlin Wall was destroyed by joyful, young people inhaling the scent of freedom. The promise of a democratic future perfumed every brick. Democracy smells sweetest when fresh. The United States, an old democracy, leaned back in its big old rocking chair and smiled, applauding the newly freed countries and the fall of an empire which had been its nemesis since the Second World War. Meanwhile back at the ranch, in San Salvador, six Jesuit priests were murdered by US trained and armed soldiers because of their opposition to the US backed government.

Noam Chomsky American philosopher and political critic stated at the time;

"Eastern European dissidents were given massive support and attention by the entire Western world, quite unprecedented support, vastly greater than the support given to people within Western domains who were suffering far worse oppression and were defending freedom and justice with far greater courage. The disparity is so extraordinary that the very word "dissident" in Western languages refers to East Europeans; no one, except those few who have extricated themselves from the Western propaganda system, even uses the word "dissident" for people like the Central American Jesuit intellectuals who were assassinated in November 1989 by elite forces armed and trained by the US. And while every word of East European dissidents is widely publicized, hailed, and treasured, try to find even a reference to the very important and courageous writings of Fr. Ellacuría and his associates, or other Central American dissidents who had to flee from slaughter or were simply tortured and killed by US-run forces."

In the UK (an even older democracy) two significant televisual events took place in the last two months of 1989. I will leave it to the reader to decide which, in their opinion, had the greater implications and importance, socially and politically.

On the November 21st, the House of Commons was televised for the first time....zzzzzzzz. Wake up! I repeat... the House of Commons was televised for the first time. Now stay awake because people are watching you!

December 8th saw an actor in a soap opera pretend to get killed, knocked over by a tram in Blackpool (yawn). Sorry, I'm not a fan of soaps but clearly there are some who are. This episode of Coronation Street attracted 26.93 million viewers. I'm not sure how many watched the House of Commons broadcast but it may have been a few less.

Finally, having previously mourned the passing of the Dusky Seaside Sparrow I feel duty bound to mention another animal made 'extinct' closer to home, in December of this year. In this month the last coypu in the wild in Britain was captured and humanely killed. This fact wasn't going to evoke the same dismay from me as the treatment of the Dusky did. The coypu is a big aquatic rodent with large, orange incisor teeth. Native to South America, coypu were brought into this country in 1929 to be bred for their soft fur. Many of these creatures objected to having their coats removed claiming, understandably, that they needed them for the British winter. Consequently, between 1929 and 1939, escapes were recorded from half of the 49 fur farms, which were mostly set up in counties in South-East England. (Most coypus dug their way to freedom but one, going by the name of Steve McCoypu, was spotted trying to leap the perimeter fence of a fur farm on a motorbike.) All farms were closed by 1945 because of their lack of profitability but not before a sizeable wild population of the rogue rodents had been established. These coypus dispersed especially rapidly along the watercourses of East Anglia. In the 1960s the wild population was thought to have peaked at around 200,000 (this doesn't include the civilised ones working as dental hygienists or running beauty parlours).

So what was the problem, apart from the fact that they looked like piglet sized rats who smoked 90 cigarettes a day? Well, to be honest, it was that they were big green eating machines. Grazing in waterways and on marshland they seriously damaged or destroyed areas of emergent marsh vegetation, such as reed beds. This removed important habitats for native animals like Bittern and other marshland birds. Local populations of the rare (and to me amusingly named) flowering rush, Butomus, were eradicated by coypu voracity. Burrowing by coypus undermined river banks, threatened flood defences and damaged irrigation systems. They also carried a parasite that could give people dermatitis. So what was to like about them unless you were a coypu's mother? They had to go; just another example of humans upsetting the natural balance of an environment by introducing alien species or destroying native species in the pursuit of profit.

(*Gurner of the year.*)

It is at this point in a chapter I usually sum up my year of running. To be honest it had been a bit of an odd one. I have no idea how many miles I had run. I didn't feel like I was making any extra effort to improve and yet I managed to start the year off with a big PB in the Helsby half marathon, I recorded a 5 mile PB of 25:53 in July and also won several team prizes with the lads. Possibly my proudest moment of the twelve months was being voted the club's 'Runner of the Year' by my brothers and sisters in legs. Mind you, looking at the picture of me receiving the trophy at the annual awards ceremony it seems I had misunderstood the category and was going for 'Gurner of the Year.'

I had also got my training grant and sixth place in the Derby Marathon but my marathon time was not improving. I didn't see how I would be able to run quicker times other than by further upping my training. I didn't feel physically or mentally capable of doing that. I did feel the overwhelming desire to simply let my running tick over. It was as if the routine of my life needed a fillip which wasn't going to be achieved by more running and as though I was subconsciously waiting for something else to happen.

On December 22nd Eileen and I went to a play at the Liverpool Playhouse. The production was, no doubt, chosen for the author's Christmassy connections but the title was also a fairly accurate description of our mood. It was 'Great Expectations' by Charles Dickens.

Chapter 9

1990 Capital Gain, Corporate Win, Prize Delight

On February 12th, just after my 39th birthday, into my 40th year and a new decade, I got a speeding ticket. I was coming out of the Wirral end of the Birkenhead Tunnel on my way to work in Rock Ferry. The route initially travels along the New Chester Road, a short section of dual carriageway devoid of houses, following the tall and grimy walls of the Cammell Lairds shipyard. I admit I was a little distracted and late for work as I took the slip road from the tunnel to join the main road. I wasn't really aware of driving particularly fast as I started to pass another car. The person in this larger, more powerful vehicle must have taken umbrage at being overtaken by a Nissan Micra because he seemed to speed up deliberately as I drew alongside him. Running out of space to pass I should have slowed down but instead I unwisely accelerated further. Suddenly my world was filled with blue flashing light. I have no idea where the other car and driver had got to. He had probably spotted the traffic cop and slowed down or turned off. I hadn't. Now I slowed and stopped. The police car (or jam butty as they were 'affectionately' called by locals) pulled up behind.

I'd read an article once about how to behave when stopped by the police. It suggested that it makes you look less guilty if you get out of the car and meet the officer half way; sad to say not in my case.

"Do you realise you were travelling 48 mph, in a 30 mph zone?" Had I answered truthfully I would have said "no" but instead, while slowly digesting the question, I shrugged my shoulders and raised my eyebrows; body language perhaps suggesting arrogance rather than contrition or innocence. "Were you racing that other bloke?" he continued. By this time I had regained the power of speech. I jerked my thumb at the Micra. "What, in this?" (My tone of voice may have suggested I was euphemistically saying; "Are you thick or what?")

"I was just trying to get past him." I feebly added trying to recover the situation.

What I obviously hadn't got past was the first paragraph of the article on how to behave when stopped by the police. I could almost see his brain assessing the validity of my reply but being strongly influenced by the attitude conveyed by its delivery. He didn't like me. To be fair I wasn't too fond of him. He shook his head in the way that policemen are trained to do. "No excuse, you can take it to court or accept a fixed penalty now?" I gave up on the recovery. "Oh, just give me the ticket and hurry up, I'm late for work." I snapped.

I took the ticket and just managed to keep "and you have a f-----g nice day too" inside my head before carrying on to school.

The truth was I'd actually thought that the stretch of road, being a dual-carriageway and non-residential, was a 40 mph area. But fair cop, seemingly, I still would have been 8 mph over the limit, even if it had been. Maybe I would have got more sympathy had I bared my soul politely to the PC. I could have told him why I wasn't as with it as I should have been. My mind was a pinball machine of thoughts, feelings and ideas. Two hours before Eileen had informed me that I was to become a father again at the age of 39.

For the first 10 years of our relationship children had not been on the agenda. Neither of us had been adamantly against the idea, it just hadn't really come up. We had been too busy enjoying ourselves. There were many occasions, when taking Laura back to her mum, I'd felt sad and had a pang of something missing; the experience of a full-time family. Frequent contact with Laura had always been my aim and I felt like I had succeeded in this but it often left me wanting more. That said, for a decade I'd had great freedom to do so many things. It was after one of our days out with Laura that Eileen felt the need to give motherhood serious consideration. Our trip to Alton Towers for Laura's 10th birthday also marked the birthday of an idea. We'd had a lovely time and Eileen, aged thirty three, felt she needed to make a decision about whether she wanted the 'joy' of being around children on a 24 hour basis.

It was after this trip she decided to move her contraceptive pills from her top dressing-table drawer to the bottom. It wasn't until some time later that she also decided to tell me about the plan which apparently had already been put into action. Until that moment I suppose I'd just been a sleeping partner! To be fair she already knew I would be in agreement, which is a good job really. So now, with a majority vote, the scheme was officially embarked upon.

An ageing marathon runner is perhaps not a paragon of fertility. I imagined my sperm being many mini-mes (which I suppose they were) in a marathon, struggling along, getting more and more knackered on the journey and being good for nothing at the end. As with marathons, it took time but we got there. The due date was late September and we knew big changes and challenges were on the horizon but for now life went on much as normal.

In January, almost in an act of prescient symbolism the tower of Pisa went too far. Its wayward leanings caused the experts to deem it unsafe and the structure was closed to tourists. It was as if a chapter of our life was being closed. By the time the tower reopened in 2001, looking at photographs of it, I noticed that a safety sign had appeared which warned; "Do not step out on to the outer walkways around each level." Now they tell us! It went on; "The Tour is not recommended for people who suffer from dizzy spells. In any case, be most prudent and orderly." I couldn't envisage anyone being imprudent enough to cavort on those outer walkways in a disorderly fashion, with disco legs and slippery sandals. You'd have to be mad.

Also in January and connected to our past freedom, the All Yugoslav Communist Party was dissolved. This decision finally removed the glue that had been barely holding together the country's disparate ethnic and cultural groups since World War Two. We had seen the splits appearing in Split in 1988. There followed years of internal conflict, carnage and genocide as the various factions fought over their versions of autonomy, freedom and democracy.

For the first two months of 1990 my running had taken a back seat while the dust from our whirlwind news settled. I did no road racing but turned out for the club in cross country events. The Northern Cross Country Association Championships conveniently took place in Birkenhead two weeks into the New Year. The venue was Arrowe Park, which is an area of parkland, woodland and leisure facilities on the Wirral to the west of Birkenhead. It comprises of approximately 425 acres of land.

In 1807, Liverpool ship owner and slave trader John Shaw bought Arrowe House farm and the surrounding land. On his death in 1829 it came into the ownership of his nephew, John Ralph Nicholson Shaw, who built Arrowe Hall in 1835, now a Grade II listed mansion. In 1908 Arrowe Hall and Park were acquired by Lord Leverhulme who was co-founder of the Lever Brothers Company and responsible for the construction of Port Sunlight Village. He subsequently sold the estate to Birkenhead Corporation in 1926. Arrowe Hall was eventually sold by the local council and became a private care centre. Built on land purchased with profit derived from a trade caring nothing for humanity, the hall had come to be used in the trade of profit-making care for humans. Also in the business of caring but, as yet, still in the public domain, Arrowe Park NHS hospital was built on 15 acres of the parkland in 1982. Happily no-one in the race needed to take the journey across the park to use this recently built National Health Service medical facility.

I remember little about this cross country race but know our team finished a creditable (for us) 59th out of nearly 140 teams. The course which followed muddy woodland paths and landscaped undulations had become briefly infamous five years previously on February 21st 1985. Then it had served as the venue for the Women's National Cross Country Championships. Anti-apartheid demonstrators forced South African-born runner Zola Budd off the course just over a mile into the race. Some people thought she was unfairly treated but, on this land with links to slavery, others thought the action against her was justified to highlight the inhuman unfairness of apartheid.

Five years later in 1990, at the same time as my cross country meeting, back in the country of Budd's birth, a man of dignity and integrity walked away from some prison gates. Leading anti-apartheid campaigner Nelson Mandela had been freed after 27 years of 'unfair' treatment. People danced in the streets all over Africa and thousands clamoured to see him at a rally in Cape Town. In our street we decorated the front of our terraced house in his honour. I think neighbours thought it was someone's birthday! Eileen and I watched his release on television. As much as I had shed bitter tears of frustration over the Zola Budd's 'nationality for medals' farce, our eyes filled joyously seeing the 71-year-old free at last. While Budd and her advisors had spent their time wheeling and dealing to get British citizenship in order to sidestep the sporting ban on apartheid South Africa, Nelson Mandela had spent his days on Robben Island, doing hard labour. While she sought personal gain, he had refused numerous offers of early release from the government in Pretoria, on principle, because of the conditions attached. Ironically it is said that Mandela had been a keen cross country runner and, when given the chance, ran in prison.

In March 1990 another travesty of athletics was belatedly put to rest. Again it was an issue of skin colour and apartheid but US style. President George Bush posthumously awarded Jesse Owens the Congressional Medal of Honor for his achievements at the 1936 Berlin Olympics calling them 'a triumph for all humanity.' It was a different story back when this black athlete was winning his medals in Germany. Then the USA was a deeply segregated society.

Owens won four gold medals at the games which, organised by Adolph Hitler and his Nazi regime, were intended to showcase Aryan superiority. On three consecutive days Owens won the 100m sprint, the long jump and the 200m sprint. Four days later, he was added to the 4 x 100 m relay team following a request by the Germans to replace Jewish-American sprinters. He won a fourth gold medal. (With regards to the long jump, he gave credit to aptly named Luz Long – a German competitor he ultimately defeated - for friendly advice which helped to improve his own performance.)

In Germany, Owens stayed in the same hotel as the white competitors but, at that time, black people in many parts of the United States were forced to use segregated hotels while travelling. Although, on his return to the US, he did get a ticker-tape welcome in New York, later in the day he was not permitted to take the main elevator in the Waldorf-Astoria hotel to reach a reception honouring him. Instead, he had to make do with the freight elevator. He received no recognition from the Head of State. Owens was never invited to the White House nor were honours bestowed upon him by President Franklin D. Roosevelt or his successor Harry S. Truman. Later Owens stated; "Hitler didn't snub me – it was FDR who snubbed me. The president didn't even send me a telegram." In 1955, President Dwight Eisenhower (himself an athlete of note) finally honoured Owens by naming him an Ambassador of Sports.

Two months after Owens had won his gold medals in Berlin, in 1936, the Jarrow March was trudging its weary way from the North East of England 300 miles to London. In March 1990 I travelled to Middlesbrough to attend the funeral of my grandfather who had reputedly taken part in this 'crusade' against unemployment and poverty during the Great Depression. I'd had virtually no contact with him during my adult life. Infrequent trips to Middlesbrough were only to keep in tenuous touch with my dad. I didn't know an awful lot about grandad apart from memories of childhood visits and unsubstantiated snippets I got from my dad. Like me, my father wasn't close to his father. They saw little of each other although they lived in the same town. Dad claimed his family hadn't supported him when my mum died and he didn't see why he should be bothered with them. With limited contact, this is what little I remember or 'learned' about my grandad Peacock.

He had worked in the steel works on what was called the "windy hammer." This was a huge pneumatic flattener which battered hot ingots into steel sheets. Time spent operating this machine had left him severely deaf. Our childhood visits for Sunday tea were formal occasions but we had to shout to be heard. I know he liked to grow rhubarb ('don't touch the leaves they're poisonous') and to sing, sometimes at the same time. When the fancy took him he gave us a deep and tremulous rendition of 'Only a Beautiful Picture in a Beautiful Golden Frame' which was a sentimental ballad about a man gazing at the portrait of a lost lover. Grandad must have heard it from his mum or dad, being only nine when it was written in 1907. As we watched him croon, at times his eyes closed and his leonine head tipped back as he strained to reach higher notes. The back of his darkly oiled, swept-back mane rested against the antimacassar, which did its job. He would also lean forwards when his voice went so fruitily low that it seemed as if he was about to retch. The sound caused his budgies to flit nervously in their cage on the sideboard.

At over six foot tall, broad and upright, he looked imposing. He was a straight laced man - a teetotaller and devoutly religious. He had become a working class Tory. It was told, however, that he had lived a far from conservative early life. Born in County Durham in 1898, apparently he had got up to high jinks as a teenager when he fell foul of the law but didn't fall, caught climbing up the church steeple in the town of Spennymoor. He volunteered for the First World War and was a horse artilleryman. Firing the big guns may have also contributed to his deafness. He survived the campaign in Gallipoli for which he was decorated. Between the wars I was told he had taken part in the Jarrow March.

What I did know for sure was that my dad didn't really get on with him and left home as soon as he could to avoid a disciplinarian regime. At 14 my father was a big lad for his age having acquired almost a stone in weight for each year. He was often in trouble at school. In the 1930s he got into a spot of bother with his PE teacher which, amazingly, resulted in a bout of fisticuffs. My dad's shirt was torn in the unseemly scuffle. He came home and related these events to my grandad who immediately took a leather belt to him, presumably to teach him not to behave so violently. Ah, the good old days.

My dad would tell this story in a matter of fact way but you could always sense the resentment. Desperate to get away from the family, he tried to join the Royal Navy at the outbreak of war in 1939 when he was just 17. He was sent home and told to come back when he was 18. This he did and spent the duration in the Senior Service, marrying my mum when he returned home after VJ day.

I had paid a rare visit to see my grandad with my dad a year before the funeral and Laura met him for the first and last time. Eileen took a photograph of us, the four generations lined up in order of age and height; like a pictograph to demonstrate the decreasing influence of the height gene in our family.

While in the Navy my dad continued his penchant for fisticuffs but this time, with gloves on, as his ship's heavyweight champion. At that time he would also have enjoyed a daily ration of rum. This naval tradition dated back to 1655 when rum replaced beer as a sailor's daily alcohol ration. The poison of choice was changed because rum survived sea voyages better than beer and, 'happily', the Brits had just captured Jamaica from the Spanish; as a result this substitute tipple was easily 'procured' from distillers in the region. The ration was an astonishing half a pint of rum, twice a day (it had been eight pints of beer). In 1740, it was reduced to an eighth of a pint twice a day, in diluted form; possibly because of the mounting expense of rebuilding piers crashed into by half-cut corvette captains and crew.

In spite of discussions in parliament in 1850 and 1881 concerning the abolition of the tradition of 'splicing the mainbrace' it carried on in the Royal Navy until 1970. The Royal Canadian Navy gave it up two years later but the plucky Royal New Zealand Navy clung on until March 1990 before they had their spirit glasses, now only awash with salty, seadog tears, prised from their trembling grasps. Spare a thought, however, for the Royal Australian Navy who never had a ration. I know... it's hard to imagine Australians missing out on the chance of a bevvy! Funnily enough the word 'grog', which originated from the tradition, came to be used colloquially to describe alcohol in Australia. It was British Vice Admiral Andrew Vernon who first introduced the reduced and diluted rum ration in 1740. He was known to wear a coat of grogham cloth (a coarse fabric of silk mixed with wool or with mohair, often stiffened with gum) and so he acquired the nick-name of 'Old Grog'. Subsequently the daily rum ration was named after him. And so after March 1990, the New Zealand navy would have no more groggy frogmen from Rarotonga; at least not while on duty.

Sticking (dubiously) to a nautical theme, at the end of March 1990 the second Battle of Trafalgar took place. This was no heroic sea battle but a conflict between police and demonstrators which erupted in and around Trafalgar Square. On a lovely spring day over 200,000 people had assembled in London to march in protest against the Thatcher government's introduction of an unpopular Community Charge (popularly known as the Poll Tax) to replace local rates. Local rates had been variable, based on notional rental value of dwellings. Protesters complained that the Poll Tax, which was a single flat rate charge per head, had the effect of shifting the tax burden from the rich to the poor. It was a hugely controversial levy and resulted in a legion of non-payers, up to 30% of former rate payers according to the BBC at the time. Enforcement was impossible because thousands of defaulters clogged up normal legal procedures. There were not enough bailiffs to enforce court orders and even the South Yorkshire Police claimed that (as much as they would have liked to, no doubt) it would be impossible to arrest defaulters because of the numbers involved. This was a classic case of an elected government going against the wishes of a large portion of electorate.

The demonstration in London was intended to be peaceful. However violence erupted on the day. Poorly prepared, the police embarked on ill-advised and at times highly aggressive tactics to control the demonstrators. This further inflamed sections of an already potentially volatile crowd. By midnight, figures released indicated that 339 had been arrested, 113 were injured; some police officers but mostly members of the public. Scuffles between rioters and police continued until 3am. Much damage was caused.

The usual condemnation of groups of trouble makers followed but a 1991 report by the police concluded there was "no evidence that the trouble was orchestrated by left-wing anarchist groups." It went on to confess that inadequate preparation by the police may have contributed to the deterioration of the situation. Afterwards, the non-aligned Trafalgar Square Defendants Campaign was established to provide committed and unconditional support for those arrested. The campaign group acquired and scrutinised more than fifty hours of police video. This was influential in the acquittal of many of these defendants when it became apparent that the forces of law and order may well have fabricated or inflated charges. This definitely sounded familiar.

The non-payment protest was strongly backed in Liverpool. In July of the following year Terry Fields, Labour MP for Liverpool, Broadgreen and Militant Tendency supporter, was eventually jailed for sixty days for refusing to pay his Community Charge. For this he was expelled from the party. The Labour Party refused to support the non-payment campaign, especially amongst MPs - "Law makers must not be law breakers" was Labour leader Neil Kinnock's catchy mantra. As misguided as some of Terry Fields' actions may have been, he was always seen as a man of principle who would back words with action. For Neil Kinnock it seemed more about the words, and not much else.

In April I was quietly working away, taxing myself on the badly maintained, due-to-under-funding, roads of Liverpool. It had been a strange few months. After the furore of our big news I had got my head down and kept it down to do a lot of 'secret training', preferring to stay close to home. Eileen had continued to run and I was back to jogging slower and slower miles with her. I was building up for yet another London Marathon at the end of the month. As impending parenthood made it likely that we would be housebound for a while after September we decided to go away with friends for a week at Easter. It was only two weeks away from the London race but we felt it might be a nice idea for both of us to wind down in different surroundings. We rented a National Trust cottage in Pembrokeshire on the Stackpole Estate.

The cottage was perched overlooking the sea on Stackpole quay. I didn't do a great deal of running while I was there but the miles I did put in were some of the most enjoyable I had ever experienced. There were more than 30 kilometres of paths around the estate, taking in everything from dense woodlands to bracing cliff tops and I sampled most of them. The paths radiated from the site of Stackpole Court, sadly demolished in 1963 before the National Trust acquired the land. Admiral Nelson had stayed there in 1803 with Emma Hamilton and now, after the second Battle of Trafalgar, Tony, Eileen and barelyabump were staying nearby, in more humble accommodation.

I concentrated my runs on the staggering coastline. My breath was taken away twice as I toiled up and down the coastal path. The cliffs rose and fell like the chest of a sleeping ogre. Below was the site of a tumultuous confluence of the Bristol Channel and the Celtic sea. It was important to tread carefully on the giant but the occasional risky glance at the swirling seascape was a must. When the path eventually dipped to sea level, it exhaled on to soft sugary coves whose surface sucked in my feet and then the air from my lungs. The effort was great but the reward was greater.

From Stackpole quay, half a mile over the cliff path and accessible only by foot, I was introduced to Barafundle bay early into my first run. This isolated cove, backed by sand dunes and pine trees, looked more like the West Indies than West Wales. The sun shone and the white sand reflected it in blinding brilliance. Reports and complaints about the tough terrain from straining muscles to the brain went unheeded as head office was flooded with surges of superlatives and waves of wellbeing.

I felt this beach was the best I had seen in the UK. (This opinion was only modified in my mind by the discovery of Achmelvich beach, in Sutherland, at the opposite northern extreme of the western British coast.) The sand was pristine. I felt a poignant euphoria as I made deep and heavy footprints in the unsullied surface. For a moment I felt like the only person on the earth. The twinkling turquoise gem-sea chewed at the strand, eager to come up and remove the mess my selfish feet had made.

I ran a similar short early morning route nearly every day of our week's stay. Each time I would cross the beach and make my marks; returning on the same route, I would only see one set of familiar footprints running towards me. As my mind and body became more accustomed to this trail, which had challenged both, I began to experience an unspecific feeling of contentment. The sun shone all week and it was unseasonably mild, warm enough to spend hours on the beach relaxing. I was in a good place. We both returned to Liverpool refreshed and happily looking forward.

In what seemed like mere moments, we were on a train to London. Eileen, Laura, me, Rugman, DJ, Grimm the Elder, the Bard and others made up our motley, merry, Merseyside company of players. The Bard wasn't running but had come as logistical support. This would involve the onerous task of checking out as many hostelries as possible. The lads were staying in some dubious hotel while we stayed at Eileen's sister's flat in Brixton. Judging by later accounts I had made a wise choice as the Bard had woken up the others, coming back into the hotel room in the early hours, 'tired' after a hard session.

I, on the other hand, had a peaceful night and felt strangely nerveless. It didn't seem to matter to me as much as previous years. The weather was cool and drizzly as I met the 'Uncoachables' at Greenwich for my fourth London Marathon. Everyone looked focussed and determined, apart from the absent Bard who probably couldn't focus at all, wherever he was. Lining up, I was aware that Rugman, DJ and Grimm the Elder had all been running well and I felt that they would probably beat me. My training had been more mythical than secret. I had put in a lot of slow lonely miles but virtually no speed work. I was relying heavily on residual fitness. Even with all this knowledge I felt uncharacteristically relaxed. The gun sounded for the start and I was running alongside Rugman. I remember waving at the cameras on the gantries at 200 or 300 metres, not something I was in the habit of doing. I then turned to Rugman, smiled and said "right, now down to business." I have no idea what that was about.

Rugman and I became separated in the crowds and I just tried to run comfortably, deliberately avoiding looking at my time early on. I eventually glanced at my watch at 13 miles after my now legendary wave to those who knew me (Laura, Eileen and her sister) on London Bridge. I was surprised not so much at the time, I had got there quicker in previous races, but at the way I felt, having got there in that time. It seemed easy, relatively. On the way back from the Isle of Dogs after 22 miles I saw Eileen again at the Tower. I waved again and smiled. She was standing next to another female spectator, who turned and said, "He must be feeling good." She was right. The expected tiredness kicked in the last three miles but it wasn't a vicious kick, more of a boot up the arse to remind me to keep going.

I lapped up the crowd's encouragement on The Mall and forged my way to the finish. I couldn't believe the time on the clock; it was just ticking towards 2:35. I crossed the line in 2:35:10, a PB of about 30 seconds. I suddenly had the feeling that this was it. Everything had come together at the right time in a way it wouldn't do again. My age and the change in my circumstances would mean I would probably never be able to be in better shape to run a marathon faster. I felt a strong surge of emotion and shed a couple of tears of joy and relief as I hobbled and rustled down the finish funnels in my silver blanket. After the tears came the endorphin rush. I felt so high and so happy. When I met Laura, Eileen and biggerbump I tried to hug all the breath out of all of them but I didn't have the strength.

We were getting the train straight back home. Our carriage was full of Scousers and cans of ale; such an unusual combination! Most of our club were in the same carriage. We swapped race stories. I had seen none of my club mates after the start, mainly because of the fact that they had all been behind me, but no one had a really disastrous race; Grimm senior, 2:37:46, DJ, 2:38:35, Rugman, 2:41:36, the Bard about 10 pints. My time was a club record which would stand for years.

The atmosphere on the train was lively but people were controlled, apart from the Bard, who was funny only just the right side of annoying. Poor Laura had to put up with him singing 'Tell Laura I love her' on several occasions and Eileen ended up with him momentarily on her lap as he lost balance, messing about in the aisle. He apologised profusely and must have wondered why I was giving him such big sharp daggers but I hadn't told any of the Uncoachables our news. I couldn't really blame him for being so bloody clumsy; this was his normal behaviour. Eileen just laughed it off. All in all it was a joyous ride home and, although I felt a bit sorry for any non-runners on the train, I needed to enjoy this moment. I had the feeling it would be my last marathon PB.

In May I continued to tot up the marathons as I returned to Derby having entered another Ramathon. I didn't have the same individual success as in 1989, I ran five minutes slower and only managed 20th place, but a few of the lads from the club had come with me this time and we were the first team. This race had been designated the Northern Athletics Association Marathon Championships and therefore we became the champions of that large area of the country sometimes described by southerners as 'the poor bit.' For our travails and in typically archaic athletic administration fashion we were each presented with a blazer badge commemorating our achievement.

If it had survived the custard, mud, gob and ink assault of the sixties I would have dug out my old school blazer to attach the badge to; I wasn't going to buy one especially. I mean, how many people under the age of 70 would have actually owned a blazer (unless of course you were an ex-mod and still had one lurking in your wardrobe)? The name of this style of jacket originated from the 'blazers' of the Lady Margaret Boat Club (1825), the rowing club of St. John's College, Cambridge. The club's jackets were called blazers because of their bright red cloth; the jacket's name survived the original red colour. Actually, if I'd had a red one in the '80s I might well have worn it, to go with my old shorts.

I had to pinch myself again to check that we were actually in 1990 when four days after the Ramathon I read that the World Health Organisation had decided to remove homosexuality from its list of diseases. Until then it had still been classed as a mental illness. How the hell had it remained on the list for so long? But at least this action was a step forward, unlike section 28.

I went in search of races during the summer and managed to fit in two 10ks, two 5 miles, a ten miler and a half marathon in June, July and August. The half marathon was The Cleveland Major, in my native Middlesbrough. It had always been my ambition to run a race in my home town and I combined it with a visit to my dad, who was back from the rigs at the time. The race encompassed two counties starting over the Tees, on Stockton High Street, in County Durham and finishing in Middlesbrough's Stewart Park, in Yorkshire. The finish area had been set up in the grassy expanse which dominated the centre of this 120 acre landscaped suburban park. It was familiar territory for me having been a visitor many times as a child with my family and occasionally with my junior school for country dancing jamborees.

Whatever happened to country dancing and its jamborees? How could such a wholesome activity and a lovely word fall into disuse? I can't imagine why the youngsters of today wouldn't enjoy prancing around in their plimsolls and sashes to amplified accordion music. It knocks spots off an Xbox and having a Wii any day. Seriously, I must confess I did actually quite enjoy these events. It was a way of meeting girls and holding hands without the necessity of going to discotheques and spending any of my half-a-crown pocket money on Babychams; aged ten that would have been slightly out of my league.

Incidentally, Stewart Park is also the site of a cottage where Captain James Cook was reputedly born. Cook 'discovered' Australia which surprised the Aborigines because they'd known about it for years. Now the possibly appropriately named Captain Cook Birthplace Museum can be found in this public space. The park was originally landscaped by one Henry Bolckow, who built himself a house there in 1858.

Bolckow is an interesting character. Stan Boardman the Liverpool comic is narrowly known for his dubious catch phrase, 'we don't like the Germans because they bombed our chippy'. In Middlesbrough it's possible that the reverse was true. Henry Bolckow was the principal person responsible for the growth of 'the Boro' as a town and therefore, I suppose, indirectly responsible for the building of fish and chip shops. He was German. Sadly, nearly a century later his compatriots tried to undo all his constructive work when the town was the first large British conurbation and industrial target to be attacked by the Luftwaffe. In May 1940 a lone bomber dropped 13 bombs aimed at the steel works and railway depots. By the end of the war over 200 buildings had been destroyed.

But back to Bolckow; born Heinrich Bölckow in Sulten, in Germany in 1806, he came over to the Northeast of England in 1827 to be a partner in a corn trading business. Here he met John Vaughn, a Newcastle ironmaster, who persuaded him to invest in iron production. I am not sure why he decided to make such a radical switch of product focus, from corn to iron. Maybe Bolckow's English wasn't up to scratch or perhaps Vaughn's writing was too scratchy on the proposal but the German signed the deal to invest in corion anyway.

Their business venture stuttered when the cost of transporting pig iron from Scotland was proving prohibitive so the pair began to search for vegetarian alternatives. This having failed they began looking for local sources of iron and found a rich seam of ore in Eston, at the foot of the Cleveland hills, just outside Middlesbrough. Because of this discovery, their iron business immediately boomed and the town expanded at a surprising speed. People came from all over the country and beyond to work in the iron works and the iron mines. The Irish and Welsh were more evident in the ironworks and in jobs associated with building up the dock area. In the mines the composition of immigrants was different.

Statistics in the table overleaf, gleaned from the 1881 census, show places of origin for people in New Marske, a village built to house the workers in the Upleatham mine near Redcar. They show an intra-national melange with an added soupcon of continental flavour.

North Riding of Yorkshire	146	Kent	10
Norfolk	87	Suffolk	10
Lincolnshire	77	Huntingdonshire	7
Northamptonshire	38	Surrey	6
Cornwall	37	Leicestershire	6
County Durham	31	Cumberland	5
Devon	27	Northumberland	4
West Riding of Yorkshire	27	London	3
Lancashire	16	Dorset	2
Wiltshire	16	Prussia	2
Ireland	14	Wales	2
East Riding of Yorkshire	13	Buckinghamshire	1
Essex	12	Middlesex	1
Hampshire	11	Nottinghamshire	1
Cambridgeshire	10	Worcestershire	1
Somerset	10	France	1

You have to feel sorry for the lone Frenchman at least the Prussians had each other. In 1829 Middlesbrough was but a hamlet of 40 souls and a few living people. It became a coal port in 1831 when an extension of the Stockton to Darlington railway was built to the river Tees. By 1841 the population was 5,400. By 1851 the first blast furnace was built and by 1861 the population was nearly 20,000.

The town received a charter of incorporation in 1853. By then Henry Bolckow had become a naturalised Brit by Act of Parliament and made a half-hearted attempt at anglicising his name. He became the town's first Mayor after incorporation. He was voted in by admirers of his mayoral qualities and the size of his bribes. By 1868 when their company was producing four million tons of iron a year, Vaughn became the town's second Mayor and Bolckow went on to become Middlesbrough's first MP when the town was granted parliamentary representation. They really had the town stitched up. Bolckow stood as a Liberal candidate and was elected unopposed. This tradition of people being handed the control of the country on the basis of their personal wealth is of course now a thing of the past. Nowadays you don't have to be a millionaire to be in government … but it helps.

Bolckow remained an MP for ten years until his death. This pair's progress politically was not matched commercially as Bolckow and Vaughn failed to move with the times, specifically the demands on the industry created by the introduction of the Bessemer Process. The iron ore from the Cleveland hills was not suitable for the new efficient Bessemer steel making process because of its high phosphorous content. The town's iron and steel industry went into decline and unemployment rose. When, in 1875, the Dorman Long Company set up in the area and started making steel from imported iron ore, the industry recovered. This was the firm both my grandfathers and my father would eventually work for.

As a child I could see the highest point in the Cleveland hills from my bedroom window. At just 1,049 feet (320m) high, Roseberry Topping may not be the biggest hill you'll ever see, but it is definitely distinctive. Its shape, caused by the combination of a geological fault and a mining collapse in 1912 made this high point a familiar landmark in the Tees valley area. With its half-cone summit and jagged cliff, some say that, in silhouette, it is reminiscent of the Matterhorn in Switzerland. All it lacks is 4158 extra metres in height. Although the hills are not alive with the sound of Alpinists blowing their horns in the climbing season a couple of Prussians did live nearby in 1881.

As a child I had often walked on this part of the North Yorkshire moors and to the top of the Topping. I was always fascinated by the abandoned mines and equipment. Shaft entrances marked the start of miles of tunnels which riddled the hillsides. These gashes in the land's skin spewed out red streams from deep inside the earth. Oxblood oxide rocks littered the slopes and rusty mine machinery mimicked the geology.

Soon after their company's demise and the relinquishing of political power, Vaughn and Bolckow were largely forgotten. Bolckow's most visible legacy can be seen in the town's two main parks. Albert Park was built by him specifically as an urban public park and, like Liverpool's docks, named in honour of Queen Victoria's husband. I had a summer job in these gardens in the sixties. Stewart Park was Bolckow's home which eventually became public in 1928. Bolckow and Vaughn were both buried in the grave yard of St Cuthbert's church near to this park. Here their graves were neglected until an overdue restoration was performed in 2009. This was the graveyard where my grandfather was interred in March 1990. Ironmaster and ironservant, from a different cast, side by side, now equals; ashes to ashes, rust to rust.

And so I got to run my hometown race on a muggy summer's day. Many people suffered running in the heat. As usual, I didn't so much suffer as slow. I was aware that my body was resisting being pushed too hard. I sauntered over the finish line in 33rd place out of 2000 and with a time of 1:15:41; a below-average time for me but understandable, considering the above-average temperatures. Eileen and gettingbiggerbytheminutebump watched me finish as did my dad and stepmother.

My dad's reaction to my performance was understated, as usual. He was good at muted reactions. I had been involved in sport all my life; football at junior school and rugby for secondary school and county in my teens. On the rare occasions he came to watch me perform he never had much to say. To me he never seemed to have it in him to openly show enthusiasm for any of his kids' achievements, or anything more than, what appeared to be, a cursory interest. I was the first person in our extended family to study for a degree but I have often joked that my dad never knew I was at university. For all I know this may well have been true because I was never asked about what the hell I was doing for three years. Maybe if I had been, I might have been able to work out what the hell I <u>was</u> doing.

Perhaps it was a generational thing, post-war dads not knowing how to relate to children brought up in the brave new world of '50s and '60s. I do believe he felt a little intimidated by his off-spring who had a radically different outlook on life to his. His typical reaction was to become self-absorbed. When my mum died it seemed he wasn't up to the challenge of helping his kids get through a difficult time. He was barely able to keep himself going. At the end of the day he decided to jump his own ship and be rescued by another. He married a woman twenty years younger who had four young children. Although he was not fully responsible for them, this family could fuss over and look after him. They seemed to speak his language. I don't think he believed he was going to get that from his real kids; not without tangled strings attached. We seemed to have become irritating thistles which he needed to remove from the lamb's wool he was trying to wrap himself up in. I wasn't destroyed by this, just disappointed.

The time I spent with him went well enough with no tension and general friendliness. He was always kind to Laura and Eileen when we visited. I always felt I needed to try to make it work but at the end of the day there was no real emotion, no deep running feelings, nothing natural. It seemed he just wanted to get on with his life and not be reminded of an uncomfortable past. We had a 2D practical relationship and I wasn't sure of its purpose. I once wrote him a letter to tell him how proud I was of him. It was a time when I was trying to rally the family troops and on reflection I was possibly writing what I thought he wanted to hear rather than what I was feeling. He never mentioned it nor did it change his emotional response to me. He just didn't get it or didn't want to.

The effect all this had on me was positive. It made me all the more determined to always encourage my own children, showing them love and giving them my attention. I was doing my best with Laura in difficult circumstances and soon I would have the chance to do it again. In a perverse sort of way my early family experiences had taught me a good lesson.

We swapped my family at the beginning of August for Eileen's at the end of the month; what a contrast! We rented a large house, former accommodation for slate quarrymen, two miles up a single-track road just outside of Coniston in the Lake District. There were eleven of us in all, including Eileen's mum and dad, two of her sisters, her brother and various partners and kids. I had spent much more time with these people over the last decade than I had with my own blood. I may have been an emotional orphan but I had been well and truly adopted.

(Come on Eileen; I know a short cut).

If there was one thing I learned from our stay in the Lakes it was this; never take a short cut over the moors, as the sun is setting, with a pensioner, a woman eight months pregnant and her sister with a broken arm, without first taking a close look at the contour lines on the map! A complicated lesson not often learnt by experience and which led me to produce a master class in appearing calm in the face of obvious danger.

One evening we decided to go for beverages. The Crown Inn in Coniston was only three miles away by road and I decided I'd like to walk it. The obvious route was pleasant for the first mile or so, following the single-track road down the secluded valley sheltering our cottages, but then it hit the A593, the main road through Coniston, which was narrow, devoid of a pavement and busy with holiday traffic. Looking at the map I could see a footpath which ran along the ridge above Coniston, parallel to the road. My desire to get to the pub on foot was echoed by three others, not so much the good, the bad and the ugly, but more the old, the expectant and the injured. All seemed to have a blind faith in my map reading which probably isn't the best kind of faith to have in any kind of reading.

We started along the little lane and soon found the rising path on to the tops. What maps don't fully inform you of is how hard or easy the going is under foot. The answer in this case was, 'not very easy.' It seemed to be taking us ages to travel those three miles which wasn't that surprising considering the state of the pilgrims accompanying me. And all the while the gloom was gathering; the moor seemed to exhale a dark breath. I was beginning to worry behind a jovial mask.

At last, good news, we came to the point where we could see Coniston. By now the lights of the houses were twinkling in the gloaming. The bad news was that all the twinkling was taking place many feet below, over what seemed like a vertical drop. I looked at Eileen's swelling belly, her sister's arm in a sling and their dad's grey whiskers and I was afeared. I went on ahead and checked the lay of the land. The lay was precipitous and precarious but what choice did we have? It would be last orders in the pub soon.

My scouting expedition had revealed a rough path which slalomed downwards, hairpinning tightly till it reached the base of the slope. It slithered down the hill like a white snake in the darkling heather. We slithered down with it. Eileen's swelling belly carried her forward as she edged down the crumbly surface. Her sister leant back almost on her backside, tentatively following with only one hand available to break her fall. Their father brought up the rear, quietly concentrating. I led this peculiar cortege, prepared to provide a poorly padded cushion if anyone fell, but praying that they wouldn't. No one complained or indeed spoke. It seemed to take as long to cover those few hundred feet as it had to walk the previous miles. By the time we reached the pub it was totally dark and the adventure had left me so scarred that I had to double up on my order of Robinson's bitter. The incident is now part of family lore.

The little road that ran past our cottage carried on up the valley and, as it came to an end, turned into a track which could be followed across a river, on a footbridge, to the neighbouring valley of Little Langdale and to the Three Shires Inn. We ventured along this flat route to the inn a couple of times. I also ran along the secluded wooded track on one of the mornings. Retracing my steps I startled a magnificent stag grazing on the other side of a dry stone wall. We were both surprised by our face to face off but I think I got more joy out of the encounter. The whole family got joy out of our stay in 'Holme Ground' and we still talk about it.

Soon the holiday ended and September arrived. The day of reckoning neared. Yes, I had to go back to school. Oh yes, and the arrival of our child was imminent. It was a relief that there was no Mersey Marathon to distract me this year. Road works by the Pier Head had meant that the usual route was not safe to follow. Back at school I had received a local newsletter from my Union, the National Union of Teachers. Three runners were looking for a fourth to make up a team to enter the union section of the Liverpool Corporate Cup. This 5k running event was designed to encourage businesses and other organisations to get their employees out to do some exercise and maybe raise some money for charity. I knew it could easily clash with another important event but my reasoning was that the course was so close to the maternity hospital that I would be able to shoot off if necessary if I received a mobile phone call. This would have been unlikely because, at that time, only about three people in Liverpool had mobile phones and I wasn't one of them. If I had been I would have needed a wheelbarrow to carry it around the course. Nevertheless, I put my name forward and became one of the Nutters

Team, warning the other members that my participation was, at present, notional.

And from my family via Eileen's family we are led to the beginnings of our own. God help the kid with that genetic mix! As the day approached we were as ready as we could be. We'd read the books. In spite of a wealth of knowledge on the subject, I still wasn't fully confident that I knew my exact role, although I did suspect I wouldn't be physically involved in the actual process.

Eileen's labour pains started and went on and on, and on. She was keeping on top of the pain although reading about them and feeling them appeared to be two quite different things. Holding it off as long as she felt was feasible, she finally made the decision that it was time to go to the hospital although we knew they were in the habit of sending you back home if they saw fit. We arrived at Oxford Street maternity hospital. 50 years previously, almost to the day, Julia Lennon had entered the same hospital doors to give birth to her son, John. Having assessed Eileen they saw fit to let us in and we sat in a delivery room waiting for things to kick off. A midwife popped in from time to time to check Eileen's vitals and seemed confident it would be a midwife delivery as everything was on track. Time dragged for Eileen as the contractions slowly got more frequent and intense. I stood by like I was waiting for a bus and tried not to say or do, or look like I was about to say or do anything annoying. For me, it was a full-time job.

Things suddenly started to speed up and Eileen was prepared for delivery. Then a look of concern which hadn't been there before formed on the midwife's face. She muttered something about the baby being distressed and hit an alarm. The calm and control went out of the window as the room erupted into a riot of people pushing trolleys, clanking instruments and jabbering medi-speak. The doctor told us that the baby had the umbilical cord around its neck and needed to be delivered immediately. He then produced the biggest pair of forceps I'd ever seen. You are probably thinking 'how many pairs of forceps has he seen?' Truthfully I had only seen one other pair when Laura was born but this type was bigger. Kielland's forceps were notoriously tricky to use and potentially dangerous for mother and baby. They terrified me and I wasn't going to be on the receiving end.

To our huge relief, the doctor did an amazing job extricating our baby girl safely and stitching up the damage done to Eileen. Once the baby had been persuaded that flesh coloured scarves were 'out' this season her APGAR score improved. The idea of a scoring system for the condition of newborns was first muted by Dr Virginia Apgar in 1952 and a backronym constructed to help midwifes to remember what to look out for.

When our newborn's APGAR was taken she was scored on Appearance, Pulse, Grimace, Activity and Respiration. Apparently a grimace is good! If you poke a baby and it doesn't grimace it isn't reactive enough. A mnemonic also used to help remember a similar assessment of a newborn's condition is 'How Ready Is This Child?' The initial letters of these words are an aide memoir for Heart rate, Respiratory effort, Irritability, Tone, and Colour. Again here irritability is a positive thing. It is natural for a baby to be a bit mardy when it is suddenly ejected from its cosy, warm hotel womb where everything is on tap, into a cold, bright, gaudy world where it has to demand everything from great galoots who haven't got a clue what it actually wants. Yes, lots of natural grimacing and irritability will ensue.

Our suitably annoyed and gurning infant was placed temporarily in an incubator and the room emptied as quickly as it had filled. Presumably everyone had been called to another difficult birth or it was dinner time or something interesting was on the telly (live coverage of Parliament perhaps).

The three of us were left alone, the previous activity still imprinted on our brains like the image of a naked light bulb suddenly turned off. Eileen asked to sit up. I helped her. She had retained a well of blood, from the birth and repair work, which dramatically decanted on to the floor as she became upright. It splattered over my shoes appearing (hopefully) a far greater amount than it actually was, a characteristic which blood has a tendency to display. I cleaned the floor with paper towels as we quietly discussed the birth, aware that little ears were twitching either side of a grimacing face in a cot in the corner of the room. The midwife then returned, checked the baby again, lifted her out of the incubator and gave her to us, to keep. We both held, Sinead our baby girl, for the first time. Many of you will know how this feels and others may not want to know, so I will not attempt to explain. Suffice it to say it is usually a positive experience!

Soon we were on our way back to the maternity ward, vacating the delivery room for another mother and father hopefully about to experience a magical feeling difficult to describe. I stayed until it was time for mum and babe to rest and then made my way home where Eileen's mum and dad waited for all the news. They would see their granddaughter for the first time at visiting hours the following day and I couldn't wait to get back myself.

This wasn't my first birth experience but it was certainly different; a different time and different circumstances. A little more than 12 years previously in 1978 I had been in Mill Road maternity hospital in Liverpool waiting for Laura's arrival. The hospital was housed in a Victorian building, which had been a 'Workhouse for the Sick Poor' administered under the Poor Law from 1884 before it became an infirmary in 1891. In 1948 its role changed again to serve specifically as a National Health maternity hospital and it was eventually closed in1993. During the Second World War, Mill Road also treated the injured from bombing raids across the city. On May 3rd, 1941 the building was hit. Many were killed as a bomb landed in a courtyard to the rear of the hospital. A maternity ward was destroyed, killing mothers and their new born babies. The ward next to maternity, full of injured soldiers, escaped the blast. Three of the ward blocks were obliterated. It was estimated that at least 78 adults and babies died.

I was unaware of the buildings tragic past as I paced up and down the waiting room, smoking an imaginary cigar. In the '70s it wasn't a given that fathers attended births. It was quite a new-fangled thing even in normal circumstances. As I wore a groove in the lino I could hear the noise of a party going on somewhere in the bowels of the hospital; the clinking of glass and the high-pitched babble of inebriated chatter. Suddenly the swing doors burst open and a man in a black suit and bow tie entered, like a gunslinger into a saloon. He nodded and disappeared through a door marked 'staff only'. The next time I saw him his dicky bow peeked over the neck of his surgical gown and beneath his mask as he wielded the forceps needed to encourage Laura to exit. The nurse had questioned the appropriateness of my presence in these circumstances. The doctor was clearly more relaxed about this and overruled her. I just hoped that his laid-back attitude was not caused by one too many Martinis at the party I presumed he had been attending. "Warning; alcohol may cause drowsiness. Do not operate machinery and definitely do not operate!"

As it was, I was the only one affected by alcohol. Laura had arrived safely and her mum was being tended to using some sort of surgical spirits. I hadn't eaten all day and fumes from the evaporating spirits went straight up my nostrils and hit my stomach with nothing to absorb them but my blood stream. It felt great but then I started to keel over, saved only by the timely placing of a chair beneath my rapidly descending buttocks.

Seeing Laura born and holding her afterwards was truly amazing but the postpartum experience wasn't. Laura's mum and I weren't getting on; a situation not improved by the fact that on being discharged from hospital she initially stayed at her mum and dad's house. Laura's maternal grandmother was a strict Roman Catholic. She wouldn't have me in the house after I had innocently confessed to being an atheist. I was banished to the wilderness, not allowed to cross the threshold. Those were tough times which failed to improve when we were eventually back together in our flat. We knew it wasn't working and I was soon moving out while making the promise to myself that I was going to try to be the best dad I could be for Laura. Post-birth Sinead was an altogether different experience for me. After over a decade of being together Eileen and I knew we were in it for the long haul well before Sinead's arrival. This was going to be an equal parent-partnership.

The day before Eileen was allowed home I took part in the first Liverpool Corporate Cup, representing the Wirral Nutters. We were 45th out of 179 teams and first trade union team. To be honest our category victory was mainly due to the fact there were only a few other teams in this section. Besides, trade unionists were notoriously unfit as a result of spending too much time in fug-filled meeting rooms plotting to take over the country with wildcat strikes and unreasonable pay demands, so I'd heard.

I enjoyed this five kilometre jaunt, winding through the impressive Victorian architecture of Liverpool's commercial district. It was a lovely way for me to mark the occasion of my second daughter's arrival. As some parents do, we created a collection of memorabilia to show her in future years (whether she was interested or not). Our collection included newspapers on the day, a vinyl record of a song we were listening to at the time (Van Morrison's 'Real, Real, Gone') and other bits and pieces appertaining to the birth. I could now add my medal from the race and a Liverpool Echo, which carried a report of the Corporate Cup containing these paragraphs.

"Other category winners included Wirral Nutters who got together through an item in the local National Union of Teachers' newsletter and had not met before. There should be a special cheer at school assembly for Mike Devitt of Calday, Lynne Kirk (Devonshire), Dave Nibbs (St Benedict's), and Tony Peacock (The Dell). But Tony could not stop and join in the presentations. He was off to see his wife and another 'prize' – a baby born on Friday."

This report was accurate except for the presumption that Eileen and I were married.

On October 1st our family was reunified. We brought Sinead back home and placed her on a big bean bag in the centre of the room and sat side by side on the sofa. We looked at her, she looked at us, Eileen and I looked at each other. No words were spoken, even by Sinead, but we were all thinking the same thing. "What the bloody hell happens next?"

Two days later, in Germany, a much bigger reunion took place when East joined West and became one. They also looked at each other and thought what happens next. Much like us, they began the long process of coming to terms with changes in their lives.

We decided we were not going to let our parenthood become a prison sentence. We wanted to get out and about. Sinead's first experience of the high life (high in more ways than one) came a little more than three weeks after her arrival. Although to some it would appear a little foolhardy, we booked a night in a hotel in the Lake District.

Checking into the Rothay Garden hotel in Grasmere on October 23rd we got some funny looks, mainly from Sinead. We were a bit concerned that she might bawl the hotel down but stopped short of booking her into a separate room on the opposite side of the building. I suppose she was our responsibility.

The weather was beautifully autumnal in that special Lake District way. An eye-defying display of reds and yellows was conveniently arranged to stimulate our newborn. This wasn't to be her only stimulation. My propensity for taking inappropriate routes at inappropriate times hadn't been suppressed by the Coniston incident, apparently. We went for a walk and I had Sinead in a front sling or papoose. We were enjoying the freedom and fresh air and the bairn was fast asleep. As we amblechatted I followed the map carelessly with my usual disregard for contour lines. As the path returned along a ridge to Grasmere we had a little bit of déjà vu. Although nowhere near as steep or high as in Coniston, the trail descended suddenly. Fairly frictionless footwear and a slippery slope meant that we hadn't learnt much since our Tower of Pisa adventure either and I had to err on the side of caution on the descent. I used the friction of my backside to grant safe passage, so to speak. I was glad the baby was on the front, as I ended up lying almost horizontal on a couple of occasions. Sleeping soundly, she came to no harm during the mini-drama, which is more than can be said for my trousers and arse.

To celebrate our survival we went to the pub for a pint. The fire was roaring in the little bar as we entered. We sat on the wooden benches along the wall and laid Sinead out, still asleep. We had a drink. Life was sweet. Walking back to the hotel we congratulated ourselves on a day well-conceived and for remembering to pick Sinead up from the bench. It has been known for children to be left in pubs (even by prime ministers). Lost property baskets are full of them. Sinead was as good as gold that night and we all slept well. The fresh air and exercise had helped us. On returning home we agreed it was an experience worth repeating. I was thoroughly enjoying these run-free weekend excursions.

It was not long before we were getting more adventurous, in November, booking a whole weekend in a cottage in Middleham in the Yorkshire Dales. The ruins of Middleham Castle dominate the town. This fortress was once the home of Richard III but he didn't die in the castle. In 2012, bones, which appear to be his, were found under a car park in Leicester. How he got there is uncertain (his car has not been found). Richard was always portrayed as a small man, hunched and stunted. The bones found suggest that at one time he might have stood at 5' 8", tall by medieval standards. This recent revelation would have immediately scotched a theory I had, in 1990, for why there seemed to be an inordinate number of exceptionally small men in Middleham. I'd thought they must all be his descendants in one way or another. They seemed to be everywhere, appearing suddenly around corners, coming unexpectedly out of doorways and equally mysteriously disappearing into them. That night I fully expected them to come down the chimney of our little rented cottage, next to the blacksmiths in the centre of the town, so I kept the coal fire burning.

I did not have to harbour this concern for too long. At daybreak the next day we were awoken by the clatter of horseshoe iron on metalled road. Looking out of the window I saw an inordinate number of small men astride the same number of large, sleek, sinuous horses. We discovered that the town was the home to the Middleham Trainers Association and several horse trainers had their stables there. The horse racing business is still the town's biggest employer and many young jockeys live in the area.

That weekend we got out and walked as much as we could in the raw and misty weather. We had both been used to running regularly and walking was one way to make lack of mileage more bearable. We also hoped that being active early on with Sinead might somehow send a subliminal message to encourage her to be active when she was older. It was hard to tell whether this was working as the lazy little bugger just snoozed away in the warmth of my jacket.
Having two daughters now made me think about changes in society which would help improve their opportunities. In the UK we had shown that we were advanced enough to elect a woman as prime minister but Thatcher's politics meant that she was not interested in

woman's rights as a whole and she merely mimicked the anti-equality, macho style of male Conservatives. She brought nothing different to the table. It was a positive thing that a woman could be voted in as PM but bad that she could still be supported while she inflicted selfish and elitist politics on the majority of society. Her policies had encouraged the gap between the rich and poor to widen. She had put the brakes on progress towards equality in so many ways. However, the Poll Tax proved to be one unpopular policy too far and the last straw that broke the Thatch. On November 28th she was shown the exit door to Number 10 and at last we were rid of her. Although this event raised the spirits, it was not an excuse for a full-blown celebration because we were not yet rid of the Tories. John Major became PM. Most Conservatives sighed with relief as they realised that this coup d'état gave them a better chance of extending their stay in power.

Also in November 1990, in the land of precise clockmakers, men were showing they were way behind the times. In Appenzell Innerrhoden, Switzerland, women were at last allowed to have a vote on local issues but only because a group of female residents had filed a lawsuit in the Switzerland Federal Supreme Court to demand electoral equality.

Once I fancied that I was a blur when I ran but, at the beginning of December, life was a blur around me as if I was standing still. We literally didn't know whether we were coming or going. I can't remember doing a lot of going (out running); too little sleep and too much to do. Babies may be mini minors but they require major maintenance. We had the same experience as most new parents with an endless stream of visitors coming to view 'her majesty' (or 'her highness' when the nappy was ripe and pendulous) enthroned. Although I may have got out occasionally for a jog (when all was quiet on the newborn front) it became a rare event.

Poor Laura was also a bit shell-shocked. She had to get used to not being the only focus of her dad's attention and just as she was going through her own experience of starting secondary school. She quickly got over being ambivalent about Sinead's arrival and was soon volunteering to help with holding and nappy changing but for her the changing didn't finish there! In a short time, she wouldn't even be able to go home and get concentrated fuss off her mum. As fate would have it, which may have seemed a little cruel to her, her mum was also due to give birth early in the New Year. From being a single child she was to have two siblings within in the space of four months. She coped amazingly well.

We all struggled bleary-eyed towards Christmas. Eileen had run until she was eight months pregnant now lack of running began to make me feel like I was expecting. (Maybe I was expecting too much.) I tried to keep in touch with my friends from the club and got a nice surprise when I went to the awards ceremony in December. I was presented with a 'Performance of the Year' trophy for my London Marathon time. I thought I deserved it more for producing another human being than for running a few miles but then I suppose I would have had to share it with Eileen.

Sinead's birth at the beginning of the '90s heralded a radical change of life for Eileen and me but globally it was also the beginning of a period of shifting political landscapes and emerging technology which would transform the world. In December Tim Berners-Lee and Robert Cailliau began to flesh out the ideas contained in their World Wide Web Project. This would change how we disseminated information and communicated ideas and knowledge for ever. At that time I had no idea what all the fuss was about. We were engrossed in our own project; 'www//gabs'. The 'when will we // get any bloody sleep' project. Communications were also at the fore of another event in December. Workers digging the Channel Tunnel from opposite directions met somewhere beneath the English Channel/La Manche. That was lucky.

Conversely, lack of communication was at the root of an amusing experience Sinead and I shared in Liverpool just before Christmas. The Merseyside Police were no different to most police forces in the country at the time, the personal touch seemed to have been replaced by an ethos of suspicion and lack of subtlety in many of their dealings with the public. On a bitterly cold December day, Sinead and I decided (it was mainly her idea) to go into town to look for Christmas presents for her mum. We took the car, I drove. Having parked the car I put Sinead in the front sling, zipped up my jacket against the icy wind and off we went (me up the road, her to sleep). In the shops I browsed and she snoozed.

I was soon returning along the back streets to the car park. Suddenly a police van screeched to a halt over the kerb, perilously close to me. The back doors burst open and the first three of an unknown quantity of officers, sardined in the van, leapt out. The first one shouted aggressively, "What have you got under the jacket?" I was quick to react and unzipped my coat. "A baby," I half apologised. He seemed disappointed. Without another word but with admirable agility, the three de-vanned PC's pirouetted on black-booted soles and pushed their other huffing, puffing, cursing colleagues back into the vehicle they were about to exit. The doors slammed and the van roared off leaving me in a cloud of exhaust, chuckling. Sinead's nose twitched at the smell of the fumes but she continued to catch up on the beauty sleep the poor pet had missed out on during the night. This was police customer service at its best; no thought of an apology or a light hearted exchange. Also, worryingly, they obviously weren't interested in the possibility of people stealing babies!

(Reality hits me)

Remembering and writing about this year was almost as exhausting as living it. My running had, for the first time in eight years, gone on the back burner. It wasn't that I was planning to give up running altogether but I knew it was going to be a challenge to keep up some sort of reasonable standard. In less than 12 months we had gone from carefree couple to a full-on family.

We went down to Birmingham at Christmas. After Boxing Day I drove back to Liverpool alone and picked Laura up to take her to Brum, as usual. We were soon in Eileen's mum and dad's house with all the family there. I took a photo of Eileen, Laura and Sinead. I'd already taken many pictures of them together but, somehow, it was at that moment that reality hit me. This was now my life. 1990 had started with a fine for speedy driving and ended with an award for speedy running but the events in between had been the real story.

Chapter 10

1991 Sleepless in South Liverpool

"In recent years there has been a marked increase in the interest shown by working class boys in running. Let us suppose that a number of lads in the heart of town wish to go in for running and decide to form a harriers' club. Of course their first consideration is a suitable dress; usually a thin vest and running pants are the only garments worn. The colours being chosen, the members then arrange some spot where they can dress and return to when the run is over. When that is settled, it is probably agreed that there shall be a run one night a week, preparatory to the greater run on Saturday afternoons. After a stiff day's work in the foundry, factory, or warehouse, the members begin to turn up about 7-30 pm, to prepare for their run and by eight o'clock some dozen lads are ready for the adventure."

Apart from the somewhat archaic language and , of course, the total lack of female representation, this could easily have been a description of how many running clubs had sprung up over the country as a result of the road running boom of the '80s. It was in fact from a 1905 pamphlet written by Charles E. B. Russell entitled 'Hare and Hounds by Gaslight.' Russell was the Hon. Secretary of Heyrod Street Lads' Club and the report was part of a survey of Manchester 'lads' at work and play. So, as you can see, the 'jogging boom' was not an entirely original idea in the 1980s. Some things didn't appear to have changed much over 80 years, except for the inclusion of lasses.

Russell describes the lads running, "through Longsight and round by Fallowfield, objects of wonder and pity to many passers-by, the scorn of others; a cause of anger, I fear, to some whose placidity is upset by the rushing past of the leaders, and whose pity is not roused by the panting, but gamely struggling lad who follows some minute or two after, hopelessly out-classed, but still determined, with healthy British pluck, to go on to the bitter end."

Although not so unusual in the eighties, the sight of people running still seemed to bring out deep-seated disapproval in some. On one occasion when Eileen was gently jogging, seven months pregnant with Sinead, a man passing called her a 'silly girl'. She didn't know whether to be annoyed by the 'silly' or pleased by the 'girl'. In a race in Crosby on the Mersey shore I was in a group of runners pelting down the promenade and we whizzed passed a couple of extra mature ladies. One turned to the other and shook her head. On the following wind I heard, 'are they trying to kill themselves?' She looked about 90 and probably hadn't done a day's exercise in her life. Maybe she had a point!

Russell's lads were obviously what we would have described as 'fair weather runners' because he describes the scene if heavy rain came on; "they beat a retreat... retrace their steps, bedraggled and muddy, threading their way wearily through the streets; and passers-by regard them as suffering from some mild form of lunacy for disporting themselves in such a fashion on such a night." In our squad we went in for the full-on madness, running in all weathers and not just twice a week like those turn-of-the-century wimps.

But fear not, for although I presume in those days it would have been pretty lethal stuff, they came to no harm having been exposed to the Manchester rain, as shown by Russell's description of the après run routine; "once in the club and after a bath and a good rub down they are all right again, recounting gaily the humours of the hunt."

His examples of 'the humours of the hunt' reminded me of my own experiences. "How B nearly fell over a perambulator in such and such a street." I was always falling over or running into things. It was quite easy to get distracted by something going on by the side of the road or inside my head which made me less aware of what was actually in front of me. Lamp posts, bollards, cans, bricks, bottles, sticks and stones had all attacked me in the past. One time I was out for a long run with the lads and we were chatting away when an unexpected child, not much more than three years old, shot out of an alleyway on a tricycle. Everybody, bar me, managed to swerve around her. I was hemmed in by my running mates. Needing to take more dramatic evasive action, I hurdled the child and, while reminding myself that I needed to work on my landings, I went a-sprawling. This amused everyone except for me and the child who, although unhurt, went a-bawling. Everyone, including me, became more concerned about her state than mine. Worried that we might be blamed for harming her and not wanting to leave a child of such tender years playing unsupervised by the side of a busy road, we collectively wondered from whence she had come. I noticed an open gate in the alleyway. Leading the child to the gate we entered the yard where a burly man was tinkering with a motor bike. We explained our presence briefly and the child went over to the man, still crying. He grunted, barely acknowledging anyone, and got on with his urgent repair job. We left perplexed.

"Or how C was nearly struck by the umbrella of an irate lady who resented his quick passage." Although suffering the occasional mild verbal abuse I had never been assaulted while out running but I knew of a few people who had been threatened, chased or attacked by groups of bored youths or interested dogs. The nearest I came to it was when five of us were running through Walton, past a big gathering of scallywags lolling against a wall. From a distance their smirking asides to one another suggested there was ill-will afoot. The boldest scally made the mistake of selecting the Bard as a target for a trip. In a flash the aggressor was pinned to the wall at the neck, attached by way of the Bard's thick brick-scarred fingers. The Rugman glared at the rest of the bristling youths, stating calmly, "I bet your mate wished he hadn't done that." Meanwhile the Bard had finished his lecture on politeness, (which may have contained some strong language) and released pressure on the jugular. We carried on as if nothing had happened.

As to the subject of people 'resenting my quick passage', most folk were generally glad to see the back of me. However, while running, I always tried not to frighten people by coming past them too close or too quickly especially when approaching from behind. I generally tried to announce my presence by coughing and where possible gave civilians, especially women, a wide berth when I found myself on quiet streets or paths. Sometimes you couldn't help terrifying people if you came on them suddenly round a corner but the shock usually worked both ways. One particular incident of this type, which could have been avoided, involved all my training squad but was my fault.

We were out on one Tuesday night doing a fartlek session. Fartlek is a Swedish word literally translated as 'speed play.' It involved going out for a longish, easy run which included harder, faster sections of varying length and intensity. We would jog along slowly but also intermittently take turns to suggest a point to run to and at what pace. For example, someone might say "to the third lamppost, up-tempo," and off we would go. Once we had reached the suggested destination we would slow to a jog again, continuing en route until we had all recovered and regathered. Then it would be a different person's turn to suggest a target and speed. This was a 'fun' way to get in the miles and some quality running. I was always trying to get brain exercise into the equation by coming up with unusual challenges. That particular night we were running on a cycle path and I spotted a man in the distance cycling at a leisurely pace. "Right," I said, "flat out until we catch the bike!" Of course I hadn't considered what effect our pursuit would have on the cyclist when he heard rasping breaths and thundering feet coming up behind him. He must have thought he was being hunted down by a pack of werewolves. Needless to say, when we caught up with him his reaction wasn't great. He took off like a rocket, legs spinning like a Catherine Wheel, muttering curses St Catherine would have blushed at. It was an unplanned fartlek session for him and he probably set a PB for the journey home but I just hoped we hadn't shortened his life by too much. As with our 1905 counterparts, these 'humours of the hunt' became well told tales embellished at each telling.

Charles Russell concluded his report by extolling the benefits of running:

"It is no bad sign, however that young lads are willing to spend their evenings in this way. There is a certain amount of moral courage required to face the streets at all, under such conditions; the practice of running merely for the sake of exercise-for there are no prizes-is turning youthful energy into a right and healthy channel."

He held up running as a more noble pursuit than football, mainly because he observed that most of the 'harriers' didn't smoke. Whereas, " in a football team of rough lads, sixteen to eighteen years of age, I have seen perhaps half a dozen of them light a cigarette at half time, or a full back even puffing his smoke during the progress of the game. But one can generally point out the moral in such cases with some effect, for a 'half-time' cigarette smoking team can rarely 'stay' the latter part of the game, if the match be at all hotly contested."

It would certainly be hotly contested if fag-ash Frank stubbed someone in the eye while going up for a header! It is sad to think that, for many of these 'lads', attempts to develop a healthy lifestyle would have been to no avail as ten years later they would be senselessly losing their young lives on the battlefields of Europe.

After the first three months of 1991, I came to feel like one of Russell's stragglers, "gamely struggling, hopelessly outclassed but still determined." Having a six-month-old excreta machine who distracted me by laughing all day and crying all night didn't help but the wood spirits of Delamere also worked against me; more of this later.

The year started with resolve which gradually dissolved in an acid bath of circumstance. I started to record mileage again in an attempt to encourage myself to get back into shape, post-Sinead. It was hard to believe it was only eight months since I had been running a PB in the London Marathon. It felt like eight years. The New Year brought a bad cold. This was the start of a familiar pattern and I only managed a pathetic 14 miles in the first week.

I was back at the club training with the blackstuff boyos. 'Sadly' I couldn't do any speed training with Rugman and DJ because I conveniently managed to tweak my ankle coming out of the sports centre; avoidance tactics if you ask me and I should know because I was doing the avoiding. I did manage to piece together 70 miles in the second week of the year. It was quite hard to get a decent weekly mileage while not doing a long run at the weekend when I was too busy enjoying fatherhood with youngest and oldest daughters.

The Helsby Half crept up on me again, which is quite surprising because you could smell it a mile off. I completed it running as hard as I could. My time indicated how much fitness and how much ground on my club mates I had lost in less than a year. My 75:20 was four minutes slower than 1990. I was behind Rugman who did 71 minutes and DJ who broke the club record again with another sub 70 minute run.

The race was also significant in that it would be my last race as a 'senior'. After this month I would be competing as an over 40 veteran. My diary announced that; "I am slowly getting back into it." Ha, so funny! I was trying to fit in the miles where I could. One day at the end of the month I ran three times; five miles early in the morning, seven miles at dinner time at work and a speed session, which amounted to eight miles, with the lads at the club; 20 miles in the day. This was after developing a stomach bug the previous weekend. I was certainly trying to look like I was being serious about my running.

The UN and the US were also 'trying' to look like they were serious about freedom. In January the UN unanimously condemned Israel's treatment of the Palestinians, but that's as far as it went. Later in the month, the US Congress authorised the use of force to liberate Kuwait from Iraqi forces. Operation Desert Storm began. Of course, the imbalance in the degree of proactive intervention in the two scenarios had nothing to do with Kuwait's oil reserves or the special relationship the US had with Israel.

February arrived and the British government were reminded, like it or not, there was still a war going on at home. The Provisional IRA launched a mortar attack on number 10 Downing Street during a meeting of the War Cabinet. Windows were blown out but fortunately no one was injured. Nearly two weeks later bombs exploded at Paddington and Victoria stations. It appeared that the Provisional IRA had changed tactics and reverted to attacking civilian targets again. They had issued warnings and the bomb exploded at Paddington without injury at 4.20 a.m. At about 7am, a man 'with an Irish accent' phoned the London Transport travel centre with a warning in which he said: "We are the Irish Republican Army. Bombs to go off at all mainline stations in 45 minutes."

Forty minutes later, a bomb hidden in a litter bin on the main concourse at Victoria exploded as police were carrying out a search.

The station had been kept open and the rush hour was at its height. Tragically, one man was killed by shrapnel and 38 injured.

The bombings were condemned from all sides of the political spectrum but Jimmy Knapp, general secretary of the rail union, RMT, also questioned the security arrangements. "There was a three-hour time difference between the explosions at Paddington and Victoria. If there was a direct warning 40 minutes before the Victoria explosion, what were the police doing?"

Home secretary Kenneth Baker called the bombings 'acts of murderous criminals' and the IRA condemned the authorities for causing casualties by "the cynical decision......not to evacuate railway stations named in secondary warnings." It was nearly twenty years since Bloody Sunday, when thirteen unarmed civil rights protesters were shot and killed by British soldiers in Derry. This had been a catalyst which played a crucial part in the onset of the IRA bombing campaign. The government still refused to recognise this political problem in their own country and the IRA still relied on violent tactics to try to force Westminster to accept their grievances.

The following month on March 14th, reminding us of the authority's previous ill-considered responses to the 'Irish problem,' six Irishmen were released from prison after being falsely imprisoned for 16 years. Their convictions, secured in 1975, were quashed by the Court of Appeal after dubious evidence and confessions beaten out of the men were finally declared unsafe and unsatisfactory. The six had been accused and convicted of planting bombs in pubs in Birmingham which killed 21 people and injured 182. In an atmosphere of anti-Irish hysteria at the time, the government wanted a conviction and the forces of law and order gave them one, albeit a bogus one. It seemed anyone would do, providing they were Irish

It had been a difficult time for Irish people living in England. Eileen's father had come to England as a young man and had lived and worked in Birmingham most of his life. In spite of this, at the time of the pub bombings, he experienced incidents of hostility and resentment from some people who had known him for a long time. It was hard to believe that in 1991 this conflict still continued.

Two weeks after the Birmingham Six were released, back in Liverpool, dismay was caused by another miscarriage of justice. The Popper inquiry into the deaths at Hillsborough announced its findings. Relatives had been hoping the jury of seven men and four women would return a verdict of unlawful killing or at least an open verdict. The jury found, by a majority of 9-2, in favour of accidental death. Families of the victims stated that they would continue to fight for "justice" and hoped to take out private prosecutions against individual police officers and the South Yorkshire force. Outside the courtroom the relatives held a press conference. Chairman of the Hillsborough Family Support Group Trevor Hicks, whose two daughters, Sarah, 19, and Victoria, 15, had died in the tragedy, said the verdict was "lawful but immoral". I thought of my own daughters and admired the dignified manner in which he continued his struggle to reveal the real truth.

The effect on the families involved in these failures of the judicial system totally put into perspective a few minor problems I was having of my own at the time. On Sunday, March 9th I ran a cross country race in the morning and produced a so-so performance. I didn't feel particularly tired so in my quest for 'fitness' I planned to do another run in the afternoon. Eileen had been invited to take Sinead to an afternoon party, celebrating the birthday of a work colleague's daughter. The problem was that this colleague had inconveniently decided to live close to Delamere forest 25 miles and a 45 minute drive from our house. It would have been a drag to drive there, come home and drive back again so I decided to drop them off for the few hours of the party and use the intervening time to go for a run in the forest. It seemed like a decent plan with a heavy stress on the 'seemed.'

Delamere forest is a remnant of the ancient greenwoods of Mara and Mondrem which, bounded by the Gowy, Weaver and Mersey rivers, covered over 60 square miles in the 11th century. As hunting grounds of the Norman Earls of Chester the area had been subject to the forest law, which had greatly limited agricultural use for many years. Ownership passed to the Crown in 1812 and then to the Forestry Commission, which now managed the woodland.

Delamere is a place of sphagnum moss, mysterious mists, will-o'-the-wisps and the occasional ice cream van. Unlike ice-cream the place can be dark and forbidding. Blakemere Moss oozes and bubbles like a primeval soup. Black Lake is a schwingmoor or 'quaking bog', a rare occurrence which can form in wetlands and sometimes around the edges of acidic lakes. The bog vegetation, mostly moss, anchored by sedges, forms a mat about half a metre thick, floating over water or wet peat. Walking on this surface can cause it to move; larger movements can encourage visible ripples on the surface and make trees sway. This bog mat can eventually cover entire bays and even small lakes. The forest was a place of mirage and illusion. That day I entered this realm in all innocence.

From the car park I set out to run four miles out into the forest and four miles back along the same route. It was pleasant to run in a different environment and the weather was ideal; still and overcast. I turned around at the approximate four mile mark, to head back, and suddenly felt tired. This was not surprising considering the number of miles I had completed and the number of sleeping hours I hadn't, the previous week. A diary entry had pleaded for understanding, "spirit weak, flesh weak, mind weak, haven't slept for a week." February had seen me run just short of 300 miles. I had reason to be fatigued but the result was that I lost concentration. Three miles to go and I was thinking about how knackered I was, how I could murder a pint and how I wasn't sure if this was the right way back. My head was a maze of tangled thoughts and under cover of this mind mess the green goblins attacked. From the pine scented forest floor a woody limb was thrust across my path. My ankle turned and, with a cracking sound like kindling on a fire, I was felled. I swear I heard a cackling laugh.

The initial electric message of pain had been received and read, leaving a dull echoing throb. I sat up and assessed the damage. I was taken back to Tenterhook football days and my 'mate' Psycho Mike. It didn't feel great. Getting up on to my feet, I knew I had to get back to the car, to get back to the party, to get back to Eileen and Sinead, to get back home. I managed to work up a painful hobble to progress and eventually reached the car park in record worst time. I fetched my wallet from the car and purchased the biggest ice lolly (or lolly-ice if you're from Merseyside) money could buy from the man in the opportune ice cream van. He looked bemused as I proceeded to attach the cold confection to my ankle with a bit of crepe bandage I'd found in my kit bag. I hopped to the car and went to pick up Eileen and Sinead.

I was lucky that the wood spirits had targeted my right leg. As I drove I could still change gear unhindered and now that the ankle was fairly numb I found I was able to brake well enough in normal circumstances. I managed to get everyone home safely although I did feel woozy on a couple of occasions. The ice lol seemed to do its job and kept the swelling at bay. I was lucky really because a little bird told me that if they hadn't got me with the tree root the hobgobshites had a schwingmoor lined up next.

It seemed running was going to be out for a while but it turned out to be a little longer than I anticipated. I limped painfully through work on Monday. If anything the ankle was worse on Tuesday, with the swelling spreading up the shin. My bloated leg resembled a Dulux colour chart for the Contusion Collection; from Pulverised Purple through Battered Blue to Gangrene Green. On Wednesday I decided to go to the doctor before school. He sent me to have an X-ray in Sefton General hospital. 'Results at the doctor's on Monday', they said as I hobbled off to work. On Thursday my leg felt better until I got home from school when the doctor's surgery rang to tell me I had a fracture of the ankle and that I needed to go to casualty the next day. This made my leg feel worse.

Friday was a momentous day as it marked the first time in the ten years I had been working at my school, that I had a 0 next to my name in the register. I had just blotted my copybook, falling down (literally) on one of my strongest professional skills; the ability to turn up! In the hospital they put a temporary back slab plaster on my leg and made me an appointment with the specialist on Monday. I hopped off on crutches and counted the two mile distance home as part of my mileage.

On Monday, a week after my arboreal attack I talked to the specialist. He showed me my X-ray and explained how the overstretching ligaments had pulled at and fractured the bone as the ankle twisted and how he would have to put a full plaster cast on to help repair the damage. I had seen the kind of muscle atrophy which resulted from wearing a full plaster and virtually begged the doctor to reconsider. I also knew that minor bone damage could heal quicker than sprained ligaments in the right circumstances. He could see how desperate I was to avoid being plastered and I could see him waver. After further discussion he consented to put an extra tight supportive bandage on the ankle instead of plaster. He also forced me to sign a contract, written indelibly on my outer thigh as a reminder, in which I promised not to put any weight on the joint or blame on him for permanent damage to it. I was pleased. However the whole experience had taken its toll. I almost immediately contracted a flu bug and, shortly after that, a urinary infection. It was as if my body was not just telling me to slow down but stop right there, right then. I obeyed.

My first post-fracture run was on April 2nd a month after the accident. In all I had one and a half weeks off work. You don't have a day off for ten years and then nine come along at once. My first week's running produced ten miles and a cold, not the return I was hoping for. In the second week in April progress was slow, I ran 24 miles. The entry in my running diary suggested how I felt about my running:

Monday 8th April <u>Type of run</u>…Easy limp <u>Time</u>…2 ½ years <u>Comments</u>…Ran at 9:30 pm after getting Sinead to sleep

The third week I ran 41 miles. I had taken my crutches back to the fracture clinic and the doctor gave me the, ahem, official green light to run again. The last week in April I ran 44 miles and finished off with a 10k race in 37: 42, which I found encouraging. I was feeling stronger by the day.

In May I managed four races, two 10ks, a five miler and a half marathon. The first run in the month turned out to be the best as I ran 35:50 and was third vet over 40. I deemed this progress. (Laura, now 12, did the accompanying 2k fun run and was fourth female, which gave her great joy). Instead of kicking on from there my racing times got worse, including a personal worst half marathon time. I just wasn't running enough mileage or quality sessions. The last race of the month was another 10k where I ran 36:40, way behind DJ and

Rugman and another member of our club who I didn't even know. How dare he? My ankle still hurt but my pride hurt more.

At the end of the month Eric Heffer, who lived at the end of our road, died aged 69. He was Labour Member of Parliament for Liverpool Walton from 1964 until his death. Born in Hertford he came from a working-class background and was previously a joiner. Seeing the Jarrow March (and possibly my grandfather) passing through Hertford in 1936 had a profound effect upon him and went towards developing his socialist ideas. He was recognised as an honest and diligent MP who stuck adamantly to his left wing views, fiercely opposing the party leader, Neil Kinnock, who he felt was attempting to strip the Labour Party of its socialism. His constituency was where my running club was based and had the largest absolute Labour vote in the country with a rock solid 23,000 majority. He defended Liverpool's local left wing politicians against the criticism of the national Labour Party, in particular Kinnock's rants. Although having been ill for some time, in January 1991 he attended the House of Commons, in a wheelchair, to vote against the Iraq war. It was a measure of the respect he had from all politicians that John Major, the Conservative PM, crossed the floor to shake his hand. In March 1991 he was awarded the freedom of the City of Liverpool.

Eric Heffer was an old school Labour politician but that didn't mean that all his ideas were unsuited for modern times. Sections of the Labour Party seemed hell bent on changing its socialist image in order to give it a broader appeal. All they were achieving was making it unappealing to everyone. Also deemed unsuitable for modern times, three days before Heffer's death, the Sutton Manor Colliery in St Helens finally closed; here the last example of a steam-driven winding engine in the country wound up for the last time.

Meanwhile I seemed to be winding down. As summer approached my running took a summarily summery approach. It has been written that Eastern European long distance running coaches in the '50s and '60s favoured visualisation techniques as part of their regimes. When training got tough, or the body started to hurt in a race, the athletes were encouraged to imagine they were somewhere else, in a comfortable place; in an armchair by a warm fire or lying on a beach in the sun. They believed that to allow your mind to dwell on your body's deteriorating condition, encouraged the body to shut down. My approach to training at this point was similar but at the same time different. I spent much of the summer lying on a beach imagining I was running.

June wasn't too bad with 54, 54, 41 and 49 mile weeks although the second 54 mile week did include a 26 mile long run. I was ticking over but not training consistently or improving after my disrupted spring training. At the end of the month I did the Selby Marathon, a flat fast course. I am not sure why I had entered. I can only imagine I was drugged and bundled into the back of a van and driven to East Yorkshire. I certainly seemed to be seeking another fix of the marathon drug. I don't know what I was thinking. I knew I was in no shape to run 26 miles competitively. It was also clear that I hadn't come with the intention of jogging around because I managed to reach 20miles in two hours and six minutes. Had I continued at this pace I would have finished in a respectable time of two hours and forty five minutes. Inevitably at 20 miles I ground to a halt. The idea of how nice it would be to end the discomfort had started to creep into my head at about 17 miles. Once inside the head the idea was unstoppable, spreading like impetigo and sending insidious messages to every extremity. Suddenly the brain shouted STOP and the body obeyed. It was like a plug had been pulled. What many people don't realise is how hard it is to start running again, in a marathon, once you have stopped. It is as if, in that split second of stopping, your mind erases the knowledge of how to run; muscles go on strike, refusing to recommence previously painful repetitive work.

I spent the next six miles jogging and walking. I had completed the first 20 miles at 6:18 mile pace; the last six were 10 minute miles. Some, who believe in its existence, may think I hit 'The Wall', but in truth I had been plastering over the cracks in my training in an attempt to kid myself that things had gone smoothly enough to complete a reasonable marathon. Twelve months after 2:35 in London I finished the run in 3:06 with a phoney smile on my face which said, 'Yeah, I am an overambitious idiot.' No wall, just lack of preparation and too much gung ho. I daresay I could have run the whole way had I selected a more realistic pace. Rugman, DJ and Testerman all finished way ahead of me and to add insult to pride injury I was the fourth counter for our club as we won 3rd team prize. We each won a splendid towel, which was handy because, at that moment, I wanted to throw it in!

My disappointment was submerged by sad news that filtered through to us after the race. A runner had died of a heart attack out on the course. The poignancy of these sad tidings increased for me when I found out that it was someone I had been chatting to beforehand. He was an acquaintance I had bumped into at many races. He was no novice but an experienced runner in his thirties. On the way home I reflected on the dangers which lurked for everyone in our sport. The incident had put my bad performance into context.

July was always a busy month at school with parents' evenings, reports to write and sports days to arrange. As the total of days to breaking up got lower and lower the kids got higher and higher (perhaps at the thought of not seeing me for six weeks or in the case of those going to secondary school, ever again). On Wednesday July 17th my diary reads;

'Type of run…? Distance run…0 miles Time…0 minutes Comments…Sports Day and disillusioned with running'

I think this statement offered a double excuse for not getting out to train. I did run a few days afterwards but my mood hadn't lightened. 'Comments…Lucky I even bothered doing it. No motivation'

What a sorry state I was in. One thing that had contributed to this mood was a recent attempt to run in a five mile race. I had stopped after 400 metres for no other reason than I didn't feel like running. Stopping in a marathon was one thing but quarter of a mile into a short race was unforgiveable. This was a first time experience and not great for morale.

August was a missing month in my training diary. We spent most of it on the beaches of North Wales and the amount of running done didn't warrant recording. Most days consisted of plonking Sinead on the sand to see how much of it she could eat, while Laura, Eileen and I played a variety of games, splashed in the sea or explored the rock pools. We occasionally checked on the baby to be sure she hadn't removed an environmentally unacceptable amount of beach. While we busied ourselves at being physically active outdoors, the electronics industry busied itself trying to encourage the young to stay inactive, indoors. On June 23rd Sonic the Hedgehog was released and proved impossible to recapture. A month later on August 23rd Super Nintendo hit the shops.

As we holidayed, The Times newspaper reported that every job vacancy was being chased by 22 people but still the Tory government trundled on. One possible factor which helped them stay in power was indicated by a poll in September which revealed that the majority of people thought that Neil Kinnock was a liability and would hinder the Labour Party's chances at the next election. What a surprise!

Too soon the summer was over and it was back to school for me and for Laura. She was starting her second year at Calderstones Comprehensive School, formerly called Quarry Bank High School. A group of young boys from the school once formed a band and named themselves the Quarrymen, after words in the first line of the school song. The leader of the band, John Lennon, was soon to form a group called the Beatles. They became quite famous in the '60s. Laura had taken up the flute but as yet had shown no desire to become a musical legend.

She had settled well at school and loved it. Calderstones' intake was from a wide and mixed sweep of South Liverpool, including inner-city areas, but its location was in the leafy suburb of Allerton, next to the beautiful Calderstones Park. In the 19th century some of the most magnificent merchant houses in Merseyside were built in Allerton, when it was still the countryside. It became one of the wealthiest Victorian suburbs of Liverpool. Many of the houses had been demolished, but the gothic Quarry Bank built in 1866-7 for timber merchant James Bland and the Italianate Hartfield mansion built in the late 1840s, now formed part of Calderstones School, sitting alongside modern buildings.

The extensive estates of these buildings and that of Calderstones House were joined to form Calderstones Park. Calderstones House was built in 1828 for Joseph Need Walker, a lead shot manufacturer. In 1875 the house and estate were acquired for £52,000 by Charles McIver, a partner in the shipping company 'Cunard'. It is a Grade II Listed building. The story (mine) goes that when McIver was showing an acquaintance around his smart new house he was asked how he could afford such a grand residence. "I work for Cunard," he stated succinctly. His friend responded, "I work f..cking hard too but I still couldn't afford this."

Most of my early morning runs consisted of a mile run to the park and a couple of laps of its mile and three quarters perimeter. The mixture of mature woodlands and grass or wood chip trails encircling the lake made it a delight to run there. Also located in the park were carefully tended, walled English and Japanese gardens and a collection of green houses with tropical plants. One of these greenhouses was home to the Calder Stones, which the park and school were named after.

It's probably true to say that most people in Liverpool are unaware that some large stones (the largest about eight feet tall) from the late Neolithic age/early Bronze age (around 2000 B.C.) can be found in their own city. They are potentially as old as parts of Stonehenge and some archaeologists believe they make up one of the most decorative monuments (or remains of) in mainland Britain. Although their existence is not common knowledge these remains have been known about for some time. It was in the early nineteenth century that the stones (along with ancient urns and a collection of bones) were unearthed and moved. One was erected in his field by a local farmer for cattle to rub up against. This was in a time when a new-found interest in amateur archaeology caused, in the words of one horrified observer, "artefacts to be picked from the ground like potatoes." People were aware of many monuments but unaware of the importance of studying their sites and carefully collecting and collating evidence to explain their function. Lack of care and consideration for ancient remains was commonplace. As recent as the early 1870s the South Western Railways planned to build a line through the Stonehenge site stating the 'fact' that Stonehenge was "entirely out of repair and not the slightest use to anyone now", in defence of the proposal,

Back in Liverpool it wasn't until the late nineteenth century that interest in the origins and purpose of our own mini-Stonehenge developed. By then only six sandstone blocks (adorned with decorative markings or 'stone art') remained and these had already been moved from their original site, the whereabouts of which experts were now unsure. Rival Victorian archaeologists got hot under their high starched collars debating whether the stones were originally part of a stone circle or the supporting structure of a collapsed tomb. Passions were aroused enough for a Professor Herdman to write to the Liverpool Daily Post on November 17th, 1896 and ask the editor to allow the newspaper to be used as a discussion forum for the raging 'Tomb or Circle' debate. There was a flurry of heated letters on the subject for several weeks afterwards. The tomb theory proved to be the most likely explanation although, when recovered, the remaining stones had been placed in a circle (and still are) because at that time it was presumed that this is how they were originally arranged.

By the time I was circumnavigating the park in 1991 the stones had been sited in a dilapidated greenhouse. They had been there since 1964. Before then they were to be found outdoors, on a circular, walled plot outside the park gates. The council moved them indoors to prevent further atmospheric erosion which had started to damage the delicate sandstone surfaces. Because of lack of funding they continued to deteriorate in damp greenhouses, neglected, unheralded and largely inaccessible to the general public.

As I ran past the stones' obscure resting place I thought about the men or women who had originally worked on their surfaces, chipping away, making the delicate designs. Maybe they had been attending a special Stone Art workshop. As they worked they might have been wondering how interested people would be in their creations, thousands of years in the future (if they could wonder up to a thousand). What they already knew was that no-one would be interested in the work of Ug, the crazy man, bashing away alone in the corner. He was making some kind of circular thing with a hole in the middle. What use would that be to anyone?

Anyway that was ancient history, as was my high mileage regime. Although I had done little or no training over summer, come September I felt compelled to continue the tradition of completing my home town marathon. It had taken a break in 1990 but was back for its 9th staging in 1991. This time I decided to approach the race sensibly and treat it like a training run. I had been persuaded by my club mates to enter a marathon in October and I needed to get some miles in before then. This was an opportunity. The course had been changed to a two lap course around the streets of South Liverpool which suited me as it meant we would miss the dreaded monotony of the dock road and I could drop out conveniently near home if the going got too tough. As it was I completed the course with relative ease at a comparatively leisurely pace.

In a time of 3:09:49, slower than my second Mersey marathon of 1983, I strolled over the line in 106th position. The positive side to this run was that, because I hadn't taken too much out of myself, I was able to run 230 miles in the next three weeks, getting some stamina into my legs before the next race which was going to be a challenge, on top of the challenge of running 26 miles; the Snowdonia Marathon. In the words of the organisers; "The course encircles Snowdon and the very hilly route is complemented by the vagaries of the Welsh weather. At 21 miles the Welsh Wall has to be experienced to be believed." Jeff Norman five times winner in the '80s and at the time a well-known figure on the national marathon running scene had this to say about the route; "The Snowdonia Marathon course is the most dramatic, most challenging, most enjoyable of all the courses I have run."

We decided to make a weekend of the trip to Wales and hired a cottage near to Llanberis and the start of the race. The timing was convenient in that half-term week followed the run, allowing us to elongate the weekend and give me more time to recover. I was looking forward to it. Annoyingly, the week before, I was accosted by yet another cold, which put a dampener on my enthusiasm. A combination of my own school's parents' evenings and attendance at Laura's first school prize-giving evening meant I had little time for running. This was probably a good thing considering the way I was feeling.

We travelled down to Wales on the Saturday, met up with one of Eileen's sisters and her family and settled in the rented cottage. We were so lucky. Sunday morning greeted us, blue, crisp and still. No need to contend with vague weather, it was making its intent clear. A few of the lads had made the trip down from Liverpool to do the race. DJ and Rugman were still running well and leaving me in their vapour trail. For a change I was sensible enough to realise that I wouldn't be competing with them that day. It would be me against the course, as it would be for most of the runners. I wanted to perform reasonably well but run easily enough to enjoy the wonderful scenery.

We gathered at Nant Peris, at an altitude of 300ft, for the start. Everyone who had read the information provided before the race would have known that in the first four miles the course climbed to 1100ft, to the top of Llanberis Pass at Pen-y-Pass. It was one thing being aware of it but another to actually experience it. There was no way to ease your lungs and legs into the race. It didn't help that my chest was tight with phlegm. The crest of the hill seemed to continuously move further away like the mirage of an oasis to a lost Legionnaire.

After much gasping and hacking, I reached the top and my lungs heaved a sigh of relief. My mind rejoiced at the visual reward for the climb; a panoramic view of rumpled hills, bobbling away to the north and east and the monstrous Snowdon looming in the west. Next came the descent, 900ft in 8 miles to Beddgelert. Just over 45 minutes of the most exhilarating running experiences I'd had in a marathon. I didn't want it to end, partly because it was so effortless and scenic and partly because I knew I would have to pay for my enjoyment. The road slipped sumptuously down the valley passing lakes Gwynant and Dinas, like diamonds in the palms of Snowdon's massif hands.

The blood rushing around my body heightened my ocular reception. Everything sharpened to pin-point clarity, focussed by sun and sensuousness. I was descending through some kind of heaven knowing that some kind of hell would follow the fall. We reached the nadir in Beddgelert which, appropriately for the race, is named after a last resting place. The English translation is Grave of Gelert and is so called because of a legendary occurrence there in the valley. A short walk south of the village, following the footpath along the banks of the river Glaslyn, is 'Gelert's Grave'. According to legend, the stone monument in the field marks the resting place of 'Gelert', the faithful hound of medieval Welsh Prince Llewelyn the

Great. On the grave an inscription tells the shaggy dog's tale. Forget that, I will give you my version.

One morning in the 13th Century (sorry I can't be more accurate) for some reason Prince Llewelyn had to leave his son at home, alone. Maybe he had to pop down to the shops for some fags or go to the pub to see a man about another dog because Gelert was getting on a bit, I don't know. I do know that Llewelyn was too tight to pay for a childminder so he left the dog in charge. Now at that time, in that area of North Wales, wolves did roam. They didn't walk or run like everyone else. Roaming was their speciality. But for now the wolves were dunroamin' because, having sniffed out baby food, they came a-knockin'.

It was obvious that the three little pigs hadn't contacted Gelert recently because for some reason he decided to let the wolves into the castle. It is said he was fooled because they were posing as double glazing salesmen and he was after a quote for the arrow slits in the South Tower. Anyway, when he found out he wasn't going to get the manager's special 'today only' bargain price, all hell let loose. The wolves were just there for a free lunch and the sad thing is Gelert probably would have cut them a deal if they'd fitted his windows.

Sometime later the room looked like a Tarantino set. The wolves were beaten and those who survived fled. Gelert had decided to have a little lie down, after all the bloody tooth and clawing. This was bad timing because just then Prince Llewlyn returned and saw Gelert covered in blood, looking sleepy and no sign of the baby. The Prince must have had too much stupid juice because, as the Welsh say, he put *dau* and *dau* together to make *pump*. He didn't ask any questions and the death of the dog by his sword was the result of his innumeracy and lack of an enquiring mind.

With the dog well dead, Llewelyn heard the baby cry and he found it behind the sofa, unharmed, playing with the entrails of a dead wolf. On finding the babe alive he was full of remorse. He had just killed his free child care. He felt so bad that he left the cat in charge and went back down the pub. When he came back that evening there was a funny smell and having checked the baby's nappy realised it must be the dead dog. He buried Gelert by the river and legend says he never smiled again... nothing could get those stains out of his favourite Persian rug.

He had even less to smile about when the baby grew up and learned to talk. The toddler reported his dad to the authorities for child neglect and cruelty to animals. Alas, Llewelyn was the authorities and let himself off with a suspended sentence. He went down the pub to celebrate and may have indulged in a sly smirk, so legend has it.

Having knowledge of the route after Beddgelert, I girded my loins, in true 13th century fashion, as the route heaved. I knew I was running within myself because I had experienced enjoyment. We pitched past lake Gadair and lake Cwellyn then through Rhyd-Ddu (a place famous as a starting point for walks up Snowdon and for consecutive d's). Salem and Betws Garmon followed as we ran northwest. Then we turned east towards the Welsh Wall. There was a rapid climb to 1200 ft. at Bwlch-y-Groes, a section of unmetalled road and then a steep descent into Llanberis and the finish.

(Overcoming Snowdon with help from family and Sugar the dog)

I was surprised at how easy I found it to get over the mythical 'Welsh Wall' and also how much I suffered on the final descent. I had to slow on the downhill section not because I was exhausted but because I thought my joints would combust from being forced to work beyond their capacity, like pistons on a runaway train. After this punishing section the last half mile consisted of a gentle incline but the sudden change to going upwards again made it one of the hardest bits of the course. I gritted my teeth and completed the course, relieved rather than distressed, and in a satisfactory time of 3:01:29 and 33rd place.

Rugman and DJ had finished 5 minutes in front of me, in that order. I found them sitting against a wall in the sunshine. I slumped next to them and we swapped stories about our individual races. An ancient local wandered up to us as we satchatted. Looking intently at us he eventually enquired, "Will yee be doing it again next year?" Rugman looked up from beneath dark brows and spoke straight-faced from under a darker moustache. "Can we have a couple of beers before we commit ourselves?" It certainly was early days to decide whether you would ever run again, never mind another marathon, never mind Snowdon. Crossing the finish line of a marathon usually evoked the thought 'never again'. To be honest as much as I enjoyed the experience it would take more than a couple of beers to entice me back to Llanberis next year (maybe three).

As I slowly recovered after the race, Sinead and Eileen contracted the throw-ups. It was the first time I'd seen Sinead vomit full on, not such a novelty in Eileen's case. There is little in this world as spectacular as an infant's vomit; so much volume from such a small container. Meanwhile I coughed my way to a 32 mile week, which looking back, everything considered, wasn't too disastrous. The next week I caught the coat tails of the family stomach bug and ceased all strenuous activity for a couple of days. I managed to sleep for twelve hours on the second night which set me right but Sinead was still unwell. I took another morning off work to take her to the doctors; she had a chest infection. Kids who'd have them? In spite of all these shenanigans I managed to run 34 miles, ending the week with a trip to Llandudno on the North Wales coast to run a ten mile race in 58 minutes and ten seconds. My diary observation was "felt comfortable most of the way round but when I tried to push there was nothing there." After the two weeks I'd just experienced I really don't know what I expected.

In the six weeks leading up to Christmas I somehow amassed some mileage. I ran just under 400 miles, averaging around 65 miles a week. This included two weekends with no running because of trips by car to Middlesbrough and Birmingham. In spite of broken sleep with Sinead's awakeness, I was still trying to fit in runs twice a day, running in the morning or dinnertime to supplement my evening run. By the time Christmas came I was running on empty. Well, that's not quite true.

On Sunday December 15th the club held their annual Christmas handicap race. Donning my Santa hat and pulling my Beano marathon boxer shorts over my purple Traksters I set off (looking like a kid's comic on legs) to run the five miles from our house to Walton Park and the sports centre. I got a few strange looks on the way there but not as many as I would attract on the way back, when my running would be more comic than my outfit. After running the five mile handicap race in sub six minute miles I popped into the sport's centre bar for a quick Christmas pint with my club mates and friends. Having been 'forced' to consume four pints of Murphy's stout, I said a slurred and seasonal farewell to "the bessie mates anyone could have in the whole wide world" (with exaggerated arm movements for emphasis) and set off home, running on a full tank.

Needless to say my speed was a little less than ten miles an hour by now. In fact, my miles were a little more than miles. I must have added an extra couple to the official distance with my meandering. It was like running with my legs in syrup trousers wearing a helmet made of Fuzzy Felt. My feet kept hitting the ground some time before my brain announced their landing. It was terribly confusing. But I had to spare a thought for the pedestrians I passed, they looked mystified. On the plus side, when I did eventually arrive home I was totally sober.

But my world was changing. Deep down I knew it but I was determined to have a go at trying to see how long I could have the best of both worlds with my running and my family. I knew in my heart I couldn't keep training at same intensity. My diary sent a short message to myself on the 18th of December. "Felt very tired, hectic lifestyle." Something would have to give.

Society was also changing but in many ways with astonishing reluctance. Prospects for women continued to improve and there had been more movements towards equality. We'd already had a female prime minister and on the December 16th Stella Rimington was announced as the first female director general of MI5. Also this year the Boy Scouts suggested maybe girls were capable of tying knots and building campfires and allowed them membership. In June, Julie Ann Gibson had become the first woman to qualify as a pilot with the Royal Air Force. And yet, it had taken until October 23rd 1991 for Law Lords in this country to change the presumption that had existed since 1736 that women agree to sexual intercourse on marriage and could not retract that consent. Spousal rape finally became a crime in England and Wales.

Princess Diana was also helping to highlight issues clouded by prejudice when in August she attended the funeral of Adrian Ward-Jackson, her friend who died of Aids. The death in December of Freddie Mercury, lead singer of the group Queen, from the same virulent disease, brought it further into the spotlight. 'Bohemian Rhapsody', a track off the album 'A Night at the Opera', had stayed at the top of the UK Singles Chart for nine weeks when first released in 1975. When rereleased in December 1991 following Mercury's death, it stayed at number one for another five weeks eventually becoming the UK's third best-selling single of all time. Proceeds from the rerelease were donated to the Terence Higgins Trust. Although not a real fan of Freddie's music, I would soon hear it again in happy circumstances, in our household.

From December the 21st to the 31st I showed extreme dedication and devoted myself to getting into the festive spirit, not to mention the ale. I did one run of 12 miles and little else. I thoroughly enjoyed the run but enjoyed the 'little else' more. I'd managed to catch another cold just before Christmas but it did not stop me having a joyous holiday. In a way it was a great relief just to say to myself 'don't even think about going for a run.' I felt I deserved a rest and fully intended to get back into it in the New Year. I never was a person who believed in being careful over Christmas to maintain fitness but now I had even stopped using the running to counterbalance the excess. Cheers.

It had been a funny running year tainted by injury and illness and yet I had still managed to run nearly 2000 miles and three marathons. My running highlight of the year had been the Snowdon experience.

The end of December would mark the end of a decade of marathon running for me. Would changes in family life reduce my commitment to running further? The likely answer was soon revealed to me.

Chapter 11

1992 Older, Wiser, More Knackered, Olympic Gold

Life is very interesting. You wait eleven years for another baby to come along and two come along in quick succession. We found out that Eileen was pregnant again just after New Year. Early August was the expected time. It shouldn't have been a surprise, in that it wasn't an accident. The plan had always been to have two children fairly close together. At the end of the day though, it's always a bit of a surprise when it happens. If everything went to plan Sinead would be in the school year above her sibling but it seemed too early and too weird to think about that. Still, we were really excited.

My racing year started slowly but early. On January 5th I went up to Beacon Park to run a cross country race. This park is West Lancashire borough council's main countryside site, consisting of over 300 acres on the slopes of Ashurst Beacon above Skelmersdale. The beacon on top of Ashurst Hill stands 173m above sea level to the northeast of the town. As one of a chain of Lancashire beacons which stretched from Everton, in Liverpool, to Lancaster Castle, it was built in the 16th Century by Sir William Ashurst to serve as an early warning system against invaders and double glazing salesmen. It now commands a magnificent viewpoint over many counties. Standing at the foot of the monument, on a clear day, you can see in the distance, the mountains of Snowdonia, the Cheshire plain, the Pennines, Blackpool Tower and the Lake District mountains. Closer at hand you can take in a splendid view of Liverpool and the Mersey. The beacon also served as the lung busting high point of the cross country course. If I'd had time to stop there and look at the panorama I wouldn't have seen much, apart from spots before my eyes and a murky mist beyond.

Had it been a clear day and had I paused for breath I might have cast my gaze into distant space and time and pondered on my past life as a marathon runner. I would have been able to see the sites of many famous and infamous runs from my back catalogue; Liverpool where it all began, the Wirral, Windermere, Blackpool, Manchester and most recently Snowdonia. With my family life looming and blooming ever larger it might have been an appropriate time to take stock on what I thought I had achieved. But not now, because as usual in cross country, my main aim at that moment was to reach the finish without throwing up. I did this successfully and finished in 13th place.

I may have eschewed the chance to reminisce on that damp, chill, open hillside but later that day, back in the warmth of my Liverpool home, I was encouraged to do so in a different way. I had an unexpected telephone call from my Wolverhampton flickering light bulb sister. We hadn't spoken in 12 years. We chatted briefly then, deciding to take the wolves by the ears, I said I would visit her and we could have a proper talk. A date was set for early February. It was going to be a strange meeting. I had met her eldest son, as a toddler in Iran and briefly in England but not her youngest son. Both my nephews were now teenagers. She had never met Laura and obviously not Sinead. For the time being, I put the whole thing to the back of my mind. The 'things to think about' section was now like a junk cupboard; it needed sorting out, but at that moment I was just going to have to put all my weight against the door and squeeze it tightly shut.

With my evening and weekend running restricted by far more important matters I was gamely trying to keep up a two-runs-a-day regime. My run at dinner time was usually five miles and involved running through the village of Port Sunlight about a mile and a half from school.

Port Sunlight is a model village originally built by Lever Brothers (now known as Unilever) to accommodate people who worked in their factory. The brothers started building the village in 1888 and decided to name it after 'Sunlight Soap', one of the firm's most popular brands, first produced in 1884. Between 1899 and 1914, 800 houses were built to house a population of 3,500, which I think was a rather extravagant way to advertise a product. Port Sunlight contains 900 Grade II listed buildings and became a Conservation Area in 1978.

Originally based in Warrington, the successful firm needed to expand. The Warrington site was unsuitable for their plans. A large, flat, unused space on the Wirral was found, ideally situated between the river Mersey and a railway line. Having built their new factory and in accordance with their vision of having a workforce living in a community close by, they built Port Sunlight Village adjacent to the factory. It had many facilities for the residents; allotments, swimming baths, a church, a cottage hospital, schools, concert halls, an art gallery and a temperance hotel. (With their beneficent paternalism they trusted their workers to enjoy the finer things in life but not to consume alcohol sensibly.) Welfare schemes and provisions for education and 'creative' recreation were made. I'm sure the Levers were not being entirely altruistic when they provided these great amenities. Many industrial philanthropists at the time believed greater contentment in the workforce made for greater productivity.

Apart from the fact that it was built on money for old soap, the remarkable thing about Port Sunlight Village was that it managed to combine comfortable living quarters with architectural richness, inspired by the Arts and Craft Movement. Many different architects were involved and many styles and materials utilised. Each house was unique. The Lever Brothers must have been like kids in a sweet shop! The extravagance involved almost raises the question; who was it really for? Was it really for the workers' comfort? Maybe it was to make the bosses' journey to work easier on the eye and their journey to heaven easier than a camel's though the eye of a needle. The Levers certainly had a vision of communal life but I reckon they were slippery soap men because it was to be a community based on and directed by their beliefs, views and taste. Yes, I know I am such a cynic. However, it was certainly a pleasantly distracting place for a lunchtime run.

The Temperance Hotel had, of course, become a proper pub/restaurant in more intemperate times and my route often took me past the windows from which diners gawped. On Friday, January 17th

I must have been in a funny mood. I suppose all the recent family news must have made me a little funnier than usual. As I ran past the Bridge Inn Hotel I suddenly took offence at being eye-balled by the folk inside the warm pub, eating their roast dinners and supping their wine and beer, so I stuck two fingers up at them. Some saw the funny side and laughed, others looked outraged. It crossed my mind afterwards that there may have been parents of my kids or representatives of the education committee having a quiet lunch in there. I hoped not; I couldn't afford to get sacked at that moment.

Two days later, I was back in Helsby to check that it hadn't dissolved in a toxic mist and to do the half marathon again if it hadn't. It was still there and I ran comfortably in a time a whole five seconds slower than 1991 but, at 41, I was a whole year older and with child (by association).

As I wandered listlessly into February I had managed three consecutive weeks over 60 miles (68, 61, and 73). In those tumultuous days that was something of a miracle. Then as is often the case with families we developed a simultaneous cold. The original source was unknown but we glared accusingly at each other through rheumy eyes. Sinead was the best glarer. There was a significant entry in my diary, like some kind of epiphany. "Week disrupted by a cold. In the past I would have run through it but now I am older, wiser, lazier and less motivated."

I managed to run 240 miles in the month but I was not at one with my running. It was as if my mind and body had different ideas about the whole project. My body thought we should just carry on and see how it went while my mind objected to this illogical approach, questioning the point of the exercise. Body struggled on with mind muttering in the background. These are the strange sarcasm tinged diary entries my mind made my hand write. "26/2. Stiff and awkward; need to see a shrink about my running. 28/2. Long run 26 miles. Almost felt I needed to run and run to justify my existence. Is it all in my head?"

Obviously too many things were in my head. I had been thrown into a temporary spin by family news. I had visited my sister in Wolverhampton early in the month, as promised, and it had been a pleasant visit, reminiscing over the olden days of childhood. I learnt things about my mother and my grandmother I didn't know, or hadn't paid attention to when I was told the first time round. My elder sister was the keeper of the family history; there often seems to be one in each family, jealously guarding the knowledge. It amazed me how, in a group of relatives, there could be so many different versions of the same past. On that visit and at subsequent get-togethers there were many things I came to discover but also many things that I sensed would never be fully revealed.

I suppose families are like snowflakes, they are all different. The cohesion of a family grouping is dependent on many factors and there can be no template for success. The history of our family indicated that we'd got it wrong. This was to be brought home to me forcefully in the months ahead.

These were some of the things I knew, or thought I knew about my family's past. My mum was married before she met my dad. She married a soldier in Middlesbrough during World War Two and had my elder sister. My mum got wind of the fact that her army husband was being unfaithful somewhere on the South Coast of England where he was posted. At about five foot tall in her stocking feet, she was a pint sized woman with buckets of pluck. She took herself down south to confront her spouse and inform the regiment's commanding officer about his infidelity. She was a proud woman. She demanded a speedy divorce which the courts granted, no messing.

Then into port came my dad, a bow-legged, suntanned, jolly Jack Tar. It was 'hello sailor' and let's 'splice the main brace'. He'd taken a fancy to my mum even though she had a child astern. What I didn't know was whether my mum agreed to my dad's proposal of marriage because of her penchant for men in uniform or because she felt that, in those less enlightened times, she wouldn't get too many offers, coming, as she did, divorced with daughter attached. Judging by their different interests and outlook they didn't seem particularly well matched but who knows, they always seemed to get on. Anyway if she hadn't agreed to wed him I wouldn't be writing this. Shame, some would say.

My brother arrived in 1949 when my sister was six, I arrived in 1951 and my youngest sister three years later to the day. Our older sister always behaved as older sisters tend to, a little aloof and dismissive of her siblings. We regarded her as snobby and tried to irritate the hell out of her whenever possible, as younger siblings are expected to. When I was about eleven, my brother and I were rooting around the family documents, without permission, and we found our birth certificates. Our attention was drawn to the section with our mother's name which read; Iris Peacock (nee Bytheway, formerly Peel). Only then, when we questioned her about the meaning of 'formerly Peel' did mum tell us that she had been married before and that our oldest sis was not our dad's daughter. We were mildly shocked at the time but soon got over it and wanted to know what was for tea.

Looking back it did explain a few things which would have been of no interest to us as young kids. After willingly taking on the whole package, it was almost as if dad came to regard our sister as a rival for mum's affection rather than someone who deserved his. He found his stepdaughter hard work. He didn't find it easy to relate closely to his own kids so it came as no surprise that he found it even harder to relate to someone else's.

Just before I reconnected with my older sister the family situation looked a bit like this. My mum had died in 1971. My dad had married a younger woman with four kids. My brother and elder sister had returned to Middlesbrough from Iran. My sister had a serious falling out with my dad and his second wife (possibly over something to do with mum). I also think she found the fact that dad's wife was a woman of her own age quite hard to come to terms with and my stepmother resented the non-acceptance. No love was lost or forgiveness found. My sister was excommunicated and she moved to Wolverhampton. Her contact with the rest of us also petered out. My brother also fell out with my dad and was 'persuaded' (I'm unsure of the circumstances) to leave the crowded family home. He stayed in Middlesbrough, married and raised bulldogs (no, he didn't actually marry a bulldog). He had limited contact with dad and I only saw him when I made the effort to pop over to his while in town. Added to this my brother's wife didn't seem too keen on him contacting us or maybe he just wasn't keen, I couldn't say. This communication also got less and less as the years went by.

My younger sister had moved to Surrey, married and had a son. Out of all the siblings, we two kept up most regular contact during the 'eighties' by visiting, phoning and writing. She had roughly the same contact with the rest of the family as me. Family relations were as tangled as steel wool.

What I wasn't sure of, being well out of it in Liverpool, was exactly why all the falling out had occurred. To be honest I didn't really want to know, skeletons rattling about in cupboards was my least favourite sound. I kept up my sporadic contact with my father and we didn't really talk family unless it was about his 'new' one. He rarely, if ever, asked about any of the others. On the face of it he appeared to have transferred his loyalties but it was hard to read him completely, because he talked so little about the past or our former family life. We certainly didn't talk about mum. New family ranks would close around him and the subject would be changed quickly. He didn't seem to have the heart or the will to pursue these matters. I gave up trying to prompt him. By visiting my elder sister I suppose I risked disturbing a hornet's nest but I did it anyway because contact with Eileen's extended family and the growth of our own made me think it might be an idea to try to draw everyone together again.

In March in spite of lack of sleep and time, I ran 300 mad miles including a 100 mile week which included a 26 mile long run. The word 'knee' begins to crop up again more regularly in my training logs usually accompanied by the adjective 'sore'. I took a night off running to watch Laura play the flute in her school orchestra's spring concert. The rest made my knee feel better. When William Congreve wrote in 1697, "Music has charms to soothe a savage breast," he was obviously unaware that it also had a palliative effect on leg joints too.

On April 9th, in our house, no music had charms to soothe us after we took a Major beating. We beat our own breasts savagely (and metaphorically) as the Labour Party led by a red-faced Neil Kinnock was defeated, yet again, in the general election; this time grey-faced John Major's Tories were the victors. It was the fourth consecutive win by the Conservatives and I for one was beginning to wonder how much damage they had to do before the electorate realised they were not good for the majority of ordinary people in this country. Labour gained 42 seats but only got 30% of the vote compared to 42% for the Conservatives. This was nowhere near as closely contested as it should have been or, indeed, as had been predicted.

Not shy in coming forward to give 'the truth' about situations, the Sun newspaper led with the headline "It's The Sun Wot Won It" and claimed that their backing of the Tories had swung the vote. The paper's political argument hinged around a semi-naked, overweight female being pictured on Page 3 of the paper with the caption "Here's How Page 3 Will Look Under Kinnock." There truly were some principled and talented people working for that paper. Thankfully, in some political quarters women were beginning to be given more respect than afforded them on Page 3 of the Sun because on April 27th Betty Boothroyd became the first woman Speaker of the House of Commons.

Labour Party politics may not have been a winner in the election but days after, Party Politics won the Grand National Steeple Chase at Aintree. A horse of that name became the tallest winner in the race's history. I didn't know what relevance its height had. From my Middleham experience I knew that in a jockey's kingdom it helped to be smaller than Richard the Third, but for a horse?

Around the same time I could also be seen galloping near to Beecher's Brook on some of my long runs with the boys from the club as I prepared for my debut in the Telford Marathon at the end of April. The week before the general election I managed to run a 102 mile week and planned to ease down from there. Telford was close to Wolverhampton so I used the opportunity to stay with my sister again, before the marathon. Although this was the first time she had watched me compete in a marathon she confessed that she had been aware that I had run in Barmy Billy Wilson's Wolverhampton Marathons because she had seen my name in the results. I found this a strange thought. She must have also found it strange.

While I was reconnecting with my Wolves sister I had encouraged my younger sister to do the same. Those two had always got on well before the family had dispersed. It didn't seem to take any time at all for the flames of kinship to be rekindled. My situation was slightly different in that I had not always seen eye to eye with my elder sibling when I was young. I railed against, what I saw as, her high-handed dealings with me. It didn't help that our political views were decidedly different. The renewed relationship between brother and older sister would not catch light so easily but we were willing to work at it.

The Telford Marathon was a dull and uninspiring affair. The course was neither flat nor particularly hilly, trolling around nondescript roads and lanes. The weather was overcast with a grinding wind. It was an out and back course. With the wind behind us at the start we all knew it was going to be a struggle on the return. I plodded around in 2 hours and 50 minutes. The first half I completed in 1:19 helped by the wind, the second in 1:31 hindered by it.

A month later I was back in Wolverhampton with my two sisters, the three of us together for the first time in so many years. The occasion was my Iranian brother-in-law's 50th birthday. Out of the blue my sister asked me to write and perform a speech for him. I suppose it was an indication of how hard I was trying to strengthen family ties that I reluctantly agreed. Having no knowledge of my credentials to complete the task, her absolute faith in my ability to do so was either a big compliment or an indication that she couldn't be arsed to do it herself. If it turned out rubbish she couldn't be blamed. It was not until I arrived for the evening's party that she gave me a scratty piece of paper with random and unconnected facts about her husband scribbled on it. In normal circumstances I would have definitely refused to write a last minute homage to someone I barely knew, to be read out to people I had never had met. Somehow I did it. The speech started; "Well, I've known Farhad for, err... let's see... at least two months."

I could see his friends thinking, *who the f---k is this?* as they politely laughed at my attempted jokes about a man they all knew so well while knowing my total knowledge of him amounted to one side of biro-scrawled A4. It was an experience for everyone. In truth, what started as a potential ball-breaker actually turned into an icebreaker, helping me get to know some of Farhad's friends.

An emotionally charged family week continued as on the Thursday following my speech I received a phone call from my stepmother in Middlesbrough. She told me my dad was in hospital with septicaemia as a result of an infected cut on his foot. Amputation of the affected leg was a possibility if treatment was not successful. I rang work, explained the situation and drove for two and a half hours straight to the hospital in Middlesbrough. By the time I got to the ward his condition had improved dramatically. He had responded well to medication. My brother was already there. I hadn't seen him for a few years.

As we chatted around dad's bed and, in my role as recently appointed ambassador for the United Families Organisation (UFO), I mentioned the previous weekend's party with the sisters and said how successful it had been. They could see I was sounding them out about a reunion but I may as well have just landed in a UFO the way they reacted to me. My brother went quiet but my dad was more vociferous. I can't remember his exact words but the gist of it, put politely, was that a reunion was out of the question. The rancorous response shocked me.

Leaving the hospital on my way home I stopped off at my old house to see my stepmother and some of her children, now all adults. I reported on my dad's condition and also mentioned his reaction to the story of the meeting with my sisters. Their reaction was equally hostile. I confess I was irked and may have pointed out to them that it was possible that some past resentment may have been caused by their sudden commandeering of our family home so soon after our mother's death. Was it possible that we, dad's original family, might have felt displaced? The step family couldn't believe I could actually think this never mind say it. The same past, two irrevocably different views of it and never the twain shall meet! Tears were shed but not by me. I felt untouched emotionally by the whole situation although my views were strong. I left my birth town that day knowing that this was one family that wasn't for reuniting. I resigned from my post as ambassador, which wasn't too difficult as I had appointed myself. I accepted my own resignation and returned to planet Liverpool by car having abandoned the UFO.

Living in Liverpool often reminded me of my Middlesbrough teenage years in the days when my mum was still alive. Music was the trigger. In the '60s I was seriously in love with contemporary music and the culture that surrounded it. I invested much of my pubescent emotion in what I suppose some would have described as hippy music. Electric blues, folk and psychedelic rock. This music transported me from a drab environment where money was hard to come by and where there was little interesting to spend it on when you had it. I would save up to make the occasional trip up the A1 to watch big bands play at the Newcastle City Hall; Jethro Tull, Ten Years After, Led Zeppelin etc.

Also, along with my brother, I had a love for the music of the Beatles. We followed and approved of the development of their style and sound. In the early days when we had similar tastes we would share the costs of purchasing music. Our parents didn't possess a record player but one Christmas my dad bought a reel-to-reel Elizabethan tape recorder. No, it wasn't that old, it was made by Elizabethan Electronics in Romford, Essex. I'm not sure if the firm were aiming at the younger market but I thought that they seriously needed to consider a name change.

The first LPs we clubbed together to buy were in the form of pre-recorded reel-to-reel tapes of the Beatles' 'Revolver' and 'Rubber Soul' albums. We were hooked.

When my dad realised Elizabethan Tape recorders weren't the way forward he purchased a stereogram, which was like a magically mysterious, musical sideboard. The first vinyl we bought was the 'Magical Mystery Tour' EP by the Beatles. I loved it and wore it out. For us stereo was still enough of a novelty for it to mess with our minds. The psychedelic sounds on this recording amazed me. We would often lay head-first in front of the stereogram, ears equidistant between the speakers. It was physically difficult for more than one person at a time to listen like this. Sometimes a bout of carpet wrestling and head bashing, between brothers, would be a prelude to the mind messing.

To answer the big question for people of a certain age, my favourite Beatles' track was the B-side of the 'Penny Lane' single, 'Strawberry Fields'. How could I know that, as I listened to these songs, which were such a big part of my teenage life, the mysterious places mentioned in the lyrics would become so familiar in my adult life? I couldn't.

When Eileen and I moved near to Penny Lane in 1985 I started having my haircut in Tony Slavin's, which is the barber's shop mentioned in the song 'Penny Lane' and where at one time some of the Beatles had some of their hair cut, allegedly. Passing by these places could still unexpectedly whisk me back to teenage days, to a time of greasy hair and a yearning to be elsewhere. I'd had a nagging, unfulfilled need to be in a more creative environment with easily accessible showering facilities and lots of shampoo.

My diary for the week after the visit to my dad states; "too many things happening this week for me to be able to do any proper running - bashing my head against a brick wall." I can't remember whether the last bit referred to family matters or running, probably both.

As I struggled to regain some sort of form, the balance of power in the club had certainly shifted. The following week on June 2nd I ran a five mile race around Walton Park, organised by our club. I was not only beaten by DJ and Rugman who finished 2nd and 3rd but also by Eyeful and Ducker. Three other club members also beat me. I was 8th from the club and 29th in all. I didn't even know some of our club's runners who were in front of me. I was one of the old guard who had let his down. Some of the young pretenders were mounting a real challenge to the established order. I had got to know one of these young lads quite well. He was a smashing fella (and he shall be called Mighty) with the potential to be a top runner. He was also a painter and decorator by trade and therefore well worth knowing.

I had already availed myself of the practical talents lurking in the marathon group. On one long run I had mentioned the need to replace our kitchen floor because of rising damp. Almost before I had finished my sentence the Bard spoke up. "Me and Rugman'll do it. Just have some sand and a bag of cement delivered to your house next Saturday." I'm not sure how keen Rugman was on the project but he didn't disagree with the Bard; people rarely did. My protests were brushed away. I knew if I'd protested longer it could have been dangerous.

When the day of the job arrived, they got cracking on removing the old floor and I was relegated to tea boy. Soon they were laying a fresh surface on top of a Visqueen membrane the Bard had 'borrowed' from work. We inconveniently ran out of cement. By chance Rugman was working at a building site a couple of miles away. "Come 'ed," he said, "I know the security guard. We'll get a bag from the site." Ten minutes later we were driving past a rather stern looking guard. Rugman nodded at him. We loaded a bag of cement into the boot of my car and drove past the guard again. He was now too busy writing in a notebook to acknowledge us. Back at my house the Bard was waiting. "Did you speak to Billy?" he asked. "It wasn't Billy. It was a new fella I've never seen before," replied Rugman casually.

The job was soon completed and payment refused. All they would accept was a bottle of Southern Comfort each for their northern troubles. For weeks after, I was waiting for a knock at the door; police, having traced my number plate, looking for stolen property. Like many guilty secrets, by then it was well hidden in the concrete floor. I never got the knock and Rugman never mentioned the security guard again.

Their unhesitating willingness to do this job was but one example of a long list of kindnesses shown to me and Eileen in our long association with these friends. Ok, so there was a borderline illegality involved in acquiring some of the materials but it was my opinion that these people worked long hours in harsh conditions and having access to resources for personal use seemed a just way to get a fairer redistribution of profits, especially when I was the beneficiary.

(The Ten Year Club.)

Getting back to the Walton Park race, I knew I would have to start to accept being beaten, not only by my old sparring partners but by runners like Mighty coming through the club's ranks. It was an indication of the lowering of my expectations that I was quite pleased with my performance of 28:35.

When I came to write this record of part of my life I decided to limit myself to the years 1982 through to 1992, which may seem like an odd choice of years. It is not a complete trawl of the '80s nor is it exactly ten years in total. For me, however the time frame presented an irresistible symmetry. Two factors steered me towards the choice. In terms of my running, the eleven years span the staging of the ten Mersey Marathons (accounting for the cancelled race in 1990) during the road running boom time. The first Mersey in 1982 was my first marathon and introduced me to the sport. The last in 1992 came at a time when my running was declining. My performances were dipping, my commitment was waning and I knew that Mr Marathon and I would soon be going our separate ways. On June 21st 1992 I became a member of an exclusive club, the ten year club. I was one of a few mad people who had run all ten Mersey Marathons.

I had tried as hard as I could in 1992 to get in as many miles as possible to finish my Mersey Marathon career on a high note because I knew full well what the birth of our child in August would mean. Clocking up a regular decent mileage with one infant in the house had been nigh on impossible, another baby would remove the 'nigh on'. This also brings me neatly to the second factor for the odd choice of eleven years. 1992 would not only see me unofficially complete my marathon career but would also see me complete my family. It would be all hands on deck for the new crew member.

On top of all this, the end of this distinct era in my life also coincided, in many ways, with the end of a distinct era in world and national politics. Many countries had seen the end of totalitarian regimes and we had seen the back of Thatcher; unfortunately she was only going to the House of Lords and not the Tower. My home would be the House of Ladies and we would be having another little dictator ruling over us. The Iron Lady had departed but for us Girl Power was alive and kicking in the '90s.

And so, as a runner, I approached my last Mersey Marathon looking back at what had been achieved rather than looking forward to what could be. Even so, I surprised myself a little. The miles I had struggled to get into my legs earlier that year served me well. I ran a relatively comfortable race and it seemed I had become old enough and wise enough (mainly old enough), by now, to run at an even pace. I actually overtook seven people in the last six miles. I finished in my highest ever Mersey position, 14th. To be honest this may not have been as a result of my time, a modest but pleasing 2:45:58, but possibly more to do with the fact that a half marathon held in conjunction with the full marathon had attracted many runners better than me, who had decided to give the full masochistic experience a miss.

This was a great marathon finale; to run in my adopted home town with those people who had become such great friends since I joined Liverpool Running Club. For some, their running careers were going from strength to strength or just beginning. I was pleased for them in spite of my declining contribution to the personal running battles. Six club members finished in the top seventeen; a great performance by all those involved which made me proud to have been associated with the club and of my friends in it.

My comments after the race also hint at what I felt I was personally up against to run a fast marathon. There was also an inherent acceptance that, as Bruce Springsteen had warned me repeatedly back in 1984, 'glory days, well they'll pass you by' and that I had done my utmost in the circumstances. I noted in my diary; "After a week of doing reports plus Sinead going to bed late and waking us up early I felt I did well in the race. In other words I was pleased."

After this race I recorded three weeks of half-hearted running before my diary suddenly stopped. Three weeks after that Eileen and I were back in a delivery room of Oxford Street maternity hospital. The last post-dated scribbled entry reads.

"Gave up recording distances - gave up serious running because of the birth of wonderful Roisin, born 10/08/92. I will try to get back into it after Christmas." I was ever the optimist.

Roisin arrived with less fuss and metal implements than Sinead or Laura but Eileen had a less than joyous birth being chivvied by an unhelpful mid-wife who we can only presume was coming to the end of her shift. She was in a hurry but Eileen obviously didn't want to be rushed and Roisin certainly had her own timetable. Instead of helping Eileen to relax the midwife was chastising her for not pushing at the right time. She kept tutting and looking at her watch. I think she must have previously worked on a battery farm or in a factory as a time and motion inspector. When the baby did finally emerge she was in the posterior position or 'sunny side up'. This was one of the reasons Eileen had found delivery difficult. As Roisin made her appearance face up it was as if she was already assessing her prospects.

You might imagine that, having had children already, the experience of another birth would be less intense. This was certainly not true in our case. Knowledge and memory of previous experiences are obscured by time. The power of the feelings generated takes you by surprise. It's as if the fact that you think you know what to expect actually makes you unprepared for the sensation again. Roisin was soon home and settling into family life with her parents and older sisters doting on her. Her knowing look said it all. "I've got this lot where I want them."

Leading up to the birth I had repeatedly whispered "the tenth, the tenth" in close proximity to Eileen's swelling belly. This date was the day after the Barcelona Olympic Games concluded. I had been following the Games with interest from the first day (including the innovative opening ceremony). Roisin obliged and arrived on cue. We purchased Freddie Mercury's single, 'Barcelona' to put into our daughter's birth bag. This was a duet with operatic soprano Montserrat Caballé, which had become the BBC's theme tune for the games. It had a rousing crescendo which was maybe a suitable musical metaphor for a dramatic year in my family's life.

The GB and Northern Ireland team won five gold, three silver and twelve bronze medals. Linford Christie in the 100m and Sally Gunnel in the 400m hurdles were our only track winners. Wirral based Chris Boardman won a gold in cycling and the two other golds were won in rowing events; these achievements indicated areas where greater Olympic success would be secured in the years ahead. The Guardian newspaper on the day, which cost 40p, reported on the Olympics but also on another sporting occasion, the Charity Shield at Wembley Stadium. Liverpool lost 4-3 to Leeds United. The star of the show was a certain Eric Cantona who scored a hat-trick for Leeds.

GB and Northern Ireland were a united team at the Olympics but at home in the same month, the divisions carried on. Hugh McKibben, according to Royal Ulster Constabulary figures, became the 3000th victim of sectarian violence in Northern Ireland since 1969; a shocking statistic. There were however signs of change even in this apparently hopeless situation. The Guardian on August 10th also covered a march of 2000 republicans in Belfast. They were commemorating the 21st anniversary of internment. In 1971 republicans, many with no connections to paramilitary groups, had been summarily arrested by British troops and imprisoned without trial. If this act had occurred in another country it would have been roundly condemned by the UK government. For republicans this was a deeply felt injustice. And yet at the 1992 demonstration, Sin Fein leaders were reported as saying that peace talks were now a possibility. At last some change seemed possible.

Even closer to home, in November Tony Bland became the 96th victim of the Hillsborough disaster when the decision was made to take him off life support. In another echo of the eighties the government announced plans to close one third of Britain's deep coal mines with the loss of 31,000 jobs. 100,000 took to the streets of London to protest but the government warned that those taking any form of industrial action against the cuts would lose redundancy entitlements worth up to £37,000. British Coal was privatised shortly after the 1992 cuts. Some things hadn't changed.

However, later in November, change was afoot in the Church of England when they voted to allow women priests; ironic really because the head of the church was apparently already a woman. So it was a good year generally for women in the church but not for the head. Queen Elizabeth had experienced an 'annus horribilis' and not the type that pile cream could ease. This is a summary of what she'd had to put up with.

In March 1992, it was announced that her second son, the Duke of York, would separate from his wife the Duchess of York. In April, her daughter, the Princess Royal, divorced husband Captain Mark Phillips. In June, a revealing book about the Princess of Wales, 'Diana, Her True Story,' was published. In November, one of The Queen's homes, Windsor Castle, caught fire. The castle was seriously damaged, and several priceless artefacts were lost. In December, the Royal Family faced further difficulties when the separation of Charles the Prince of Wales and his wife Diana the Princess of Wales was announced. To cap it all, heavens above, it was announced that for the first time since the 1930's the monarch would have to pay income tax like the rest of us.

(The House of Ladies....and a lad)

If I was head of the church I'd be having a word with the Boss Upstairs about all this unpleasantness to see if he (or she) could pull off a few miracles. The disaster I sympathised mostly with was the fire tragedy. I don't know which of my many homes I'd least like to go up in smoke.

Nonetheless with Roisin's birth, for me, the year had been mirabillis not horribilis. At the age of 41, I had also managed a satisfactory marathon performance, as a last hurrah in my running story. In the months leading up to Roisin's birth I had run nearly 1500 miles, completing two marathons, a half marathon, four 10k's, and a five miler. Unlike HM, as the year drew to a close I was happy. I was in a loving relationship. I had three amazing daughters, none of whom were old enough to get divorced, and I lived in my small terraced house, with smoke alarms fitted, in a fascinating city.

This 11 year period of my life had been nothing like a marathon. Firstly, it seemed to have gone in a flash, secondly, I had enjoyed virtually all of it and thirdly, when it had come to an end, if you had asked me, would I do it all again, I wouldn't have needed a few beers before saying, 'yes'.

Epilogue

Hillsborough and the miner's strike were in the news. The country was in the throes of a recession and the Conservative led government had responded to the economic situation by punishing those who had least money and were least to blame. They were making swingeing cuts to public services and trying to introduce an unpopular tax penalising the poor. I had run the Liverpool Half Marathon in March. You could be forgiven for thinking that this was a description of a year in the late eighties. Actually, it describes 2012, 20 years after my last Mersey Marathon and ER's horrible annus.

Many things had changed in the intervening years but some things just seemed to keep repeating, like a stuck record or more topically, a damaged CD. As I write in 2013 the UK has a Conservative government, cunningly disguised as a coalition. We are still in a double dip, somersault with pike, recession. Yet again, it would appear that the people who brought this upon us have not been selected to bear the brunt of the government's austerity measures 'to get the economy going again'. As George Orwell or George Osborne didn't say, "We are all in this (shit) together but some of us are in it more than others." We can only presume that the government's main reason for wanting to crank start the economy is to help supporters and friends who had to postpone the building of an extension on their second home or the redecorating of the south wing.

This supposition leads us neatly to the unpopular tax proposed by a government, whose cabinet, incidentally, is still awash with smug millionaires. It bears an eerie similarity to the Poll Tax. It is certainly targeting the same people. It is a Bedroom Tax, to try to discourage people on housing benefit, in social housing, from living in anything bigger than a matchbox. Apparently it is not enough that many of those targeted live in crappy accommodation in run-down areas; now it has to be smaller, crappier accommodation or alternatively a move to private rented accommodation with the uncontrolled rents and insecure tenancy agreements associated with non-social housing. I wonder which way most landlords vote!

With this Bedroom Tax the government plans to cut the housing benefit of those in social housing by 14% if they are deemed to have one spare bedroom and 25% if they have two. All couples, even if ill or disabled are expected to share a room and kids up to ten, or 16 if the same sex, are also expected to share, two to a room. The size of the bedroom is irrelevant. You can understand the government's thinking here. How dare the plebs have a bedroom each or god forbid one spare? In fact, they should all sleep in the same room or even better, two families to a room like in the good old days of Victorian values.

The cabinet's enthusiasm for these measures must, I feel, either be a result of fond memories of the dorm at public school, where they had such jolly japes, or because of their obsession with the sport of "sponger" bashing. Although less than 1% of the welfare budget is lost as a result of fraud, they seem to think it more important to reduce this budget rather than chase their tax evading contemporaries who cost the country far more. For them it makes sense to stop giving money to those who need it rather than take money from those who can afford it. The tax does not apply to private rented accommodation and so it is also a convenient way of driving tenants into non-social housing; a beneficial tax for the poor private landlords in times of economic need and another attempt to diminish the public sector. As many as 660,000 people in social housing stand to lose £728 a year. The government aims to save £465 million a year. This is fair enough. Just imagine how unfair it would be to ask anyone with more than three bedrooms earning more than £75,000 per annum to pay tax for each extra bedroom; unthinkable. It would be especially hard on certain members of the cabinet who might struggle to remember how many houses they have, never mind bedrooms.

In Liverpool the majority of the social housing stock is three bedroom or larger and so families with two children or less will theoretically be forced into the rip-off world of private renting or to have more kids. It will be interesting to see how this unjust law is 'fairly' enforced. In the blustering blind crusade against 'benefit scroungers' it is often not mentioned that most people on housing benefit are actually in work but in jobs which do not pay enough to allow a decent standard of living.

The Tories just don't seem to get it or don't want to. In the economic system we live in, they are rich because so many are poor. They talk about hard working families as if hard work is a cure-all for poverty. Surely they realise that only a few people can escape penury this way. Most people on the breadline could work 24 hours a day and still not have enough to live on because they earn a minimum wage not a living wage. In a humane society these 'have-nots' should be helped by the 'haves', not hindered.

While writing this epilogue, reports came through that Margaret Thatcher had died. It was interesting to read reactions in the press. Prime minister, David Cameron and many others, including ex Labour PM Tony Blair, eulogised about her contribution in shaping modern Britain. It is true that we still live in Thatcher's Britain. The question was whether this was a thing to celebrate or not. My view, shared by many others, was that she destroyed communities and promoted personal wealth.

She cared about freedom but it was only the freedom to allow a few people to make money on the backs of many others. She had supported Zola Budd's right to be free to run for the UK but had also supported the apartheid regime in South Africa which denied the freedom of millions. The individual was put before the community. If people didn't agree with her nation view they were crushed. Thatcher was willing to let Liverpool go into decline because she and her cronies didn't think they would get anything back from any money put in and also because the city had the audacity to stand up to her. In my opinion the only positive thing to be said about her was that she was the first woman PM but that was not good enough. Some people talk of her as a force in world politics. She did not have a world view. Her view was narrow, blinkered and bigoted. She was a parish pump thinker who got credit for her inflexibility, mistaken for steely determination. She was unable to consider the other side of any argument. As you can see I wasn't a fan. I believe her legacy is that the present leaders of her party still think that looking after themselves and their own kind is a satisfactory way to run the country for the rest of us.

And on the theme of fighting injustice in Liverpool, more than twenty years on, the Hillsborough tragedy was not consigned to history as the establishment, led by Thatcher, would have liked. The families refused to allow it to be. At last the real truth has been revealed. A new independent panel found the supporters blameless and pointed the finger of blame in the right direction; the police, the politicians and the press, three P's in a pod. The original inquest findings were quashed in 2012 and a new inquest ordered. The home secretary also announced a new police enquiry into the disaster.

Taking the lead from the Hillsborough Families' example, after 30 years, there was also a growing demand for an investigation into the actions of the police at Orgreave coking plant during the miner's strike. The Guardian Newspaper reported in December 2012; "Last month, in the wake of a BBC documentary and mounting pressure for a thorough account of events in the summer of 1984, the South Yorkshire (Police) force referred itself to the policing watchdog over Orgreave. The Independent Police Complaints Commission has confirmed it is looking at allegations of assault, perjury, perverting the course of justice and misconduct in a public office. A new group, the Orgreave Truth and Justice Campaign, has begun orchestrating support for a public inquiry into the policing of the bloody confrontation on 28 June 1984."

One miner speaking to the Guardian explained how a dubious conviction for obstruction tarnished his reputation and ruined his employment chances. His reason for continuing the fight for truth was simple. "All I want is for somebody to say: I'm sorry, you have not got a criminal record any more, you were fitted up." He added, "I don't want compensation or anything else, just somebody to say sorry."

Looking back, the '80s were a hard time for Liverpool, but the problems were rarely, as some would have us believe, of the city's own making. The starting point of this account of my running was a year after the Toxteth riots. During that disconcerting time I was living in Liverpool 8. We were less than half a mile from the flaming buildings and burning cars. We could hear the clatter of looters, with their full shopping trolleys, rattling down our street. When we ventured out the next morning many of our local shops had disappeared. They seemed to have sunk into the melted tarmac, the surface of which was whirled and swamp-like, transformed by the fierce heat of the previous night's flames. Stepping on to Lodge Lane in Liverpool 8, was like being hurtled back four decades to the 1941 Blitz.

That week, as I travelled to work by bus, police in pairs stood 20 yards apart for the whole of the three quarter mile length of Princes Avenue. Reinforcements had been bussed in from all over the country, like an army of occupation.

The press portrayal of the city was of one plagued by lawlessness. My experience was different. At that time the black population of the city was concentrated in L8, but the area was not exclusively black. As with many other things in Liverpool, its black community was distinctive. A great proportion were Liverpool born and of mixed heritage. In many ways this could have been seen as a paradigm for social integration. As a white person living in the area I detected no particular antagonism because of my skin colour.

Early in our relationship Eileen and I had enjoyed many post-pub drinks and dances in the African clubs which could be found in the crumbling Georgian terraces clustered around Princes Boulevard. The Ibo, The Yoruba, The Somali, The Nigeria; these names tell of the African roots of many of the locals. White faces were rare in some of these clubs but we were never made to feel unwelcome. Nearly all the antagonism and prejudice, at the time, came from outside the area. Racists in other parts of the city and country dubbed the area 'The Jungle' and many refused to venture into Toxteth. It was almost as if they resented the area more because it was mixed. I have heard people with this attitude, even in the 21st century, telling stories of how "it wasn't safe to walk the streets" or of how "muggings happened all the time." When I hear this talk I have to interrupt and point out I lived in Toxteth for ten years. I'm sure muggings did occur, as they did in other parts of the city and in every other city in the country but for the decade I regularly walked the streets at all times of the day and night I never witnessed or was ever subjected to this type of crime. And I don't think I was just lucky. It was as if Merseyside's attitude to Toxteth almost mimicked the rest of the country's view of Liverpool.

There was, at the time, a presumption in the city that if you were black or mixed race you were guilty of something. As an ethnic group the Liverpool Black Community were excluded from the social and commercial life of the city centre. There was an informal apartheid culture in operation. The police reinforced it. They singled out many innocent Liverpool born black kids for some outrageous treatment. If there was a mixed group of teenagers in trouble, the black youths would be selected for special attention by the forces of law and order. The riots were not initially caused by lawlessness but by a reaction to injustice.

Labour Councillor Margaret Simey, who died in 2004 aged 98, was a friend of Eileen's and an unlikely advocate for the black community. From an affluent academic background, tall, upright, pale skinned and white haired she looked like the stereotype of a 1930s school Ma'am. She could often be seen striding purposefully around the inner-city streets. She became chair of the local police authority in 1981 and wasn't afraid to speak out in her refined accent about the unacceptable treatment of black youths in Toxteth. She predicted trouble. She famously said, referring to local people's confrontations with the police, "they would be apathetic fools ... if they didn't protest." She saw the riots from the view point of the residents and spoke about them saying, "I am a dogged woman. I never condoned violence but I warned of it. I saw people being neglected and disenfranchised: a community being subjected to dependence."

After the riots, some money was diverted into the city for regeneration. Generally it seemed to flow past L8. By 2012 it appeared to have dried up altogether with a Conservative led government in power and austerity very much on its mind, development quangos were among the first to suffer the coalition axe .The racism which was so evident in the '80s is still here but not so overt. Post 1981, there were some changes, policing improved and local public bodies opened up their recruitment processes. However by 2012 all the African clubs had gone as had many of the terraced streets, demolished or waiting to be. The neighbourhood was a shadow of its former self and many of the locals had been dispersed and were no better off.

On the whole Liverpool is still a poor city but also continues to benefit from a cultural richness. For a little city it has much to offer. It now appears that more people are sharing my enthusiasm for the place if the number of tourists it attracts each year is anything to go by. Obviously there are still plenty of detractors but the granting of World Heritage status for the iconic waterfront buildings and the awarding of European Capital of Culture to the city in 2008 undoubtedly enhanced its national and global standing. It has always been a vibrant and fascinating city but now more people were 'daring' to experience this first hand. I am also pleased to say that a section of the Festival Gardens, including the Chinese Garden, has been restored and reopened to create a peaceful haven by the Mersey. It is a wonderful addition to Liverpool's impressive green spaces. Now we can take the blindfolds off visiting Chinese delegations.

I still get my hair cut in the barber's shop in Penny Lane. They actually started selling souvenirs a few years back. People now come into the shop to take photos and they are asked to donate to The Linda McCartney breast cancer centre. I think I should be in the Guinness Book of Records, in the category for 'the largest number of appearances (back of the head only) in Japanese photo albums'. The Magical Mystery Tour buses, which take tourists around all the old Beatles' haunts, now often park outside just to snatch a glimpse of my noble profile.

The hairdresser who cuts my hair was telling me recently that a builder, who had knocked down a wall in some student flats above the shop, took all the bricks away and tried to sell them on the internet. He was especially trying to offload them, so to speak, in Japan, as 'bricks from the Penny Lane Barbers'. It appears he was actually implying that the shop had been demolished. The proprietor was none too pleased about the effect this might have on business.

I am still reminded of my youth occasionally when I sit waiting to be shorn. The mirror shows all my hair is still there but unlike Paul McCartney's it has greyed. Somewhere, beyond the salt and pepper crop (increasingly more salty) and the baggy eyes, a long haired lad from Middlesbrough still lurks. My family never did fully reunite. My dad died in 2009, my elder sister wasn't at the funeral. In some ways she was lucky. I didn't really know the man being buried. It was someone else's dad. I met my brother at the ceremony. I'd hardly seen him this century and haven't seen him since. On the positive side I keep in regular touch with my sisters. My daughters have grown up in close contact with their aunts and cousins and I have close relationship with my nephews. Along with Eileen's tribe, we were all together at my 60th birthday party in 2011 at the Everyman Theatre; a genuine family.

2012 was another Olympic year but this time on home soil for team GB. A stunning effort by the home team saw 29 gold medals won and a third place in the medals table, a far cry from the less than inspiring performances of the eighties. GB dominated the cycling and rowing events. On the track, Mo Farah rejuvenated the country's reputation for long distance running by winning both the 5,000m and the 10,000m. I ran every yard (in my head where I easily kept up) with Mo and whooped at his success. I also listened with interest as commentators raved about his 100 mile a week training regime. (I do admit to thinking, yeah, but try to do that while just about holding down a job and running all the miles like a donkey.)

And on the subject of donkeys, the ass had fallen out of my running soon after 1992. I ran one more marathon in 1993 for old time's sake. I'd got an automatic entry to London thanks to my 2:45 over 40 qualifying time at the 10th Mersey. It was my 5th marathon in the Capital. When I was finally forced to stop running completely, people who knew me as a runner would ask whether I was still bashing the blackstuff. I would reply, "No, when the kids arrived, my knees went." This statement had a great deal of truth in it. Cartilage wear and tear in my right knee made it impossible to run long distances. I wouldn't have had the time anyway. Family life had taken over. I tried to keep fit by going back to football, playing five-a-side once or twice a week. It was like I had almost come full circle. My knee was always stiff after playing but I had time to recover between games.

As my kids grew up my knee seemed to go into remission or maybe kneemission. With less time needed for parental input I started jogging a little. I found it hard, initially, but my troublesome joint, although not perfect, seemed to cope as I got fitter. Approaching 60, I started training a little more. I ran a few half marathons. I was still managing around 90 minutes for a half and 40 minutes for a 10k. As I turned 60 I went into a different Veteran's age category and was first in my age group in races on a number of occasions. It was amazing to be able to come back to the sport after nearly 20 years and still be able to compete. It reminded me of how inclusive it was.

I was like the Rip Van Winkle of running. It was a different world to me with 'Garmins', 'chip timing' and 'parkruns'. I met up with old club mates again at events but couldn't bring myself to rejoin the club. I felt that would be a throwback rather than a comeback. DJ, Mighty, Testerman and the Brothers Grimm were all still going strong(ish) although many others, including the Bard, Rugman and Whistler, had fallen by the wayside, mostly side-lined by injury. I flirted with the idea of trying another marathon but common sense, for once, got the better of me.

Sadly, my comeback was short-lived. My knee started to feel more uncomfortable again and after just managing to complete the Liverpool Half in 2012, I could hardly walk afterwards. I eventually had an arthroscopy. This procedure inserts a camera into the knee to try to detect the problem while simultaneously clearing out any troublesome debris. After taking holiday snaps of a trip behind my kneecap the specialist gave me his opinion. Trying to baffle me with his medical terminology he declared that my knee was 'shot'. The grainy images he showed me looked so much like a pregnancy scan that I thought he'd picked up the wrong ones from the chemist but, no, it was my ugly knee not a beautiful baby. He pointed at where the cartilage should have been. "This is supposed to be white, like a piece of...err... white cheese. Now it looks like... err I don't know what it looks like." Descriptive prose is obviously not a unit on the university knee specialist degree course. "Gorgonzola," I offered, hating to see a brainy man struggle for words. 'Yes', he smiled; he could afford to, it wasn't his knee.

And so I limped home with my wrongcheese knee and decided it was, in fact, time to hang up the running shoes (again), stop running and start to write about it. Some who had read my stuff said, "Isn't it a pity he couldn't have run a bit longer."

Laura, now married with two children, was talking about my predicament (the running one not the other one I keep secret) with her husband. He said, "I bet your dad wishes he hadn't run all those miles, now." Laura replied, "I bet he doesn't." She knows me. I am the Edith Piaf of marathon running and not because of the skinny legs, troubled personal life and French accent, because none of those apply (apart from the legs). I had no regrets in '92 and now that my headless chicken legs had come home to roost again I still did not. I'd had a second shot at getting an endorphin buzz and had enjoyed the return trip.

I also managed to achieve a partial ambition. My comeback coincided with the arrival of 'parkrun' in Liverpool. This organisation is amazing. Started in Bushy Park in 2004, it now organises, with the help of an army of volunteers, free, timed and accurately measured 5k runs every Saturday morning in over 170 locations in the UK and also many worldwide. The Liverpool run takes place in Princes Park and I managed to complete 50 of them before my knee said, 'no more, thanks very much.' I have such polite knees.

Before I stopped I had the pleasure of completing a run with two of my daughters, Laura and Sinead. They both actually like to run. Now, when they tell me about their running or when I watch Eileen going out the door for a couple of jogs a week, I feel a little envious but also proud at the thought that I may have influenced them to take up the sport. (Just for the record and so I don't get into trouble, Roisin, the youngest, would always rather have a set of wheels beneath her, bike or skateboard.)

And so we have come to the end of the story of this Rip Van Piaf of running. After all said and done, in many ways, this has been a love story. Firstly, the love of my family, Eileen, still happily unmarried to me after nearly 35 years, and my three daughters, Laura, Sinead and Roisin still happily taking the mickey out of me; secondly, the love of Liverpool an enigmatic and special city; and finally, the love of running and my memories of being buoyant on the blackstuff.